SR SUPPLEMENTS

Volume 20

The Social Uplifters

Presbyterian Progressives and the Social Gospel in Canada, 1875-1915

Brian J. Fraser

Published for the Canadian Corporation for Studies in Religion/Corporation Canadienne des Sciences Religieuses
by Wilfrid Laurier University Press

1988

Canadian Cataloguing in Publication Data

Fraser, Brian J. (Brian John), 1947-
The social uplifters

(SR supplements ; 20)
Bibliography: p.
Includes index.
ISBN 0-88920-972-3

1. Sociology, Christian – Canada. 2. Presbyterian Church – Canada – History. 3. Social gospel – History. 4. Church and social problems – Presbyterian Church. 5. Presbyterian Church – Canada – Biography. I. Canadian Corporation for Studies in Religion. II. Title. III. Series.

BT738.F73 1988 261′.0971 C88-094298-3

88 89 90 91 4 3 2 1

The Social Uplifters: Presbyterian Progressives and the Social Gospel in Canada, 1875-1915 has been produced from a manuscript supplied in camera-ready form by the author.

Cover design by Michael Baldwin, MSIAD

Order from:
Wilfrid Laurier University Press
Wilfrid Laurier University
Waterloo, Ontario, Canada N2L 3C5

Printed in Canada

TABLE OF CONTENTS

Preface vi

Introduction ix

1. The Intellectual Roots: Scottish Evangelical Liberalism 1
   - British Idealism 3
   - Biblical Criticism 8
   - Urban Revivalism 12

2. The Theology: Evangelical Liberalism 23
   - Educating Six Progressives 23
   - The Theology of T.B. Kilpatrick 27
   - Kilpatrick on Evangelism 33
   - Kilpatrick on Character and Reform 38

3. The Institutional Framework: The Growth of a Canadian Denomination 49
   - A National Denomination 50
   - A New Metropolitan Centre 56
   - New Frontiers 66

4. The Suburban Base: The Presbyterian Critique of Canadian Society 77
   - The Problem of the City 78
   - The Pre-Assembly Congress, 1913 84
   - The Urban Core and Settlement Work 90

5. The Strategy: Creating of a Christian Collective Conscience 99
   - The Christian Home 100
   - The Pulpit and the Platform 105
   - The Press 109
   - The Public School and the Sunday School 114

6. Implementation: Mobilizing a Christian Nation 127
Mobilizing the Church 128
The Illusive Alliance with Labour 132
Legislation 137
Law Enforcement 142

7. The Testing: The Ordeal of World War I 155
Progressive Peacemaking 156
Presbyterian Progressives at War 160
Progressivism in Crisis 165

8. The Social Uplifters in Perspective 173

Selected Bibliography 181

Index 207

TABLES

Table 1	Statistics of the Uniting Presbyterian Churches	57
Table 2	Metropolitan Statistics of the Presbyterian Church in Canada in 1987	58
Table 3	Metropolitan Statistics of the Presbyterian Church in Canada in 1913	59
Table 4	Metropolitan Statistics of the Presbyterian Church in Canada in 1875 - 1881 - 1891 - 1901 - 1911 - 1913	60
Table 5	Urban Growth in Canada and the Urban Growth of Presbyterianism	62
Table 6	Financial Support for Social Service and Evangelism	167

PREFACE

This book is a study of the Social Gospel among Canadian Presbyterians. It focuses on six leaders who shaped the way in which the Presbyterian Church in Canada responded to social developments in Canada at the turn of the twentieth century. By examining their intellectual roots, theology, institutional and social bases, and strategies, the study seeks to provide a comprehensive look at this particular wing of the Social Gospel in Canada.

My interest in the subject was sparked first by Trevor Wigney, then at the Ontario Institute for Studies in Education. It was furthered by John Webster Grant at Emmanuel College and the late Allan Farris at Knox College. The original draft of the book was written as a doctoral thesis under the direction of Ramsay Cook at York University.

In addition to these teachers, several individuals and institutions have offered help and encouragement. The librarians and archivists at the Presbyterian Church Archives, the United Church Archives, the Ontario Archives, the Public Archives of Canada, the University of Toronto Archives, Caven Library at Knox College, the Toronto Public Library, and the Vancouver School of Theology Library have all been most generous in assisting this research. Parts or all of the manuscript have been read by Richard Allen, Viv Nelles, Clara Thomas, John Moir, Marg Prang, Bob Stewart, Phyllis Airhart, and Robert Handy and I am grateful for their critiques and suggestions. Invaluable editorial advice and guidance came from Tirthankar Bose. Deserving of special gratitude as a mentor, critic, and friend is Keith Clifford. The strengths of this book are due to the community of scholarship these people and others too numerous to name have created. The weaknesses are my responsibility.

This book has been published with the help of a grant from the Canadian Federation for the Humanities, using funds provided by the Social Sciences and Humanities Research Council of Canada. Thanks are due to the Publications Committee of the Canadian Corporation for Studies in Religion for their support. Sandra Woolfrey and the staff of Wilfrid Laurier University Press have been helpful and patient. Gratitude also should be expressed for the encouragement from my colleagues at the Vancouver School of Theology in the final stages of the redrafting of this book and for the financial assistance I received from the Macmillan Fund. None of this would have been possible without the love and support of Joan, to whom this book is dedicated.

INTRODUCTION

Progressive Christians of all denominations, gathered from across Canada in Ottawa for the Social Service Congress in 1914, heard the following poem:

The Ignorant Masses

The Social Uplifters, those eminent sifters
Of merit and poor people's needs,
Went down to the slums to regenerate bums,
And do meritorious deeds.
We washed them, we dressed them,with libraries blessed them,
We prayed with those ignorant mobs,
And the wretches were hateful and vilely ungrateful
And said what they wanted was jobs.

Our noble committee then searched through the city
To find all the fallen and lost;
We learned how they came to be living in shame,
This, mind you, at no little cost.
We swamped them with tracts and statistical facts,
But the creatures were terribly rude.
They acknowledged 'twas nice to be freed from all vice,
But said what they wanted was food.

They're just as God made them, it's useless to aid them,
The brutes do not ask for reform;
Intellectual feasts are all wasted on beasts
Who want to be fed and kept warm.
Let them keep their allotted positions, besotted
And blind, when you bid them advance.
Those ignorant asses, the underworld masses,
Will say all they want is a chance.[1]

The social uplifters in the audience would not have agreed with the negative bias of the poem towards their efforts, but it did capture much of the irony to be found in the thought and work of the progressives on whom the focus of this monograph rests. Convinced that the values and culture of Anglo-Saxon Protestantism were the key to moral and social progress in Canada as it entered the twentieth century, the leaders studied in this volume carried their ideals to the frontiers of the city and Western Canada. Their ideas became the accepted orthodoxy in church colleges and courts by the first decade of the new century. But their efforts to mobilize the church to create a Christian nation met with limited success in the church and much indifference in society at large.

This book examines a particular group of Christian progressives within a particular denomination clustered in a particular region of the country at a particular time in the nation's history. Charles William Gordon, John George Shearer, James Alexander Macdonald, George Campbell Pidgeon, Robert Alexander Falconer, and Thomas Buchanan Kilpatrick were all Presbyterian clergymen who rose to prominence in the Presbyterian Church in Canada in the 1890s and became central figures in articulating and implementing a social Christianity within their denomination. All exercised their ministries in close connection with the metropolitan centre of Canadian Presbyterianism, Toronto. They formed the core leadership of the Board of Social Service and Evangelism which co-ordinated efforts in moral and social reform on a national level between 1907 and 1915, the latter being the year when the pressures of war led to amalgamation with the Board of Home Missions. The group represents what Richard Allen described as the progressive wing of the Social Gospel in Canada,[2] which held together the personal and ethical emphasis of the conservative wing of the movement and the organic social philosophy of the radical wing.

In *The Social Passion*, Allen also argued that the history of the Social Gospel in Canada was best understood from an ecumenical and national perspective. Allen believed that the work the social reformers did in interdenominational coalitions on issues that affected Canada as a whole provided the key to understanding the movement. Such an approach, he was convinced, was a more promising way to understand the movement than an examination of the structures and thought forms of the denominations from which the proponents of social Christianity came.[3] Since Allen's pioneering work appeared in 1972, a variety of studies have appeared that examine phases of the movement in their denominational and regional contexts.[4] Without detracting from Allen's contribution, they are creating a clearer picture of the variety of perspectives that made up the broad coalition of progressive forces that united under the Social Gospel movement. This study is a contribution to that process.

As for the men chosen for this study, the denominational influences that shaped their careers, the institutional bases from which they worked, and the network of colleagues that supported their work can be seen most clearly within the context of Canadian Presbyterianism. It is true that all were fervent supporters of church union and saw their work as part of the broader ecumenical mission of evangelical Protestantism in Canada, but their foundations lay deep within the Free Church Presbyterianism of central Canada.

Chapters 1 and 2 examine the ideas these men espoused. Born in the 1850s and the 1860s, our subjects grew up amid the Victorian crisis of faith. Philip Hefner has argued that the church formulated three reactions to this crisis of authority in the nineteenth century — pietism, dogmatism, and liberalism.[5] Pietism created a war-free zone in the realm of feelings. Dogmatism did the same in the realm of the mind. Liberalism represented the attempt to come to grips with modernity and to restate the essentials of the Christian faith in terms the modern world could understand and accept. Sidney Ahlstrom has identified two schools of liberalism in nineteenth-century theology — a modernist school in which the new social sciences became the point of departure in the reinterpretation of Christianity and an evangelical school which took for its slogan, "Back to Christ."[6] In James Hastings' *A Dictionary of Christ and the Gospels*, W. Morgan pointed out that the Back to Christ school attempted to get behind the Christ of the creeds and the dogmatists to the Christ of history[7] and was itself divided into three distinct wings — a conservative wing which sought continuity with earlier forms of Christianity through revision rather than reconstruction of doctrine, a progressive wing which focused its attention on the religion of Christ rather than a religion about Christ, and a radical wing, associated with the German theologian Albrecht Ritschl, which focused solely on the person and ethical work of Christ.

Richard Allen and Ramsay Cook identified as formative for the Social Gospel in Canada the Ritschlian theology that provided the dominant intellectual framework for the movement in the United States.[8] Presbyterian progressives drew on different theological sources found in Scotland. Our focus on the denominational sources of social Christianity in Canada produces a clearer picture of the specific influences from Great Britain and the United States.[9] The conservative wing of Back to Christ liberalism, represented in Scottish Presbyterianism by A.B. Bruce, George Adam Smith, and Henry Drummond, seemed to the Presbyterian reformers to provide the most effective apologetic to the modern world for the essentials of Christianity; it interpreted the supernatural power of God through the consciousness of the historical

Christ who was, at one and the same time, the Jesus of history and the divine Christ, the Saviour of the world.

Such an evangelical liberalism solved the crisis of faith for our subjects and allowed them to see the advance of Anglo-Saxon Protestantism during the nineteenth century as the providential progress of the Kingdom of God on earth. The recognition of the social significance of the teachings of the Old Testament prophets and of the social conscience of Jesus completed their understanding of the revelation of God's will in the Scriptures and now had to be applied to every field of human existence. Their confidence in the advance of Christendom through the agencies of Anglo-Saxon Protestantism remained unshaken until World War I created a crisis of culture that no adaptation of Christian thought and life to modernity could solve.

Chapter 3 deals with the institutional base and chapter 4 with the social bias from which these Presbyterian progressives worked. By the time the Board of Social Service and Evangelism was established in 1907, the Presbyterian Church in Canada was the largest Protestant denomination in the country and was well on its way to establishing a sizeable bureaucracy, centred in Toronto, to co-ordinate its efforts to Christianize Canadian civilization. As suggested by the bit of doggerel recited at the Social Service Congress, our subjects were all part of the growing urban middle class which enjoyed the fruits of an expanding Canadian economy in the first decade of the twentieth century. Their perspectives and strategies both reflected and shaped that bias.

Unlike the more radical Methodists in Western Canada who have attracted most attention from historians of the Social Gospel in Canada, the Presbyterian progressives who are studied here sought to legitimate and perfect the social culture and system in which they were raised and which they had come to see as the means of their success in life. They welcomed alliances with Canada's business and professional communities, in which new wealth was being generated, and sought reforms that would make the social and economic system work more harmoniously and efficiently. If their moralism was at times passionate and strident in seeking the complete realization of their ideals, it nevertheless did not involve any fundamental critique of the values and institutions that had been the vehicles for the providential progress of Anglo-Saxon civilization throughout the nineteenth century. The key to national righteousness, in their minds, was the assimilation of the poor, the immigrants, and those who engaged in the business of vice into their middle-class Protestant culture.

Chapters 5 and 6 discuss their strategies and examine some of the efforts to implement them in Canada. Our subjects relied heavily on character formation and persuasion as the primary means of bringing about their vision of a righteous nation. It was only as individual consciences were revived and reformed by the evangelical witness of the church that the structures of Canadian society were shaped by the spirit of Christ. Exercising this uplifting influence within an organic society, the church would provide the central moral dynamic for a collective Christian conscience which would guide Canada to assume its destiny as a model for the world.

World War I shattered their vision of providential progress. Our subjects responded in very different ways to a war that did not fit into their scenario of increasing harmony and co-operation among the nations of the world. For some, the vision died. For others, the war was the final time of testing. For all, it marked a watershed in their crusade for a Christian Canada. I have chosen to terminate this study in 1915, the year that the Board of Social Service and Evangelism ceased to exist and a year after Richard Allen's *The Social Passion* picks up the story. Chapter 7 examines the reasons for the Board's merger with the Board of Home Missions and indicates the various ways in which World War I affected these Presbyterian progressives. Their careers continued long after the war, but the cohesiveness of their efforts to create a Christian Canada disappeared after 1915. The reasons for that and the dynamics of their continuing careers are addressed by Allen but also call for further study within the denominational context.

The Presbyterians examined in this monograph, like their Scottish mentors, strove for an ethical Christian community characterized by those vital virtues they felt necessary for the regeneration of the world — a strong work ethic, sobriety, probity, thrift, charity, and duty informed by a democratic Christian conscience. They united evangelical zeal with moderated reason in their attempt to establish a universal consensus on individual morality and social responsibility. Taken together, these qualities of character would reform, in an ascending pattern, the family, the city, the province, the nation and ultimately the world.

It was moral character, on both a personal and a communal level, that would ensure the regeneration of social existence and the continuance of providential progress. Presbyterian progressives were concerned about employment, food, and opportunities for the poor and the immigrants in Canada's cities and on the Western frontiers, but they believed that the elevation of human existence depended on something deeper and more intangible within the person, something they identified as the spirit of the Jesus who embodied a social Christianity.

NOTES

1. S.W. Dean, "The Church and the Slum," *Social Service Congress, Ottawa, 1914* (Toronto: Social Service Council of Canada, 1914), p. 133.

2. Richard Allen, *The Social Passion: Religion and Social Reform in Canada, 1914-1928* (Toronto: University of Toronto Press, 1971), p. 17.

3. *Ibid.*, pp. 16-17.

4. On Methodism, see W.H. Brookes, "The Uniqueness of Western Canadian Methodism, 1840-1925," *The Bulletin* 26 (1977):57-74; N. Semple, "The Impact of Urbanization on the Methodist Church in Central Canada, 1854-1884," (unpublished Ph.D. thesis, Victoria University, 1979); and P.D. Airhart, "The Eclipse of Revivalist Spirituality: the Transformation of Canadian Methodist Piety, 1884-1925" (unpublished Ph.D. thesis, University of Chicago, 1985). On Anglican social Christianity in Canada, see E. Pulker, *We Stand on Their Shoulders: The Growth of Social Concern in Canadian Anglicanism* (Toronto: Anglican Book Centre, 1986). On regional context, most of it Western Canada, see R. Allen, "Salem Bland: The Young Preacher," *The Bulletin* 26 (1977):75-93; R. Allen, "Salem Bland and the Spirituality of the Social Gospel: Winnipeg and the West, 1903-1013," in D.L. Butcher *et al.* (eds.), *Prairie Spirit: Perspectives on the Heritage of the United Church of Canada in the West* (Winnipeg: University of Manitoba Press, 1985), pp. 214-232; B. Smillie, "The Woodsworths: James and J.S. — Father and Son," in Butcher, *Prairie Spirit*, pp. 100-121; R. Cook, "Francis Marion Beynon and the Crisis of Christian Reformism," in C. Berger and R. Cook (eds.), *The West and the Nation: Essays in Honour of W.L. Morton* (Toronto: McClelland and Stewart, 1976), pp. 187-208; R. Allen, "The Social Gospel as the Religion of the Agrarian Revolt," in Berger and Cook, *The West and the Nation*, pp. 174-186; and I.M. Manson, "Serving God and Country: Evangelical Piety and the Presbyterian Church in Manitoba, 1880-1900" (unpublished M.A. thesis, University of Manitoba, 1986).

5. Philip Hefner, "The Real Challenge of the Nineteenth Century," *Dialog* 22, no.1 (Winter 1983):35-41.

6. Sidney Ahlstrom, *A Religious History of the American People* (New Haven: Yale University Press, 1972), pp. 763-784.

7. W. Morgan, "Back to Christ," in James Hastings (ed.), *A Dictionary of Christ and the Gospels* (Edinburgh: T. & T. Clark, 1908), pp. 161-167.

8. Allen, *Social Passion*, pp. 4-8; and Ramsay Cook, *The Regenerators: Social Criticism in Late Victorian English Canada* (Toronto: University of Toronto Press, 1985), pp. 44-46.

9. The question of the trans-Atlantic connections that influenced the Social Gospel is brought into focus by W.R. Hutchinson, "The Americanness of the Social Gospel: An Inquiry in Comparative History," *Church History* 44, no.3 (1975):367-381. Scottish and American links are explored in B. Aspinwall, "The Scottish Religious Identity in the Atlantic World, 1880-1914," in S. Mews (ed.), *Religion and National Identity* (Oxford:

Basil Blackwell, 1982), pp. 505-518. Canadian and American connections in the related area of social work are examined in T.K. Hareven, "An Ambiguous Alliance: Some Aspects of American Influences on Canadian Social Welfare," *Social History/Histoire Sociale* 3 (June 1969): 82-98. Some of the intellectual cross-fertilization is discussed in A.B. McKillop, *A Disciplined Intelligence: Critical Inquiry and Canadian Thought in the Victorian Era* (Chico, California: Scholar's Press, 1984), describes the international connections in a field of seminal importance for the Social Gospel movement among Presbyterians. R.Carwardine, *Transatlantic Revivalism: Popular Evangelism in Britain and America, 1790-1864* (London: Greenwood, 1978) bears examination for the clues it might provide for connections within evangelical Protestantism that influenced the Social Gospel movement. As yet, however, no one has attempted a synthesis of international influences on the Social Gospel in the North Atlantic triangle.

CHAPTER 1

THE INTELLECTUAL ROOTS :

SCOTTISH EVANGELICAL LIBERALISM

Queen's University in Kingston, Ontario, was the institutional base to which social Christianity in Canada has been traced. Of particular importance in studies of leading figures in the movement were the alumni conferences at Queen's where the social issues of the day were discussed in the light of the new philosophical school of Idealism represented by John Watson and George Munro Grant.[1] Both were graduates of the University of Glasgow, where they had studied under John and Edward Caird, leading figures in the intellectual revival of the established Church of Scotland.[2] But Queen's did not represent the Free Church tradition that came to dominate Canadian Presbyterianism following the union of Presbyterian groups across the country in 1875. The liberalization of Free Church theology, with its sources in developments in Scotland, proceeded at a slower pace and was influenced by movements that focused on the Bible and on religious experience as much as on philosophy.[3] It was from the Free Church tradition in Canada that the acknowledged leaders of the institutional and programmatic implementation of social Christianity among Canadian Presbyterians came. The Free Church progressives were not immune to the influence of Watson and Grant, and accepted their contribution to the defence of Christianity in the modern world with enthusiasm, but their institutional roots were in the Free Church colleges — Knox College in Toronto, Presbyterian College in Montreal, and Presbyterian College in Halifax. Professors, visiting lecturers, student conferences, alumni journals, and their denominational press exposed them to a broader and more international network of liberal apologists for the faith which addressed the society emerging in the wake of industrialization and urbanization.

Canada was still an intellectual colony of Scotland in the late nineteenth century, and Presbyterians were certainly no exception.[4] Free Church theology in Canada was a mirror image of Free Church theology in Scotland, taught and preached by Scottish-born, and often Scottish-trained, ministers. P. Carnegie Simpson,[5] himself a Free Church theologian at the turn of the twentieth century, described three sources of liberalization within the Free Church tradition and identified the decade of the 1880s as the crucial turning point in the transition from an evangelical conservatism to an evangelical liberalism. Edward Caird, Scotland's leading Idealist philosopher under whom many of the Free Church's most promising students studied moral philosophy in the 1870s, changed the way people viewed the world; William Robertson Smith, who was removed from his chair in Old Testament studies in the 1880s after a series of heresy trials over Higher Criticism in biblical studies, changed the way people read the Bible; and Dwight L. Moody, the American evangelist who conducted triumphant crusades in Scotland in the 1870s, especially among Scottish college students, changed the way people understood religion. Simpson's classification provides a convenient framework within which to examine the intellectual roots of social Christianity among Canadian Presbyterians.

The underlying motivation of the liberals within the Free Church in Scotland was the defence of the faith in the face of the challenges posed by science and philosophy and the failure of the church to convince more people of the validity of Christianity. One of the most influential of the apologists for this school was A.B. Bruce, Professor of Apologetics and New Testament Exegesis at Free Church College, Glasgow. In his widely used textbook, *Apologetics, or Christianity Defensively Stated* (1892), he set forth both the purpose and the audience of Christian apologetics in the late nineteenth century. Bruce tried to do three things in his book: first, he sought to defend the eternal truth of Christianity as it had been tested by the facts of nature and of human consciousness; second, he presented Christianity as a historical fact to be viewed in its relationship to the general history of religion; finally, he attempted to gain for Christianity a fair hearing in dealing with anti-Christian prejudices. The discipline of Apologetics was intended as an aid to the faith wherever doubts arose and challenges were presented, especially those raised by philosophy and science.[6] Bruce's perception of his audience was broad. It included those with "a sincere sympathy with the good, an implicit rudimentary faith in God, a spiritual receptivity that would readily respond to such teaching as that of Christ, a vague, restless longing for light on the dark problems of life that under proper guidance might ripen into Christian faith."[7] Such audiences might include, Bruce offered, students of theology who were fresh from philosophical study and no longer comfortable with the faith of their childhood and young men in all ranks and professions who were seeking the will to live more moral and socially useful lives. The impact of Bruce's *Apologetics* suggests that the importance of the three movements Simpson saw as the roots of liberal theology among members of the Free Church was proportional to the usefulness of the movements in providing a defence of the faith in the social and intellectual climate of the late nineteenth century.

British Idealism

Moral philosophy was the crown of the Scottish university curriculum. Normally taken in the third and fourth years of the programme, it sought to bring all the knowledge acquired in a person's studies into the proper moral focus for the individual and thus define the social obligations attendant upon enjoying the privileges of higher education. The avowed aim of this structuring of education was to produce an educated class of people capable of exerting responsible moral leadership in society by using their influence to promote strong moral character among their fellow citizens. These views characterized both the Scottish Common Sense school and its successor in the 1870s, British Idealism.[8] Edward Caird's influence spread primarily through his teaching of moral philosophy and his work as a social reformer in Glasgow, both through students who entered the ministry and through those who themselves became professors of moral philosophy and theology. By the 1880s, a new generation of theologians, biblical scholars, and philosophers had passed through the classes of Caird and had their world-view shaped by his Idealism.[9]

Caird's initial awakening to Idealist thought came, not from philosophy, but from poetry and literature, specifically from the writings of Thomas Carlyle. He credited Carlyle with establishing an important connection between the Idealism of German literature and the "religious and moral principles which all in this country — and especially we Scotsmen — had received into ourselves almost with our mother's milk." Carlyle's discovery of the significance of the revival of German literature for the failing faith of men and women resulted in a "Puritanism idealised, made cosmopolitan," and Caird claimed that he had changed "the old banner of the Covenant into a standard for the forward march of mankind toward a better ideal of human life." Carlyle not only revived the essence of faith for readers like Caird, but also pointed them towards a better social philosophy. He did much to banish the eighteenth-century theory which limited the functions of government to "a grand policeman" and to revive the Platonic idea of the state as a social and ethical force in the life of the nation. The most glaring weakness of Carlyle's thought on this subject, according to Caird, was his lack of understanding "of the organic unity or solidarity of human life, or of the creative powers of those social forces which arise, not from individuals taken separately, but from the way in which they act and react upon one another in society."[10] If Carlyle had been a lonely prophet protesting against the materialism and moral shallowness of his age, Caird and his disciples were the priests of a new generation of ministers, educators, politicians, civil servants, and social reformers who were convinced that the principles they learned in their moral philosophy classrooms had to be put into practice if Anglo-Saxon Protestantism and civilization were to survive.

Caird's romantic Idealism was broadened and deepened during two years of study at Oxford under Benjamin Jowett, the leading figure in the nineteenth-century revival of Platonism, and in company with those who were to form the nucleus of the British Idealist school — T.H. Green, F.H. Bradley, R.L. Nettleship, Bernard Bonsanquet, and William Wallace. The seminal intellectual influences on this group were Kant and Hegel. Two editions by Caird of *A Critical Account of the Philosophy of Kant* (1877 and 1889) and his popular introduction to Hegel in the Blackwood series (1883) displayed the extent to which these philosophers shaped Caird's thinking. Hegel, claimed Caird, was the pinnacle of the movement of nineteenth-century thought from subjectivism and pessimism to organicism and reconstruction. Its leading thinkers were those who had not lost their faith in the spiritual powers and destiny of humanity. In this movement Caird found "a way through the modern principles of subjective freedom — the very principle which produced the Reformation of the sixteenth and the Revolution of the eighteenth — to a reconstruction of the intellectual and moral order on which men's life had been based in the past."[11] The whole of human history, intellectual and moral, revealed the unfolding of the ultimate principle of unity.

Philosophy and religion, according to Caird, were the only adequate means of satisfaction for the higher needs of humanity. Philosophy sought to find the principle of unity that underlay all the manifold particular truths of separate sciences and disciplines. Religion was also concerned with the absolute principle of reality, but it was not primarily theoretical. Rather, religion provided the conviction as to the ultimate basis of existence which allowed people to find "an adequate object of affection and a sufficient aim for all practical endeavours."[12] Caird saw philosophy and religion as complementary endeavours, the former providing the theories and the latter the motivation to lead socially responsible lives.

At the centre of Caird's thought lay an immanental view of the relationship between God and the world. Reality was the expression of a rational principle that was God. Everything, in its proper proportion, was a vehicle for the self-expression of the divine, and humanity was the highest and most fitting. By virtue of their self-consciousness, men and women offered the best means for the progressive realization of truth and goodness. Evil arose through an ignorance of the true nature of reality, and as such it was relative.

Through positive corrective action, often educational in nature, evil could be overcome and transformed into good.

Living a moral life was directly linked to awareness of one's relationship to the organic whole from which one has come. Caird argued that all individual consciousness emerged from an organic whole that remained the basis of all life. This organic whole assumed form as the social community, represented historically by the state. The reconstruction of a healthy community required the recognition of the organic relatedness of all persons. Contract theories of society which had emerged from the eighteenth century were too mechanical in their stress on the reciprocal actions of independent individuals. The organic theory of society that Caird was proposing saw each member of society as simultaneously dependent and independent. Primarily a member of the whole, each individual had a unique place and function within the social order. The purpose of society was to provide each individual with the greatest freedom of opportunity to develop his or her capabilities. At the same time, an enlightened view of the common good would evoke devotion to the well-being of the whole society and understanding of the proper place for the talents each citizen possessed. The social philosophy articulated by Caird and his colleagues, sometimes called "the higher individualism" or "collectivist liberalism," sought to offer a middle way between individualism and socialism. The most important implication of this philosophy for political thinkers and actors was the justification it provided for greater state intervention. Law and authority in the social order had the positive task of providing proper conditions for the full development of each individual. The state had the moral responsibility and right to emancipate citizens from those forces that denied human development and to eliminate forms of competition that allowed the strong to exploit the weak. The competitive process was to be regulated in such a way that the rights of individuals and groups would be protected and people would be able to take their proper place in the social organism as instruments of social harmony. In the two essays that Caird published on political and economic topics, he argued that change took place through a slow evolution based upon the essential goodness of human reason. Human nature, characterized by an extraordinary flexibility, could be remoulded by new ideas. Significant social changes, he concluded, "cannot be the creation of a day or a year but only of the slow working of man's new circumstances on his thoughts and of the continuous reaction of his thoughts upon his circumstances."[13]

Edward Caird's work outside the classroom reflected the collectivist liberalism of his social and religious philosophy. He was active in the University Extension Movement and the University Settlement. These ventures sought to provide the moral, intellectual, and spiritual influences their founders thought were lacking in the poorer sections of Glasgow, where traditional family life was weak and adequate educational and church facilities and workers were absent. Caird felt that the life of the poor could not be raised unless they were given "the opportunities of social and intellectual progress and of contact with things that are beautiful," opportunities enjoyed by the middle and upper classes. The heritage of humanity should not be the possession of the few, and those who enjoyed these advantages "should do their best to bridge the gulf that separated the well-to-do from the poor, and foster mutual understanding and goodwill by social intercourse; so that the nation might be one body and its members bound together in one fellowship."[14] What the poor needed most, in Caird's mind, was the moral uplifting provided by the cultural heritage of Western civilization offered by the universities. Equipped with such enlightenment, they would find their place in the social order and contribute to the social harmony of the community.

Caird also spent considerable time working for the improvement of conditions for women and children in industry. Attempts to organize unions among women failed, but more success was achieved in lobbying for legislation to regulate working conditions; the results included investigations of specific sites which were published in the press to arouse public opinion and influence legislators. If disadvantaged groups, such as women, were unable or unwilling to organize to protect themselves, the government had the right and the responsibility to regulate the activities of some of its citizens for the protection of others.

The questions that Caird and his colleagues sought to answer through their social and religious philosophy were those of the educated and the cultured. In the realm of religion, their ideas sought to affirm the rationality of God in the face of growing tendencies towards agnosticism and atheism, immortality in the light of an aggressive naturalism, and the freedom of men and women in the context of a society structured on mechanistic lines and leaning towards determinism. In the realm of social theory and practice, these men sought to give sense and direction to the changes and innovations that had collectivized everyone's life. Their emphasis on evolutionary progress, whereby the good in traditional things was preserved but synthesized with new discoveries and accomplishments, gave to many a sense of continuity and order when the old and the new seemed locked in mortal combat. Finally, the ideal of social harmony opened the way to extensive reforms in education and welfare which were designed to create greater opportunity for those who wished to work within the system and greater protection for those at a disadvantage in it. At the same time, these efforts did not pose a threat to the status and wealth that had become symbols of success for the middle classes. The aims of reform were character formation and social opportunity, elevating and integrating the lower classes into a social order determined by the ideals of the educated and progressive middle classes.

Edward Caird considered Christianity to be the most important movement through which the progressive interaction between thought and environment took place. The Idealist interpretation of Christianity was more fully developed by his older brother John, Professor of Divinity and Principal of the University of Glasgow, and by Edward's foremost student, John Watson, Professor of Mental and Moral Philosophy at Queen's University in Kingston, Ontario. The religious interests of humanity, Watson believed, could be preserved only by a theology that affirmed that all forms of being were manifestations of a single spiritual principle, identification with which the true life of humanity consisted. "Religion," he wrote, "is the spirit which must more and more subdue all things to itself, informing science and art, and realizing itself in the higher organization of the family, the civic community, the state, and ultimately the world, and gradually filling the mind and the heart of every individual with the love of God and the enthusiasm for humanity."[15] The heritage of the whole of Western civilization, according to Watson, was synthesized in the Christian ideal — the Greek ideal of clear thought and love of beauty, the Jewish ideal of righteousness, the Roman ideal of law and order, and the Teutonic ideal of freedom, all harmonized by the divine spirit of love of God and humanity.[16]

In Jesus, the Idealist religious philosophers found the highest form of religious consciousness and morality. Jesus saw with absolute clarity that nature and humanity were identical in their essence with God and grounded his moral teaching in that principle. The authority of Jesus and the faith that flowed from his life and teachings was found, not in the externals of creeds or ecclesiastical structures, but in the consciousness of unity and reconciliation with God and in the enthusiasm for humanity that issued from such awareness. Faith, John Watson suggested, "is the personal side of the whole consciousness of the 'kingdom of heaven', as Jesus understood it: it is the spirit which operates in every member of those who are reconciled with God, and are therefore at unity with themselves and with one another."[17] Watson and his fellow Idealist philosophers of religion saw the vacillation between transcendence and immanence in religious consciousness in the centuries following Christ as the result of the dualistic categories imposed by Greek and Roman philosophy. It was only with Hegel that the spiritual and ethical monism of Jesus was recovered, locating the true principle of life, art, and religion in the idea of a self-manifesting, self-knowing spiritual unity.[18]

A.B. Bruce and other Free Church apologists found important resources for the defence of the Christian faith among the Idealist philosophers and agreed with them that philosophy raised the questions that only theology could answer fully. But Bruce insisted that there was more to the power of Christianity than a few ethical or philosophical ideas. Christianity had its centre in a person, not in a philosophical principle. The ultimate vindication of Christianity, in Bruce's mind, was religious experience, based on a personal encounter with Christ which conveyed the passion in the heart of God for saving lost men and women, rather than an abstract principle. Such cautions about the adequacy of Idealist philosophy as a full expression of Christianity resulted from the emphatic recognition of a biblical grounding of the faith and of the importance of an evangelical experience that complemented the Idealist framework among Free Church thinkers. Higher Criticism, that is, new historical methods of biblical study, within the Scottish context provided the tools for a reinterpretation of the witness of Scripture that recovered the consciousness and the teachings of the psalmists and the prophets and, of ultimate importance, rediscovered the historical Jesus.

Biblical Criticism

Higher Criticism became the most controversial focus for the clash between the old Presbyterianism and the new. The heresy trials of William Robertson Smith, A.B. Bruce, and Marcus Dods in Scotland, of Charles Briggs and Henry Preserved Smith in the United States, and of John Campbell in Canada all centred on their interpretation of Scripture and the methodology they used to reach their conclusions.[19] Higher Criticism was the critical study of a text in Scripture in its original historical setting, as distinct from Lower Criticism, which endeavoured to arrive at the original text. It had its modern origins in the rationalist environment of German universities in the eighteenth century, where biblical scholars tried to establish a pure science of biblical research which would yield impartial, objective answers to the questions posed by repetitions, discrepancies, and contradictions in the canonical arrangement of the Scriptures. They developed an historical-critical method of research that used scientific methodology to analyse historical and literary sources. In the atmosphere of free inquiry provided by the loose ties between the German churches and the universities, many German scholars followed their conclusions to the point of abandoning belief; they were unable to reconcile their critical understanding of the Bible with the Christian orthodoxy of their day.[20] In other parts of the world, therefore, the new critical methods arrived with the reputation of destroying the faith. J. D. Smart has noted, however, that the environment within which the new methods took root had much to do with the conclusions reached by scholars and the reception they received.[21] The Scottish scholars within the Free Church grew up in the atmosphere of evangelicalism, especially under the influence of the local revivals of 1858 and

Moody's campaigns in the early 1870s. Their evangelical piety shaped their defence of the faith and led them to find in Higher Criticism a powerful method for reconstructing Christianity to appeal to a questioning and critical age.

George Adam Smith was representative of the combination of evangelical piety and liberal scholarship that gained Free Church biblical critics a sympathetic ear among many Scottish and Canadian Presbyterians. He had studied under Edward Caird at Glasgow and A.B. Davidson at New College, Edinburgh, and became a colleague of A.B. Bruce on the faculty of Free Church College, Glasgow.[22] Smith's clearest defence of the critical methods and their beneficial results came in 1901 with the publication of *Modern Criticism and the Preaching of the Old Testament.* Criticism, he argued, was an important means of bringing the Bible to life by helping people discover its essential quality of faith. The critical conclusions that had changed people's understanding of the history, order, and composition of the Bible had also unveiled its humanism and its faithfulness in recording the development of Israel's experience and perception of God. The Old Testament was now seen to be the record of progressive revelation from primitive beliefs to ethical monotheism, best seen in the Psalms and the Prophets. Critical study had confirmed that the Bible was written with a religious purpose and that its writers were faithful to their experiences of God and the human heart. As seen through critical eyes, the Scriptures spoke of the reality of God much more convincingly to a generation raised on science than did the doctrines of orthodoxy. While the latter called for mere assent, the former, according to Smith, led to genuine religious commitment. Modern criticism of the Bible made it a much more effective instrument for accomplishing the evangelical task of winning the minds and the hearts of the nation for Christ.[23]

The impact of Smith's book was both immediate and lasting. The degree of acceptance that Smith's views had won within the Free Church by 1901 was indicated by the soundness with which a conservative attempt to have him tried for heresy was defeated in the Free Church General Assembly of 1902. The motion to dismiss the charge carried 534 to 263.[24] Smith's ideas became part of the accepted orthodoxy within the church, and thus an active component of Presbyterian liberalism in Canada.

Just as John Watson carried the thought of Edward Caird to Canadian shores, so John Edgar McFadyen disseminated the attitudes and teachings of his mentor, G.A. Smith. Higher critical scholarship had been introduced earlier to Canadian Presbyterians in the person of J.F. McCurdy, a Presbyterian who taught at University College, Toronto, and published frequently in the Canadian Presbyterian press.[25] But McFadyen was the first prominent Scottish scholar to teach the newer views in a theological college. He had studied under Caird at Glasgow, then at Oxford. He took theology at Free Church College,

Glasgow, under Smith, Bruce, and other evangelical liberals on the Glasgow faculty. A semester was spent in Marburg, and in 1898 he came to Knox College in Toronto as Professor of Old Testament Languages and Literature.[26]

McFadyen's appointment did cause some concern among Toronto Presbyterians,[27] but his inaugural lecture sought to assure them that he believed that biblical criticism strengthened rather than threatened the Christian faith. Sound criticism did not seek, nor could it, to deprive Christians of the substance of revelation. Criticism was a means subordinated to moral and religious ends. The end of the rigorous scientific reconstruction of the historical context and sequence of the Scriptures was the increase of Christian faith.[28] "The specific object of Biblical criticism," McFadyen wrote later in *Old Testament Criticism and the Christian Church*, "is to put us in possession of the mind and spirit of the men who wrote the Bible, to help us to understand the history in which they took part, and which they and their books helped to mould, and to make plain the divine purpose which unfolded itself in their history."[29] McFadyen's emphasis on a biblical faith open to and enhanced by modern thought expressed the apologetic intention of Free Church scholars. The sections of the Bible that attracted most of his attention — the Psalms and the Prophets — revealed to McFadyen the ideas of men who felt that the best way to influence the life of the nation was to shape the minds of its people with the religious and moral principles of ethical monotheism. McFadyen justified his interest in the Old Testament by saying that everything that was deepest and dearest in the New Testament found its historical preparation in the Old. The Psalms and the Prophets were especially important because they represented the highest spiritual development of the faith of Israel, that which prepared the way for the coming of Christ. McFadyen's treatment of the Psalms showed his affinity with the evangelicalism of the Scottish revivals and his interpretation of the religion of the prophets disclosed the extent to which his reading of their writings was shaped by the social philosophy of the British Idealists.

The Psalms, McFadyen claimed, taught people "to enter into the sanctuary of our hearts and commune with God as a friend."[30] He always introduced his junior classes to Old Testament criticism by studying the Psalter. In *An Introduction to the Old Testament,* written in 1905 as a popular introduction to the constructive results of biblical criticism, he argued that the piety of the Old Testament as expressed in the Psalms was austere in its spiritual tone, simple in its passion for God, and bracing in its sense of fellowship with the eternal. For McFadyen, the men who wrote the Psalter exemplified a liberal evangelical spirit. They emphasized the centrality of their relationship with God and

> counted God their Friend; and although they never forgot that He was the infinite One, whose home is the universe and who fills the vast spaces of history with His faithfulness and His justice, He was also to them the patient and loving One, who preserves both man and beast, under the shadow of whose wings the children of men may rest with quiet and confidence, and before whom they could pour out the deepest thoughts and petitions of their hearts, in the assurance that He was the hearer of prayer, and that His tender mercies were over all His works.[31]

The social vision that emerged from such piety was, McFadyen thought, best seen in the writings of the prophets.

The prophets were equally important to William Robertson Smith, who wrote about his views in an article in the *Encyclopedia Britannica* that led to his first heresy trial, found in the prophets the culmination of the historical evolution of Israel's religious consciousness. They were the key leaders in the development whereby the religious ordinances and beliefs of the old covenant were transformed from a crude and imperfect form to a more mature expression of the spirit and purpose of God. Through spiritual intuition, they apprehended the essence of religious truth and remoulded religious doctrines and institutions to conform to that truth.[32] George Adam Smith credited the interest of Robertson Smith and A.B. Davidson in the prophets with the revival of ethical preaching from the Old Testament, which he found among late nineteenth-century preachers. As leaders of the revival of religion among the Israelite people, the prophets presented a clear analysis of the social conditions of their day and directed their ethical teachings at those who abused the resources of the nation for their selfish ends. Their chief contribution to social ethics, according to George Adam Smith, was the concept of righteous patriotism. Faith in the essential sacredness of their national history was combined with a consciousness of past failures and present opportunities.[33] Ready parallels were found by these biblical scholars between the divine mission and destiny of Israel in the prophetic age and the responsibilities of the Scottish race at the end of the nineteenth century.[34]

McFadyen actually went so far as to claim that the prophets stood closer to modern needs, and therefore closer to modern preachers, than the apostles because they expected to have some practical effect on the politics of their age. The conservation of national morality and the possibilities of redemption through the action of a people called by God to provide the nation with moral and spiritual leadership gave a sense of mission and urgency to the message of the evangelical liberal biblical scholars. They found in modern civilization the same ills they discovered in the society that had produced the prophets. In the fiery rebukes and the burning words that the prophets hurled

> at the carelessness and licentiousness of society, at the heartless ceremonialism of priests and people in their worship of God, at the polished selfishness and cruel luxury of the rich, we might almost fancy we hear the voice of a nineteenth-century preacher whose heart was aflame with love to God and people.[35]

Scottish evangelical liberals, with the aid of biblical scholars who reconstructed the historical context of the prophets, found in the writers of the prophetic books kindred spirits whose concerns were the same as theirs: moral laxity among public officials and the populace; dogmatic and formal religion that did not touch the minds and hearts of people in a practical and social way; and individualistic economics and politics that destroyed the harmony and co-operation that should characterize an organic society. Further, the solutions that the prophets offered — dedicated moral leadership in the reform of social and religious institutions in the nation, and increased practical knowledge of and commitment to love for God and others — coincided with the perceptions held by these Christian apologists in the fifty years before World War I.

Urban Revivalism

George Adam Smith admitted that he was unable to convince Dwight L. Moody that Higher Criticism was a proper and constructive approach to the study of the Scriptures.[36] But Moody did acknowledge that it was content rather than authorship that mattered most in communicating the gospel. That was enough to allow Smith to advocate the use of critical methods to see how the message of the Scriptures arose from real life, addressed living people, and spoke to the essential problems of human society at the same time that he worked with Moody's organization in Scotland.

In 1873 Moody, a relatively unknown Chicago evangelist, was invited to conduct a series of crusades in Great Britain. Accompanied by his musical director, Ira Sankey, he spent two years in England and Scotland, returning to the United States in 1875 with a rapidly growing reputation as one of the great popular evangelists of the century. Moody became the best organized and most influential evangelist of his age. By the time of his death in 1899, he had built an efficient and extensive organization which supervised crusades, ran schools and conference centres, published periodicals, pamphlets, and Sunday School materials, and co-operated with an international network of voluntary Christian organizations serving people from cradle to grave.[37] Moody's message was an elementary one of forgiveness and love from God in Jesus Christ, with an emphasis on the practical morality of the Christian faith as an everyday discipline. It was, as one American religious historian concluded, "a simple and relatively innocuous blend of American optimism and evangelical Arminianism" that provided many Christians from pietistic and traditional rural backgrounds with a sense of continuity and security in the midst of urban and industrial conditions.[38]

Between November of 1873 and March of 1874, Moody and Sankey toured Scotland, where their crusades generated an enthusiastic response from all corners and at every level of Presbyterianism. Their stress on experiential religion, a loving God, the moral and spiritual essence of the gospel, and the unity of all Christians struck a responsive chord among the Scots who had been divided so long by academic theologies and schismatic church courts.[39] Attempting to explain Moody's appeal in Scotland to his generation, George Adam Smith claimed that his preaching won the hearts of the Scots because of its loyalty to the Bible and its expository character. Further, the centrality of biblical instruction in small classes appealed to Smith. And finally, the practical spirit of Moody's preaching offered a religion that was related to the actual life of people. "His gospel," Smith wrote,

> which had its centre in the Atonement, was the gospel of an Incarnate Saviour: no mere voice, but hands and feet with heart and brains behind to cleanse the cities of their foulness, organize the helpless and the neglected, succor the fallen and gather the friendless into families. . . . there was no preacher more civic or more practical among us.[40]

Moody was an apologist for the common person. He proclaimed the gospel with intellectual simplicity, emotional passion, and ethical clarity. His campaign during the early 1870s had a special appeal to a younger generation of college students who found their own needs for spiritual roots nourished by Moody's approach. At the same time, they discovered an experiential and practical faith which might shape the minds and hearts of a nation destined by God to make a significant contribution to the Christianization of civilization.

Outstanding among this generation of students influenced by Moody's evangelism was Henry Drummond, a student of theology at New College, Edinburgh, when he first encountered Moody and later Professor of Natural Science at Free Church College, Glasgow.[41] Drummond's most influential contribution was his apologetic writings in response to Darwin's theory of evolution, in which Drummond posited an ascent of humanity based on the evolutionary principle of self-sacrificing love rather than a descent of humanity from lesser species through a random process of the survival of the fittest. In addition, published versions of his evangelical addresses, which focused on the love of God in Christ and the way in which nature mirrored this benevolent power, were popular throughout the Anglo-Saxon Protestant world.[42]

"The one great need in our Christian life," wrote Moody, "is love, more love to God and to each other." That message, in a multitude of forms, was at the heart of the evangelical revivals of the nineteenth century. The seeds of such a faith had been sown in Scotland in the early part of the nineteenth century in the writings of Thomas Erskine and John McLeod Campbell, but they had fallen on the rocky soil of dogmatic conservatism within the Free Church. They lay dormant until the revivals of the late 1850s and Moody's visit in the 1870s.[43] Few tracts on the theme of evangelical love were more widely distributed than Henry Drummond's *The Greatest Thing in the World.* Its origins are obscure, but it was reputed to have been delivered as an exposition on I Corinthians 13 to guests of Lord and Lady Aberdeen in 1884.[44] The tract was originally published by the Moody organization as a Christmas pamphlet, but soon appeared in several editions and languages, with a circulation in the hundreds of thousands. In format it exemplified the expository preaching favoured by Scottish evangelical liberals, and in content it presented the heart of the gospel applied to the practical concerns of life.

Faith, Drummond insisted, was a natural part of human life. The business of the Christian life was to apply the elements of love — patience, kindness, generosity, humility, courtesy, unselfishness, good temper, guilelessness, and sincerity — to the needs and problems of everyday life. Love developed through practice. Using images from the natural sciences that characterized his writings, Drummond argued that the soul developed according to the same laws as the body and the mind.

> If a man does not exercise his arm, he gets no biceps muscles; and if a man does not exercise his soul, he has no muscle in his soul — no strength of character, no robustness. Love...is a robust, strong, manly, vigorous expression of the whole character and nature in its fullest development.[45]

His version of muscular Christianity was aimed at the young men and college students with whom he did most of his evangelistic work. It was intended to shape the characters of these men who would become leaders in a society that sought to spread the evangelical liberal religion and reform throughout the world.

Character formation was a key factor in the evangelical strategy to Christianize civilization, and Jesus exemplified the perfect character. He was the source and the model for all the virile qualities of love that would reshape the social order of the nation and the relations within the world community. The personal influence of a person who had been shaped by the example of Christ was the most powerful force Drummond could imagine in the church's mission to reform the world according to the moral and spiritual laws revealed in the Scriptures and found in nature. Again drawing the parallel between the natural and the spiritual laws that governed the universe, Drummond wrote:

> You put a piece of iron in the mere presence of an electrified body, and that piece of iron for a time becomes electrified. It becomes a temporary magnet in the presence of a permanent magnet, and as long as you leave the two side by side, they are both magnets. Remain side by side with Him who loved us, and gave Himself for us, and you too will become a permanent magnet — a permanent attractive force; and like Him you will draw all men unto you.[46]

Religion did not come to people by chance or mystery, according to Drummond. Rather, it came by natural law and by supernatural law, for both were identical since they originated with God. Drummond's apologetic was grounded in the conviction that natural and spiritual laws came from the same source and followed the same principle. In 1883, this view was expounded in a book that made Drummond's name a household word throughout the Anglo-Saxon Protestant world. *Natural Law in the Spiritual World* sold 34,000 copies by the end of 1884 and an estimated 130,000 were in print by the end of the century.

In *Natural Law in the Spiritual World,* Drummond dealt with a topic that not only had interested many people but had brought large numbers of the educated classes raised on traditional religion to a crisis of faith which led to a rejection of Christianity. His main thesis was simple: physical law continues to apply within the spiritual realm of human existence and both realms are governed by the benevolence of God. Whatever the experts on either side of the Victorian battle between science and religion thought of Drummond's apologetic for religion in terms of natural science — and few were satisfied[47] — his effort to expound, defend, and enforce the deepest human religious experiences on the basis of the dominant scientific methods and ideas of the age was welcomed by many. For traditional Christians, the most threatening of the scientific theories to emerge in the nineteenth century was evolution.[48] Drummond welcomed it and argued that the development theory in natural science had given theology a vastly more reasonable body of truth about God and humanity and sin and salvation than it had had before. Further, evolution provided Christianity with a new and improved understanding of the Bible. "The new Bible," he wrote in a paper on the contribution science had made to Christianity,

> is a book whose parts, though not of unequal value, are seen to be of different kinds of value; where the casual is distinguished from the essential, the local from the universal, the subordinate from the primal end....It is not an even plane of proof text without proportion or emphasis, or light and

> shade; but a revelation varied in its nature, with the Divine in its hidden parts, in its spirit, its tendencies, its obscurities, and its omissions. Like nature, it has successive strata, and valley and hilltop, and mist and atmosphere, and rivers which are flowing still, and here and there a place which is desert, and fossils too, whose crude forms are stepping-stones to higher things.

In all, Drummond argued, the Scriptures offered "an ascending series of inspired facts in a matrix of human history."[49] The idea of religious truths growing through a natural process to reveal a higher expression of the essential and universal truths of religion made Drummond a welcome member of that company of Free Church apologists who found the same basic thrusts in the religious philosophy of the Idealists and the biblical theology of the higher critics.

In his other major work, *The Ascent of Man* (1894), Drummond sought to define the guiding law of evolution that expressed itself in all life, both natural and spiritual. The central thesis of the book was a response to the popularizers of Darwin's theory of the struggle for life and the survival of the fittest. Drummond countered that this law, valid though it was, was not the primary agent in the progress of evolution, especially in relation to human development. The law of the struggle for the life of others was equally important, especially in the higher human and social stages of evolution.[50] The supreme law of evolution was altruism or love and the most important event in the process of evolution was the emergence of motherhood, the highest symbol of the self-giving love necessary for the survival of others. Drummond brought the whole weight of natural science and evolutionary theory to bear in support of the traditional structures and values of evangelical Protestant Victorian family life, especially with respect to the role of women as mothers and moral guardians. Further, he placed the evangelical gospel of love at the very heart of the natural world. Although Drummond did not trace his theory in detail beyond the emergence of family life in the evolutionary saga, he promised a second volume that would follow the ascent of humanity through its higher potential in social organization.[51] His death in 1897, at the early age of forty-five, prevented the completion of this project.

Drummond presented an apologetic for Christianity that centred on a social, as well as a personal, ideal of love, service, sympathy, sacrifice, co-operation, and world community. He highlighted the rationality of faith; the ability of men and women to shape their social environment, each in his or her appointed ways; the inevitability of evolutionary moral progress if Christian leaders accepted their responsibilities in the new social order emerging with urbanization and industrialization; and reforms designed to create opportunities for self-help and upward mobility for the lower classes and the disadvantaged.

Whatever effect his evangelism had on the lower classes and the urban population of Scotland, it did provide moral and religious fervour to a generation of university and theological students on both sides of the Atlantic who sought to preserve the essentials of an evangelical Protestantism in the midst of social and intellectual change. Drummond's blend of the world-view of the Idealist philosophers, the critical perspective of the biblical scholars, and the religious enthusiasm of the revivalists offered to the educated in search of a modern Christianity a comprehensive and convincing defence of the faith.

* * * * *

The intellectual framework described in this chapter formed the front-line defence for the garrison mentality found among Presbyterians in Canada from the 1890s until the 1920s. These three movements — Idealist philosophy, Higher Criticism, and Moody's revivalism — provided a guiding light to evangelical Protestants at a time of social and religious ferment and transition. The men who assumed leadership within Canadian Presbyterianism at the turn of the century were dedicated to preserving their version of a Christian civilization in central Canada and to extending it across the country as Canada assumed the responsibilities of nationhood. The Free Church spirit had come to dominate the Presbyterian Church in Canada in the years following 1875 and the apologetic articulated by a new generation of Free Church scholars in Scotland in the 1880s exerted a powerful attraction on theological students who would rise to positions of national prominence by 1900.

NOTES

1. McKillop, *Disciplined Intelligence*, pp. 217-224.

2. On the significance of the Cairds within the Kirk, see A.L. Drummond and J. Bulloch, *The Church in Late Victorian Scotland* (Edinburgh: St. Andrew Press, 1978), pp. 235-258.

3. *Ibid.*, pp. 257-271.

4. John Irving, "The Development of Philosophy in Central Canada from 1850 to 1900," *Canadian Historical Review* 31, no.3 (1950): 252-287. See also D.C. Master, "The Rise of Liberalism in Canadian Protestant Churches," *Canadian Catholic Historical Association Study Sessions, 1969*, p. 409.

5. P.C. Simpson, *The Life of Principal Rainy, Vol. I* (London: Hodder and Stoughton, 1909), p. 409.

6. A.B. Bruce, *Apologetics, or Christianity Defensively Stated* (Edinburgh: T. & T. Clark, 1982), pp. 35-37.

7. *Ibid.*, pp. 38-39.

8. The social impact of Common Sense moral philosophy was felt on both sides of the Atlantic. For Scotland, see G.E. Davis, *The Democratic Intellect* (Edinburgh: Edinburgh University Press, 1961); for the United States, see D.H. Meyer, *The Instructed Conscience: The Shaping of the American National Ethic* (Philadelphia: University of Pennsylvania Press, 1972); and for Canada, see McKillop, *Disciplined Intelligence*.

9. For a partial list of those influenced by Caird, see H. Jones and J.H. Muirhead, *The Life and Philosophy of Edward Caird* (Glasgow: Maclehose, Jackson, 1912). For the reform movements in which he was involved, see C. Harvie, *The Lights of Liberalism: University Liberals and the Challenge of Democracy, 1860-86* (London: Allen Lane, 1976).

10. E. Caird, "The Genius of Carlyle," in *Essays on Literature* (Glasgow: James Maclehose and Sons, 1909), pp. 221-249.

11. E. Caird, *Hegel* (Edinburgh: W. Blackwood and Sons, 1892), pp. 1-3.

12. E. Caird, *The Social Philosophy and Religion of Comte* (Glasgow: James Maclehose and Sons, 1893), p. 99.

13. Quoted in Jones and Muirhead, *Caird*, p. 330.

14. Quoted in Jones and Muirhead, *Caird*, p. 330.

15. J. Watson, *The Interpretation of Religious Experience, Vol. II* (Glasgow: James Maclehose and Sons, 1912), pp. 327-328.

16. J. Watson, *Christianity and Idealism* (New York: Macmillan, 1897), p. 216.

17. For Watson's views on Jesus, see *Ibid.*, pp. 60-109.

18. Watson, *Religious Experience, Vol. II*, pp. 318-326.

19. On the Scottish trials, see Drummond and Bulloch, *Late Victorian Scotland*, pp. 40-78 and 264-270. On the American trials, see L.A. Loetscher, *The Broadening Church* (Philadelphia: University of Pennsylvania Press, 1954), pp. 18-29; and W.R. Hutchinson, *The Modernist Impulse in American Protestantism* (Cambridge: Harvard University Press, 1976), pp. 91-94.

20. On German biblical criticism, see H.F. Hahn, *The Old Testament in Modern Research* (Philadelphia: Muhlenberg Press, 1954); E.G.H. Kraeling, *The Old Testament Since the Reformation* (London: Lutterworth, 1955); and J. Rogerson, *Old Testament Criticism in the Nineteenth Century: England and Germany* (Philadelphia: Fortress Press, 1985).

21. J.D. Smart, *The Interpretation of Scripture* (Philadelphia: Westminster Press, 1961), p. 242.

22. On Smith, see L.A. Smith, *George Adam Smith* (London: Hodder and Stoughton, 1943).

23. G.A. Smith, *Modern Criticism and the Preaching of the Old Testament* (London: Hodder and Stoughton, 1901).

24. R.A. Riesan, "Higher Criticism in the Free Church Fathers," *Records of the Scottish Church History Society*, 20 (1980), pp. 119-142.

25. On McCurdy's central role in introducing Higher Criticism into Canada, see Moir, *Sense of Proportion*.

26. J. Maclaughlin, "McFadyen, John Edgar," *Dictionary of National Biography (1931-1940)*, p. 572; and D. Lamont, "John Edgar McFadyen, 1870-1933," *The Expository Times*, March 1934, pp. 261-264.

27. *The Westminister* (Toronto), May 21, 1898; June 11, 1898; July 9, 1898; and Aug. 27, 1898. McFadyen's appointment was made by the college after the General Assembly had been unable to find a suitable replacement for G.L. Robinson, who went to McCormick Seminary in Chicago. One can only speculate as to whether the choice would have been challenged on the floor of Assembly.

28. *The Westminster* (Toronto), Oct. 8, 1898.

29. J.E. McFadyen, *Old Testament Criticism and the Christian Church* (London: Hodder and Stoughton, 1903), p. 94.

30. *The Westminster* (Toronto), Oct. 8, 1898.

31. J.E. McFadyen, *An Introduction to the Old Testament* (London: Hodder and Stoughton, 1905), pp. 238-255.

32. J.S. Black and G. Chrystal, *The Life of William Robertson Smith* (London: Adam and Charles Black, 1912), pp. 183-185.

33. G.A. Smith, *Modern Criticism*, pp. 217-281.

34. The centrality of a moral nationalism for Scottish identity in the late nineteenth century is discussed in Aspinwall, "Scottish Religious Identity," pp. 505-518.

35. *The Westminster* (Toronto), Oct. 8, 1898.

36. G.A. Smith, *Modern Criticism*, p. 217.

37. On Moody, see J.F. Findlay, Jr., *Dwight L. Moody: American Evangelist, 1837-1899* (Chicago: University of Chicago Press, 1969).

38. Ahlstrom, *Religious History*, p. 745.

39. Findlay, *Moody*, pp. 153-163.

40. G.A. Smith, *The Life of Henry Drummond* (London: Hodder and Stoughton, 1899), pp. 57-58.

41. On Moody's impact on Drummond, see *Ibid.*, pp. 93-100.

42. See, for example, Henry Drummond, *The Ideal Life* (London: Hodder and Stoughton, 1898); and *The New Evangelism* (London: Hodder and Stoughton, 1899).

43. On Erskine, see J.B. Logan, "Thomas Erskine of Linlathen: Lay Theologian of the 'Inner Light'," *Scottish Journal of Theology*, 37, no.1 (1984):23-40; and S. Gowler, "No Second-hand Religion: Thomas Erskine's Critique of Religious Authorities," *Church History* 54, no.2 (June 1985):202-214. On Campbell, see J.B. Torrance, "The Contribution of McLeod Campbell to Scottish Theology," *Scottish Journal of Theology* 26, no.3 (1973):295-311.

44. Lord and Lady Aberdeen, *We Twa, Vol. I* (London: Collins, 1925), p. 205.

45. H. Drummond, "Love: The Supreme Gift: The Greatest Thing in the World," in *Addresses* (Chicago: Fleming H. Revell, 1891), p. 36.

46. *Ibid.*, p. 39.

47. Smith, *Drummond*, pp. 212-214.

48. On the impact of evolution on Christian thought, see B.M.G. Reardon, *From Coleridge to Gore: A Century of Religious Thought in Britain* (London: Longman, 1971), pp. 285-302; G. Himmelfarb, *Darwin and the Darwinian Revolution* (New Your: Norton, 1962); and W. Irving, *Apes, Angels, and Victorians: Darwin, Huxley and Evolution* (New York: McGraw-Hill, 1955).

49. Drummond, "The Contribution of Science to Christianity," in *The New Evangelism*, pp. 183-184.

50. H. Drummond, *The Ascent of Man* (London: Hodder and Stoughton, 1894), pp. 16-17.

51. *Ibid.*, pp. vii-viii.

CHAPTER 2

THE THEOLOGY: EVANGELICAL LIBERALISM

In *A Disciplined Intelligence*, A.B. McKillop drew attention to the close connection between the spirit of Queen's University in Kingston and the Social Gospel in Canada. An exception to this generally tenable observation is the group of Presbyterian clergymen we are considering here, for none of them studied at that institution. They came from widely scattered locations and studied at different schools, universities, and theological colleges. But whether in Canada (as was the case for J.G. Shearer, C.W. Gordon, J.A. Macdonald, and George Pidgeon) or in Scotland (as was the case for R.A. Falconer and T.B. Kilpatrick), all received their formative education in high schools that stressed classical studies in Greek and Latin, at universities where Idealism had replaced Common Sense as the integrating philosophical framework, and in theological colleges where evangelical liberalism was making its impact felt. In addition, the Scottish influence was significant: Canadian Presbyterians were keen observers of the religious scene in Scotland through family ties and the religious press. Not only in their educational institutions, but also in their homes and congregations, this new generation of leaders became convinced of the soundness of the apologetic for their religious and social values provided by Scottish evangelical liberalism.

Educating Six Progressives

Shearer, Macdonald, and Gordon had the most in common in background and education. All were raised in western Ontario within the tradition of Free Church Presbyterianism which was closely allied with the political liberalism of one of its most prominent laymen, George Brown, proprietor of the powerful Toronto *Globe* and its publishing empire.[1] Shearer was born into one of the pioneer families of the region in 1859 and raised on Sprucedale Farm near Bright, Ontario. He began his higher education at the Brantford Collegiate Institute. Macdonald was born in 1862, grew up on a farm in Middlesex County, and attended Hamilton Collegiate Institute. Although Gordon was born in Glengarry County of eastern Ontario, an area made famous in his Ralph Connor novels, he moved with his family to Zorra in 1870 at the age of ten.[2]

Western Ontario was directly affected during the early nineteenth century by the revivals of the Second Great Awakening in the United States, especially through Methodist and Baptist groups.[3] Presbyterian leaders were suspicious of, if not antagonistic toward, the theology and methods of the early frontier revivalists. The vehemence of their protests, however, suggested that the awakenings had considerable appeal among Presbyterians in western Ontario. By the 1860s Methodists and Baptist groups had modified their revivalism as they became concerned with social respectability and stability, while the Free Church split among Presbyterians had heightened the importance of evangelical experience among the majority of Presbyterians west of Toronto.[4] Several revivals were experienced within the Free Church of Scotland during the 1840s and 1850s, which were followed with considerable interest among Canadian Presbyterians.[5] This gradual acceptance on the part of Presbyterians of a moderate form of revivalism was reinforced by the detail with which Dwight L. Moody's Scottish campaign in the early 1870s was reported in the Canadian Presbyterian press. Western Ontario also proved to be a centre of missionary enthusiasm, providing more missionaries for the home and foreign fields of the Presbyterian Church in Canada than any other region of the country.[6] Shearer, Macdonald, and Gordon came, then, from a region of Ontario where evangelical enthusiasm was an important element of their Presbyterianism.

There is no evidence that this trio met before they attended the University of Toronto and Knox College in the 1880s, but during that decade a lasting bond was formed among the three. The intellectual tone of University College, where Free Church students took their arts courses, was set by George Paxton Young, Professor of Metaphysics and Ethics since 1871. What has been written of Young has focused on his career as a teacher of philosophy and superintendent of education, but it is also important to remember that he remained an ordained Presbyterian minister active in the courts of the church until 1877 when he withdrew, probably as a result of the Macdonnell heresy trial.[7] Young came to Canada in 1847 with the first wave of Free Church ministers who followed Robert Burns to serve the new congregations in the colonies. After a brief pastorate in Hamilton, he came to teach at Knox College, spent four years as provincial inspector of grammar schools under

Egerton Ryerson, and returned to teach at University College in 1871. Some indication of the continued respect for Young and his views following his departure from Knox College in 1864, the date commonly given for his demission as a minister, was the invitation to become Principal and Professor of Theology at the new Free Church seminary in Montreal in 1868.[8] By the time Shearer, Gordon, and Macdonald studied under Young, his ethical teaching was firmly grounded in the British Idealism of T.H. Green, whose *Prolegomena to Ethics* (1882) reportedly led Young to abandon any plans he had to publish in the field.[9] Shearer graduated with a first-class honours degree in mental and moral philosophy and civic polity, gained largely under Young's influence.

Another source of Idealist influence at University College in the 1880s was Maurice Hutton in the Classics department. Hutton had studied under Benjamin Jowett at Oxford, and his social philosophy was a synthesis of Platonism and Christian beliefs. Within the framework of his Idealism, true democracy was thought to prevail when, through equality of opportunity, individuals with character and talent rose to positions of social leadership and regulated society on the basis of Christian morality.[10]

William Caven, Principal and Professor of Biblical Studies at Knox College at the time the trio studied theology, had not moved as far from the old philosophical and theological moorings as George Paxton Young, but neither was he as entrenched in the rational orthodoxy of the Princeton theology as his colleague in systematic theology, William MacLaren.[11] Caven's own roots were in western Ontario, where his father had been a teacher and where he had studied with William Proudfoot at the United Secessionist Divinity Hall in London, Ontario. His theology was conservative, but open to the progressive advance of knowledge. A balanced Christian mind, he wrote in 1891, was "conservative of everything good which comes down to us, while it seeks by careful investigation to enlarge the boundaries of ascertained truth and to purge away errors and mistakes."[12] What impressed Macdonald most about Caven, however, was his social and political activism within the Liberal Party, which was based on "the fundamental principles which lay at the very heart of national greatness and upon which a country's enduring institutions must be based."[13] In his teaching, as Macdonald remembered it, Caven presented a liberal social stance justified from Scripture and presented as essential to the moral rectitude of the community.

Upon graduation from Knox in the late 1880s, Shearer went to serve a congregation in Caledonia, Ontario, while Gordon and Macdonald left for a year of study and travel in Scotland and on the Continent. Gordon's account of this period in his autobiography paid tribute to the influence of a long list of leading figures in the evangelical liberal movement in Scotland, including Henry Drummond, George Adam Smith, A.B. Davidson, and Marcus Dods.[14]

Soon after Gordon and Macdonald returned to Canada in 1889, another Canadian arrived in Edinburgh to continue his studies. Robert Falconer, the son of a Trinidad missionary, was born in 1867 in the Maritimes where the connections between the Free Church and political liberalism were as strong as in western Ontario and the impact of American revivalism as great.[15] Following a high school education at Queen's Royal College in Trinidad, Falconer won a scholarship to attend London University, from which he graduated with an Honours B. A. in classics and philosophy in 1888. In Edinburgh, he received an M. A. in classics before taking three years of theology at New College from the leading Scottish liberal apologists. Biblical studies attracted Falconer as a field of specialization and a post-graduate tour took him to Berlin, Marburg, and Leipzig. The major figure in biblical studies at Leipzig was Franz Delitzsch, "a conservative higher critic who set the tone for biblical studies for most Canadian scholars and for most Canadian Presbyterians."[16] Falconer returned to Canada in 1892 as lecturer, then Professor, of New Testament Exegesis at Presbyterian College in Halifax.

Few Canadian Presbyterians had Falconer's wide experience in biblical studies outside Canada. Like Shearer, George Pidgeon did not go to Scotland until much later in his career. He was born in 1872 in the Eastern Townships of Quebec and raised in a devout Presbyterian home by a mother of Methodist background. He took his arts degree at McGill, where John Clark Murray, another of Canada's leading Idealist thinkers, taught mental and moral philosophy.[17] The strongest influence on Pidgeon during his theological education was Donald MacVicar, Principal of Presbyterian College in Montreal and the model for the university professor who sparks the Glengarry revival in C.W. Gordon's semi-autobiographical novel, *The Man From Glengarry*.[18] Although MacVicar had been a student of George Paxton Young in Toronto, his theology had remained much more conservative than his mentor's mature thought. Pidgeon found MacVicar's evangelicalism a powerful and lasting influence. "No student passes through our principal's classes without having awakened in his soul the spiritual earnestness, the evangelical fervour, the deep-seated love for God and man that characterize the life and teachings of him whom we delight to honour," Pidgeon wrote in the *Presbyterian College Journal*. "The study of theology has often been regarded as the investigation of doctrine isolated from practical life. But here we find the life brought into living connection with the truth on which it rests, and are taught that as in Christ was the truth incarnate, so every preacher of the gospel must live and know experimentally the truth he teaches."[19] Pidgeon studied apologetics with John Campbell during the time Campbell was charged with heresy for agreeing with some of the conclusions of those who practised Higher Criticism in biblical studies. Campbell's basic contention was that the loving Father portrayed by Jesus represented a higher stage of the historical evolution of the faith than the angry judge represented in parts of the Old Testament. Although condemned by the Presbytery of Montreal, Campbell was cleared of heresy in an appeal to the Synod of Montreal and Ottawa.[20]

The only non-Canadian in this sextet of Presbyterian progressives was Thomas B. Kilpatrick. He was one of a trio of young Scottish professors trained under the Scottish evangelical liberals who were invited to teach in Canadian colleges in the late 1890s. John Edgar McFadyen arrived at Knox College to teach Old Testament in 1898, after gaining the approval of William Caven in interviews in Scotland.[21] Kilpatrick was appointed to Manitoba College in Winnipeg in 1899 as Professor of Philosophy and Apologetics, as well as lecturer in Old Testament. John Mark King, Principal of Manitoba College who was Caven's minister at Toronto's St. James Square Presbyterian Church between 1873 and 1884 and C.W. Gordon's father-in-law, played a central role in choosing Kilpatrick.[22] Just before Kilpatrick arrived, however, King died and was succeeded in 1900 by William Patrick.[23] All three had been educated at the University of Glasgow under the Cairds and at the Free Church College in Glasgow under A.B. Bruce and George Adam Smith.

The appointment of these three young Scots to important teaching positions within the Presbyterian Church in Canada indicated the extent to which their evangelical liberalism had gained widespread acceptance among Canadian Presbyterians. Kilpatrick emerged very quickly as a popular speaker, preacher, and teacher throughout the church. Not only did his background and career illustrate well the various influences at work in the emergence of evangelical liberalism, but his writings also provided the most articulate statement of that apologetic among Canadian Presbyterians.

The Theology of T. B. Kilpatrick

Thomas Buchanan Kilpatrick graduated with first-class honours in mental philosophy from the University of Glasgow in 1877. Canadian legend has it that Edward Caird considered him and John Watson to be the two finest minds to pass through his classes.[24] Idealism, as taught by Caird, was essentially a philosophy of religion. It served educated Christians in the late nineteenth century, who were troubled by the assaults of science, philosophy, and social indifference, by its apparent success in explaining reality without explaining away humanity's religious consciousness. For someone from Kilpatrick's evangelical Free Church background, it legitimized his basic emotional sympathies and moral values by rooting them in what appeared to be the very nature of reality itself. At the same time, it affirmed the identity of enlightened Christians as the moral cultural leaders of society by assuring them that their work in evangelism and moral and social reform was at the cutting edge of the advance of the Kingdom of God. Kilpatrick found in Idealism the resources needed for a reinterpretation of evangelical Christianity in contemporary terms that answered what he considered to be the fundamental threats of the age to Christian faith — individualism, scepticism, pessimism, and materialism. It was an apologetic aimed at confirming the confidence and allaying the fears of educated Anglo-Saxon Protestants as they faced a fragmented and secular society.

Kilpatrick's early attention as a writer focused on the relationship between philosophy and religion. In 1883 he contributed the concluding essay, "Pessimism and the Religious Consciousness," to *Essays in Philosophical Criticism*, a volume which represented the philosophical manifesto of the younger generation of Scottish and English Idealists. Edward Caird wrote in his preface that the authors in the volume believed that the most important contributions to the contemporary intellectual life of humanity would be made by following the lines of investigation opened up by Kant and that no one had followed those lines more successfuly than Hegel. The collection, he continued, would "serve the purpose of its writers if it shows in some degree how the principles of an idealist philosophy may be brought to bear on the various problems of science, of ethics, and of religion which are now pressing upon us."[25] The idea that lay at the root of many of the problems of the nineteenth century, according to Kilpatrick in his essay in the volume, was individualism. Individualistic philosophical theories had left people alone in the universe, without any assurance of support from a superior power and separated from nature and the rest of humanity. Scepticism and anarchism resulted, leaving the world in fragments, setting individual against individual, class against class, and nation against nation. The root of all evil, he contended, was the perception of the world as a collection of disconnected phenomena, with the only motivation for morality being self-interest. But history proved, to Kilpatrick's satisfaction at least, that people reached their highest achievements when they became aware of the single principle that reigned supreme throughout the world, a principle that brought the conflicting elements of experience into a harmonious whole and provided a comprehensive basis for morality. The search for that principle constituted the perennial quest of philosophy; religion provided the solution which philosophy sought.[26]

The central role assigned to philosophy by Kilpatrick rested on his view of human beings as self-conscious creatures. The essence of the human constitution was thinking about the life people lived. For humans alone was experience a problem and philosophy was "the activity of thought brought to bear on experience as a whole."[27] Self-consciousness brought an awareness of an object beyond the thinking subject, Kilpatrick posited, but further reflection convinced the consciousness that subject and object were related by a deeper principle of identity. Following Kant and Hegel, Kilpatrick called this principle "Thought" and defined it as the universally determining principle of both knowledge and its objects. "It is implied," he wrote, "in the very fact of experience being a problem that, without its manifold and diverse elements, there is a unity of thought, reason or spirit. . . . It is the task of philosophy to make explicit this unity which is implicit in human experience."[28] Yet philosophy was doomed to failure in its search for the ultimate synthesis of the elements in human experience. It might, for a time, reach a harmony satisfactory to thought and stimulating to action, but in the end it raised questions that only religion could answer.

It was the task of religion to proclaim the synthesis that gave human existence its ultimate meaning and offered it the power to realize that meaning. "Religion," Kilpatrick contended, "discovers the principle for which Philosophy has been seeking, and exhibits it, not as a theory, but as a power, in the freshness and originality of actual life, transforming character and inspiring service." The harmony that triumphed over the discords of life was not found in intellectual formulae, but "in the verifiable realities of spiritual experience."[29] Philosophy and religion were never opposed to each other in their inner meaning. Both were necessities of the human spirit. "Both alike," Kilpatrick concluded, "presuppose the spiritual unity which pervades experience, and makes possible both thought and life. Each has its special function in apprehending and realizing this unity; and in their respective functions each is essential to the other."[30] Hence, religion and philosophy were not in conflict, for the former called people to an awareness of the power that unified life, while the latter provided an apologetic for such a faith and a critique of inadequate forms of religion.

The Idealists continued to teach philosophy in the two traditional Scottish categories — mental and moral. The first dealt with the discernment of the principle underlying all reality, and the second treated the ethical consequences of that principle. In the evolution of both, Kilpatrick was convinced,the crux of the philosophical problem came when the thinkers involved became aware that individualism offered no adequate answers to the needs of humanity.

For mental philosophy, the crisis came in the post-Aristotelian period, which Kilpatrick found to have a marked affinity with the modes of thought and attitudes of the late nineteenth century. The dominant thought of the period, represented by Stoicism, Epicureanism, Scepticism, and Neoplatonism, was intensely and increasingly occupied with the needs of humanity. With the advent of Neoplatonism, the life of humanity seemed hopeless, and the demand of the age was for salvation as an escape from the dissatisfactions of this life. In Neoplatonism, "Thought, the mighty force that had led the human spirit in its quest for unity, breaks down, and gives up the reins of government."[31] It was Christianity, in Kilpatrick's version of the evolution of thought, that succeeded Greek philosophy and eventually redeemed Western civilization from barbarism. He found many parallels between the Greek solutions to the problems of human experience, namely, ethics or religious escape, and the various ethical and religious movements of his own day. Both worlds had been torn by divisions and were desperate for moral and intellectual stability. Christianity had rescued the Greek world and could do the same for Anglo-Saxon civilization by redefining the problem of human life and offering a different solution to it.

Christianity, as Kilpatrick understood it, found the essential human problem which brought pain and unrest to the world in an antagonism of personal wills between humanity and God. It "boldly grasped the fact of personality; had for its goal the fullness of personal life in communion with a personal God; and saw the hindrance of this consummation within the personal life itself. Evil, the barrier to unity of God and man, is not outside of man, in the material framework in which he finds himself, but within man, in the determination of his will against the divine will." The solution to this antagonism, Kilpatrick maintained, was Christological. Christianity "approaches the human spirit, not with a theory, scheme, or process, but with a gospel, a declaration whose sum and substance is Christ Jesus, incarnate, crucified, risen. Holding steadfastly before the eyes of men, as the ultimate problem of life, the reconciliation of wills, human and divine, it proclaims the problem solved, the reconciliation achieved through Christ."[32] Christianity located the problem of evil in the will of humanity in revolt against the will of God, not in the senses as elements in human experience, as was claimed by the sensationalist philosophers of the post-Aristotelian period. Kilpatrick argued that the British moralists had similar problems in finding an adequate basis for morality in their individualistic and sensationalist psychology.

Ethical theory in England encountered the problem of individualism in the thought of Thomas Hobbes, the first of a long line of British moralists who sought the source of moral obligation and the faculty of moral judgement within human subjectivity. This tradition included the Scottish Common Sense school and culminated in the Utilitarianism of John Stuart Mill. These philosophers, as Kilpatrick interpreted them, posited a moral sense, be it reason, virtue, or some other faculty within the individual, that functioned as moral motive and guide. Self-interest was seen to be the spring and standard of action and the chief end of human existence was happiness. In Kilpatrick's understanding of their philosophy, "The moral faculty is a variously described compound of feelings, whose fluidity is stiffened by the sanctions and punishments of society." Kilpatrick saw this moral and social philosophy as having allied itself with the hypothesis of organic evolution, so that "draughts of illimitable time aid in establishing its conclusions."[33] Kilpatrick countered the sensationalism which had dominated British moral philosophy with the intuitionism which he found in Bishop Butler and which was most fully developed in the ethical Idealism of T. H. Green's *Prolegomena to Ethics*.[34]

Kilpatrick's own moral philosophy defined human beings in a different way. They were selves or personalities who were rooted in an infinite self or personality. Individual self-consciousness derived from and was maintained by an infinite, eternal, universal self-consciousness. Human knowledge was the gradual discovery of this eternal mind or spirit in things and people. It involved the discovery of the world as "the self-manifestation of an infinite personality, with whom the finite intelligence of man is one."[35] Morality, then, was "the progressive accomplishment of an eternal purpose, with which the individual is and ought to be one, whose goal is the perfection of man," wrote Kilpatrick. "The good for man is self-realization; but it is the realization of an infinite self, and is thus identical with the widest possible range of good for others, and is attended by the profoundest self-surrender."[36] Kilpatrick identified the infinite self or personality with the Christian God, whose historical self-manifestation was recorded in the Scriptures of the Old and New Testaments. This viewpoint grounded the Christian ethic in the very nature of reality and saw its influence progressively realized in history, culminating in the personality and character of Jesus Christ. "The Jewish race," Kilpatrick explained, "charged with the special function of guarding and transmitting the spiritual heritage of humanity, has appropriately a special revelation of good, explicitly bearing the stamp of superhuman origin. Finally, when the fullness of time in the moral discipline of mankind is reached, the good finds complete revelation in a person, the man Christ Jesus."[37] The solution to the problems of moral philosophy, as it had been for mental philosophy, was Christological.

It followed then, Kilpatrick contended, that the church, which had been entrusted with the teachings and work of Christ, was a necessary part of the mental and moral education of humankind. But it was not alone in bearing the task of personality formation. Character and conscience were educated by the entire social environment, as Green had emphasized. Hence, efforts through education, organization, legislation, and law enforcement to ensure that the purity of the social order be protected were central to civic responsibility. Such activity was the duty of all citizens and contributed to the progressive realization of the Kingdom of God in all facets of human life. "The ethical functions of parent, teacher, pastor, employer, statesman," Kilpatrick insisted, "are seen to be of the highest and most sacred. Under their influence, the conscience of the individual receives its revelation of duty, and its preparation for the exercise of its legislative and judicial vocation."[38] A moral citizenship, aware of belonging to both the nation and the Kingdom of God, the one a means of realizing the other, worked for an harmonious realization of the common good. In this evangelical version of collectivist liberalism, the cardinal virtues were service and self-sacrifice as exemplified in Christ and to be embodied in the lives of leaders in society who followed him.

When churchmen like Kilpatrick came to use Idealism as a prolegomenon for their evangelical apologetic, substantial changes took place in the traditional formulations of the Christian faith. God's activity was seen as immanent in nature and history rather than transcendent. God's power was realized in the transformation of character and history through education and moral persuasion rather than in miraculous interventions in personal lives or social institutions. God's will was manifest in those movements for moral and social reform that promoted harmony and personal virtue. The virtues of character that would nurture social harmony would then reflect the unifying principle that defined all reality. The growing commonwealth of humanity resulted in the progressive realization of the Kingdom of God on earth.

Kilpatrick's perception of the problems of his age and his solutions reflected the interests of the educated middle classes, which comprised the membership of the mainline Anglo-Saxon Protestant churches in the North Atlantic triangle. To the intellectual problem of scepticism, his evangelical liberalism offered a definition of reality that confidently proclaimed that all the world an arena for and means of God's self-realization; the Kingdom of God could advance only with moral people, such as his readers, as its pioneers. To personal problems of despair and pessimism, his apologetic offered an optimistic assurance of reconciliation with God and a meaningful moral life through identification with the divine will and purpose. To the materialism of his age, his theology offered an interpretation of reality that saw the world as the manifestations of Absolute Spirit and, thus, spiritual in its very nature. To the social problems posed by fragmenting individualism, his liberal Christianity presented a vision of an organic society best served by a collectivist liberalism which, while defending the liberal ideal of self-realization, insisted that it be done through collective responsibility for the harmony and order of the whole of society. Against the background of such a theology, evangelism became a way of promoting the Kingdom of God and calling on people to participate in that reality where they would find their ultimate self-realization.

Kilpatrick on Evangelism

Kilpatrick was two years old when the Revival of 1859 swept Glasgow. His father, at that time minister of a Glasgow working class Free Church congregation, was actively involved in this indigenous awakening which preceded the revival of Moody and Sankey in the early 1870s. Kilpatrick remembered his father as a man who combined a devotion to evangelism with earnest study and deep thought, a combination not uncommon in Free Church manses during the nineteenth century. In a reminiscence published after his father's death, Kilpatrick spoke of the leading ideas that had characterized his father's ministry. Kilpatrick senior stressed the divine indwelling, implying that all of life was of God; the oneness between Christ and the believer as the heart of faith and theology; the Atonement, as understood in the light of this divine-human identification rather than commercial or forensic images; Christ as the head of church and state, and as an active presence within the church as a vehicle of his work; and denominationalism as a human and dispensable concept. Kilpatrick commented that, though modern thought may have modified the expression of these ideas, their evangelical power and truth remained.[39]

Kilpatrick was sixteen when Moody and Sankey came to Scotland in 1873. In a textbook on evangelism written for the Board of Moral and Social Reform and Evangelism in 1911, he remembered the impact of that visit on the religious life of Scotland as a deep and permanent one. "Theology," he recalled, "became more experimental, and without losing hold of the doctrines of grace, was less bound by the ideal of systematic wholeness." Moody shaped the religious convictions of a younger generation of Scottish students who would rise to positions of power and influence in the Free Church in the 1880s. "In the persons of well known modern Scottish scholars," Kilpatrick continued, "keenest scientific spirit and scrupulous scientific methods are combined with an unfeigned acceptance of the Bible as the Word of God, and with a very earnest evangelism." Exemplary of this generation was Henry Drummond, whom Kilpatrick encountered during his student days. Kilpatrick acknowledged that Drummond had a keener insight into the difficulties of the modern mind than into the permanent value of older doctrinal statements, but the Christological focus of his evangelism derived from solid New Testament roots.[40]

In 1908, three years after Kilpatrick had moved from Manitoba College to Knox College, he and Principal Alfred Gandier, who had been a gold medallist under John Watson at Queen's, tabled a report for the Knox College Senate which was based on visits to American cities and colleges to examine their efforts in introducing courses in practical theology. Following their advice, the Senate approved the addition of religious education, missions, sociology, homiletics, polity and organization, evangelism and pastoral work to the traditional four-part curriculum of Old and New Testament, Church History and Systematic Theology. Initially, each professor was to incorporate lectures on these topics into his regular courses, with Kilpatrick given responsibility for evangelism.[41] By 1911, changes had been made to provide for a fuller training in these areas. The reforms in the curriculum marked a significant shift in the course design of the college and owed much to Kilpatrick's insistence that ministers be educated in a manner that prepared them for moral and social leadership in modern society.[42]

Also in 1908, Kilpatrick became an active member of a special committee on evangelism appointed by the General Assembly and convened by C.W. Gordon of Winnipeg. The acknowledged model for this national work was the Wilbur Chapman organization which worked within the Presbyterian Church in the United States. Chapman had been a protege of Moody and, following a successful evangelistic campaign in Winnipeg in 1907, he had been invited by Gordon to address the Assembly in 1908, with the result that the special committee to promote Canadian evangelism was appointed. The committee followed closely the Simultaneous Evangelism model developed by Chapman in which travelling evangelists worked in close co-operation with local churches and ministers.[43] During the first year of the committee's activities, Kilpatrick and Shearer travelled to British Columbia to speak in such a campaign in the Kootenay district. Their report, *The Kootenay Campaign: Evangelism and Moral Reform,* was published by the committee to promote the programme across the church.[44]

Kilpatrick's *New Testament Evangelism,* first delivered as a series of lectures to an alumni conference at Knox College, outlined the theology that had grown out of Kilpatrick's early experiences of revivals and that guided his current participation in campaigns. He dedicated the book to his father, "my best teacher and friend, who, after seventy years in the service of evangelism, still lives to bear witness that the Gospel is the power of God unto salvation." The book's central argument was that evangelism was the church's primary work. Kilpatrick grounded his ideas in the Bible, illustrating them from history and applying them to the circumstances of the modern church.[45]

Evangelism, Kilpatrick began, was quite simply the declaration of God's purpose and power to redeem and save. The coming of Christ marked the culmination of a long history of increasing human awareness of the depths of the world's need for salvation. God answered by reconciling the world to himself in Christ. Salvation was "a divine power, operative upon man's spiritual being, and effecting therein results, which correspond to man's constitution, as made in the image of God, and meant for God's fellowship."[46] Through experiences of salvation, which Kilpatrick refused to stereotype, God manifested himself as a personal, ethical energy working to redeem people from evil by raising their consciousness to a redemptive awareness of being children of God and brothers and sisters within the human race. God had accomplished salvation through the cross of Jesus Christ and it was the energy of the crucified Christ that flowed through all life as its unifying principle and power. The church's primary duty, and the source of its real power, lay in the declaration of this principle through evangelism.

Kilpatrick was emphatic that evangelism should precede the church's work in moral and social reform. Salvation, he acknowledged, had a real and effectual bearing on the social and political relations of humanity, but not until "the saving power of God be admitted to the depth of man's being, and be permitted to control the ethical forces, which, in real, though unseen ways, govern all social and political relations, can the Gospel have, in these directions, its normal and designed results."[47] The church's responsibility, however, did not end with the proclamation of salvation. As Kilpatrick's comments on evangelism and reform suggested, the announcement of salvation was but the beginning of an extended process of moral and religious education and activity that were essential parts of the church's mission. Evangelism planted the Christian principle "deep in the finest faculties of human nature, mind, conscience and will," making it "the creator of all great and worthy civilization."[48]

When the Presbyterian progressives for whom Kilpatrick spoke talked of the Christianization of civilization, they had in mind a comprehensive vision of the transformation of individual characters into the likeness of Christ and the gradual permeation of society by the moral and social values perfectly manifested in his character. But at which locus of the social structure might such a permeation begin? Could existing society offer a base? Kilpatrick's conviction that no great civilization could be built on the foundations of individualism led him to search for a collective base for the creation of character. He found that fundamental social organism in the Christian family.

God, Kilpatrick pointed out, worked according to human nature, and the home was where the long process of character formation began. From earliest childhood to adolescence, the task of parents in the divine economy was to tell their children about God's grace in Christ. The home was the starting place in the campaign to defend the faith and win the world for Christ. No amount of supplementary activity, be it Sunday School, the Boys' Brigade, or any other Christian education organization, could replace the influence of the Christian home in building the character of the nation through its citizens.

Because of its character-building power, the Christian family formed the basic ethical unit of society. Not only was it the chief instrument of evangelization in the early years of life, but it remained the best means of regenerating society by challenging the individualism that Kilpatrick found to be the greatest weakness of church and society in the early twentieth century. The Christian home was not an aggregate of individuals but an organism, "living in its head and members by the communication of the Divine Spirit, and manifesting, according to the various place and function of its constituent elements, the graces of the Christian character."[49] In the family lay both the proof and the power of humanity's social nature. Therefore, Kilpatrick and his fellow progressives stressed the protection of the well-being and influence of the family against the assaults of the liquor traffic, organized vice, and wasteful entertainments, as well as against greedy employers and landlords. Preventing the fragmentation of the family and reversing its declining importance in urban and industrial society were of central importance in their reform efforts.

Kilpatrick used military language to describe the need for evangelism and reform. Enemy forces were concentrated in the city."Its position in the nation is one of commanding influence," Kilpatrick wrote. "Here is the strategic point. Hold this, and the campaign is won. Lose it, and defeat is inevitable. The modern Church must betake herself to city evangelism with an intensity and skill which have scarcely yet been applied to the problem."[50] The troops in the war against the forces threatening Anglo-Saxon civilization and causing social fragmentation were to be sought among the youth in Canada's schools and colleges. "The battle of Christianity in Canada," Kilpatrick urged,

> will be won in the playing fields of our schools and colleges. Give us young men of our middle class, clean limbed, well groomed, athletic, energetic. Give us their sisters, elegant, accomplished, high spirited. Fill them with the Christian spirit. Dedicate them to the Christian ideal. Subdue them before the Figure of the Crucified. Inspire them with His love, quicken them by His power, and we have won Canada for Christ, fairest realm within the Empire of Britain.[51]

The battle cry was for muscular, manly Christianity from the young men and virtuous, elevated Christianity from the young women of Canada. The battle plan depended on maternal influence shaping Christian character in the home and young men carrying these values into their professional lives and voluntary efforts throughout society. The enlightened leadership that would guide Canada to its divine destiny would come from the homes of the Anglo-Saxon Protestant middle classes.

Kilpatrick's description of his regular courses in Systematic Theology at Knox indicated the way in which he tried to continue the process of character formation and the central place he accorded evangelism in his liberal apologetic:

> The point of view adopted in the work of this department may be described as soteriological or Christological. The subject of the study is, broadly expressed, the fact of Salvation. The organizing principle is that stated in 2 Cor. 5:19, "that God was in Christ reconciling the world to himself." This leads to the great topics: the Source of Salvation — God; the Object of Salvation — Man; the Work of Salvation — Christ; the Appropriation of Salvation — the Holy Spirit; the Perfecting of Salvation — the Last Things. The endeavour is made in handling these subjects to present them in their Biblical origin, their historical development, and their constructive statement. The result aimed at throughout is not merely intellectual, but above all personal and practical, the deepening of experience, and the strengthening of conviction, together with an increase of power to proclaim the message of Salvation clearly, fully and persuasively.[52]

The course description also illustrated the different paths that Kilpatrick and John Watson had travelled since they had sat in the classroom of Edward Caird. Both centred their interpretation of Christianity on the reconciliation of the divine and the human and both reflected the influence of Caird's social philosophy. But Kilpatrick stayed much closer to the traditional expression of the Christian faith than Watson, which reflected the lasting influence of his evangelical roots. Throughout his writings, he was more evangelist than philosopher, an apologist for a return to Christ as the unique incarnation of the divine principle that governs the world.

Kilpatrick's understanding of evangelism encompassed all the means used by the church within its own structures and in its social environment to convey its message of salvation. He fervently believed that humanity needed that message and that humanity was incomplete without the relationship with God that was promoted through evangelistic work. Evangelism worked closely with moral and social reform movements to transform character and to elevate the ethical conscience of the nation. But the transformations sought were not aimed at substantial change in the social or economic systems operating in Canada at the turn of the century. Indeed, the values Kilpatrick found in the character of Jesus — spirituality, courage, patience, and self-sacrifice — contributed more to the harmonious running of the system than to fundamental social change.

The kernel of the message of salvation was the person and character of Jesus Christ. The personal and social morality that arose from Christ's example was outlined in a volume based on Bible classes given to Kilpatrick's Aberdeen congregation and published as *Christian Character: A Study in New Testament Morality* (1904). The ethical power of Christianity was manifested through the creation of individuals and social organisms that had in them the mind of Christ, a mind that thought remarkably like that of a liberal Protestant theological professor whose identity was rooted in the culture of the Anglo-Saxon Protestant middle class.

Kilpatrick on Character and Reform

T.B. Kilpatrick was no social radical. Whether speaking to a Bible class of young men drawn from the middle classes of Aberdeen, or to an assemblage of Toronto's leading citizens, or to his neighbours in the affluent residential district surrounding the Kilpatrick home at 128 Spadina Road in Toronto, he articulated a social ethic that legitimated the power and values of the middle classes. Elevating the lower classes to that standard was but an extension, an important but not a revolutionary one, of that ethic.

Character was the pivotal ethical concept that Kilpatrick drew from his study of the Bible. Building character was central to God's work of redemption, and the manifestations of character in all dimensions of human life were the essential means for the spread of Christian civilization. "Character," Kilpatrick asserted, "is the highest achievement, the mightiest influence, amid the thousands which enter into the complex life of man."[53] The destiny of the Anglo-Saxon race depended on the successful formation of Christian character.

Christian character dated from the person of Christ. It came into the world with him, was maintained by a personal relationship with him, and received its inspiration and power from him. "Christian character," wrote Kilpatrick, "declares the mind of God in the creation of man. This is man as God meant him to be."[54] The character of Christ was absolutely unique in the moral history of the race. It brought together the greatest of previous moral types and added the genius of universality. "From the elements of grandeur and beauty presented in Greek sage, Roman soldier or statesman, Hebrew psalmist or prophet," Kilpatrick noted as he described the evolution of Christian character, "we pass to the New Testament with the distinct conviction that here we have a type congruous indeed with the others, and gathering into itself their excellencies, yet supreme in its own loveliness, attracting to itself as they never did the admiration and loyalty of heart and intellect, perpetuated as they never were, nor could have been, in the lives and deaths, not of a select few, but of unnumbered multitudes."[55] Inasmuch as this moral perfection was unique to Christ, Kilpatrick saw Christianity as the universal and ultimate religion, alone capable of satisfying the human needs expressed in all other forms of thought and religion.

The question of character thus became the cornerstone in Kilpatrick's understanding of humanity's relationship with God. In traditional evangelical fashion, Kilpatrick saw sin, the revolt of the self against God, at the root of all evil. Beneath the evils of political corruption, of degraded surroundings, and of intellectual ignorance was sin. More imperative than political purity and enfranchisement, social reform, and education was redemption. The atoning death of Christ, in which he assumed the sin of humanity, established the moral fact that God and humanity were reconciled, the consequences of sin undone, and the possibility opened for the creation of the Kingdom of God. Such redemption, at its heart, was "a new relationship between God and man, according to which they are organically one in full moral accord and deep vital union; and this involves also a new relationship between man and man, in which they are in the fullest sense members of one organism, and therefore, of one another."[56] Identification with God in Christ came in and through character and the human mind was the most powerful faculty in character formation.

Humans were endowed with reasonable souls, created in the image of God and responsive to his presence as absolute mind or spirit. Participating in the divine mind through reason, imagination, and memory, the human mind was the most powerful force in the world. "Mind," Kilpatrick argued, "is the mightiest influence in the world. It can bend nature to its purposes, and make material things bear the impress of its conceptions, and carry out its designs. It sways the history of nations, constrains the most turbulent fury, compels the most tumultuous force to obey its purposes."[57] Whether confronted with the harshness and isolation of the Canadian frontier or the forces of evil that had collected in Canada's cities, Kilpatrick and his colleagues maintained an unquestioning faith in the power of Christian character guiding a moral mind to solve the problems the nation faced. Such character was not that of the individual alone, but an element of the community as a whole.

The individual, as Kilpatrick saw it, existed only in relationship to an organic whole. The community itself had a personality and a public conscience, "the conscience not merely of this man or that, but of the body of men living together as a moral organism."[58] The state was one expression of this moral organism, and the laws of the state, for the most part, were to be obeyed as expressions of the mind of God. Deviations from this law of obedience occurred only when the leaders of the state perverted the institution for personal or class gains. In Kilpatrick's own mind, the liquor interests and commercialized vice had so corrupted various parties and governments in Canada that active opposition was the only ethical path to follow.[59] But the most important issues of personal and social morality were beyond the reach of the legal and administrative power of the state. They were in the sphere of the public conscience. "No Act of Parliament," Kilpatrick stated, "can make the country sober; but the conscience of the community, awake, enlightened, active, in all ranks and classes could do it. No legislation can cleanse Scotland of the taint of impurity which makes domestic life so dismal, and often so tragic; but the public conscience, operative in every social circle and in every home, could do it."[60] This view of the power of public opinion lay behind various efforts at moral persuasion that Kilpatrick and his colleagues adopted as the major strategy of the Presbyterian Social Gospel. It led several of them into professions other than the ministry because they thought they would be better able to shape the public conscience of their nation from the editor's chair, the organizer's office, or the professor's desk, and so help Canada fulfil its destiny as the bearer of Christian civilization.

The values to be upheld by the public conscience were those Kilpatrick found in the character of Christ: faithfulness, courage, calmness, and self-sacrifice. These, in turn, guided life in the family, the workplace, the state, and the community at large. In his discussion of these social institutions through which the conscience of the community was formed and expressed, Kilpatrick considered the church to be the cornerstone. "The Christian Church," he said, "is the crown and consummation of all organic relations which link men together in moral and spiritual fellowship. Without the Christian Church, society would be in perpetual danger of falling back into the anarchy of mere selfishness."[61] Such a view of the central importance of the church led those ministers who chose occupations outside the institutional church to remain active as churchmen in the courts and committees of the church. Further, the Presbyterian progressives placed great hope in the consummation of a union among the Protestant churches in Canada as a means of increasing their power and influence within the community.

Kilpatrick's discussion of the labour question showed the way in which the values found in Christ's character and entrusted to the church were to be enshrined in modern society. Work was a necessary element in the education of a human being. Like suffering, it contributed to the growth of character, Kilpatrick argued, however hard and difficult to bear. A proper humility came from the necessity to observe the laws of nature and work in harmony with the natural order, both physical and social. "To be part of an infinite whole," he suggested, "to be an intelligent citizen in an ordered universe, to be a willing agent in its great design, is the highest dignity of man; and this dignity work enables him to attain." Work also taught people that they were instruments of a wider good than their own and that "selfishness which sets man against man, trade against trade, men against masters, is not only a crime but a blunder, and entails endless loss to those who make selfish gain the sole end of labour." There was no higher morality for Kilpatrick than "absolute fidelity to our station and its duties."[62]

The central issue in the labour question, as far as Kilpatrick was concerned, was motivation. Were workers simply dissatisfied with their conditions and seeking to amass wealth, or were they motivated by an inner desire to improve the collective well-being of the community? If the movement for higher wages and shorter hours was aimed at providing the workers with greater opportunities for social and moral progress in their lives, it was to be applauded and supported. If, however, the agitation arose out of distaste for work or love of money and ease, it stood condemned. "Many economic problems," in Kilpatrick's view, "run up for their solution into the moral sphere. If throughout the workers of our country there be maintained a genuine love of work, an honourable pride in it, and a perception of all its gains, moral as well as material, the standard of efficiency will be well maintained, and as a nation we shall have nothing to fear from the competition of rival races."[63] Such an attitude proceeded from a genuine moral position, but easily provided a rationalization for opposition to any demands from the ranks of labour.

Kilpatrick condemned much of the socialism he found in the labour movements of his day for its selfishness, materialism, and militant atheism. In their report on the Kootenay evangelistic campaign, he and Shearer listed socialism "of the anti-religious and fanatical type" as one of the difficulties they encountered in the district. It was more common among the miners than the farmers or fruit growers. It did not, in the view of the clergymen, seem to be based on any understanding of economic laws nor on any deep consideration of social problems. However, "it prejudices those who are possessed by it against religion, and makes them bitterly hostile to the Church, which is regarded by them as the ally of the hated capitalist."[64] Had the miners so "possessed" read the report, they would have had their suspicions of the alliance between capitalism and the church confirmed. Kilpatrick and Shearer told, with obvious satisfaction, of a banquet for the campaign workers hosted by the Fernie Board of Trade and attended by one hundred of the town's most prominent citizens. "The hard-headed business men," the report noted, "whether themselves religious or not, felt called upon to openly express their high estimate of the 'economic value of character' of the type produced by the religion of Jesus."[65] The businessmen evidently recognized and acknowledged that the campaign sought to perfect rather than to transform a social and economic system that valued efficiency, acceptance, and harmony above all.

The attitudes of many socialists were seen by Kilpatrick to contribute to the fragmentation of society and violate the principles of community and harmony that should govern social relationships. Legitimate claims for improvements in working conditions and wages within the nation were to be settled "by wise statesmanship, supported by enlightened and Christianized public opinion."[66] The best arbiters in labour disputes were thought to be members of the impartial middle-class professions, such as the clergy, who had the interests of the whole community at heart. Kilpatrick also feared that socialism, as a political alternative that gave the state possession of all the means of production, all means of employment, and all distribution of goods, ran the risk of violating the rights of citizens to a free, intelligent, and moral life. The function of the state, in his social philosophy, was to provide each citizen with the opportunity for full human development within the community. The overarching concern of the state's legislative and administrative policies would be to promote morality and harmony throughout the social order, thereby creating an environment in which people could develop their fullest potential as citizens. In doing so, the state would restrict some individual liberties, but only for the benefit of the greater social organism.[67]

Kilpatrick's advice on career choices to the young people in his Bible classes showed his preference for traditional middle-class occupations — commerce and the learned professions. Commerce, he concluded, had been a humane and benevolent influence in the history of the race, "a leading factor in subduing savagery, restraining the hostilities of nations, encouraging peaceful arts, raising degraded peoples, and giving them a place in the organism of humanity, and, in general, ameliorating the lot of millions of mankind." The moral qualities that made the merchant a valued member of the community were those Kilpatrick thought essential in any righteous nation — "intentness and earnestness of mind, breadth of interest in all matters affecting the welfare of society, fixedness of purpose which does not relax till it has gained its end."[68] Commerce might be degraded by the scramble for wealth and the fierce selfishness of rivals and enemies, but Christian character would ensure that higher moral values would prevail.

While those pursuits that ministered to the material wants of humanity and built the material fabric of the nation were important, and increasingly attractive to young people, the highest calling was still the learned professions — medicine, law, education, literature, and the ministry — which served humanity's higher mental and moral constitution. "The results they gain," Kilpatrick believed, "are the direct heritage of mankind. They demand for their discharge the highest qualities of mind and heart; and afford a vocation which the brightest and the worthiest may be proud to follow."[69] Such men, together with the few women who were just beginning to enter the professions, would be the leading bearers of the culture of evangelical liberal Protestantism. These were the people Kilpatrick hoped would shape the mind and the morality of the nation.

Imitating the character of Jesus would demand from the young men and women of Canada considerable will and effort. Their relationship with God would produce a transformation in character that would lead them to identify their wills with the divine will in all their activities. Kilpatrick's vision of the divine will was a perfect reflection of the will of the Anglo-Saxon Protestant middle classes of the late nineteenth century. Evangelical conversion of the kind he advocated led to no radical assault on the social values or structures of the nation, but rather to an energetic attempt to defend those values and propagate them among those whose ethnic or economic background had not provided the advantages of a middle-class, Protestant upbringing.

* * * * *

In *The Modernist Impulse in American Protestantism*, W.R. Hutchison summarized in a cluster of three beliefs the liberal theology that informed much of the American Social Gospel: the conscious and intended adaptation of religious ideas to modern culture, the belief that God was immanent in human cultural development, and the belief that human society was progressing towards the realization of the Kingdom of God on earth.[70] The Social Gospel added its own emphasis to this religious progressivism, namely, that social salvation, as opposed to individual salvation, was the essence of Christianity and the primary task of the church.[71] The Canadian Presbyterians for whom Kilpatrick spoke shared the assumptions of adaptation, cultural immanentism, and Christian progressivism that Hutchison found among liberal Protestants in the United States. But the Canadians were unwilling to accept the insistence of American Social Gospel leaders that social salvation must precede individual salvation.

Within the collectivist liberalism of their theological and social apologetic, which drew on sources different from those that shaped the American Social Gospel, the question was one not of either/or but of both/and. If pressed, however, they would come down on the side of character development as the primary emphasis of the church's work. There was no doubt in their minds that an improved social environment would better the quality of personal and social life in Canada. But the new society would take shape only as Christian citizens brought their values and beliefs to bear on the affairs of the nations. Progress in the Christianization of their civilization depended, not on structural changes in the institutions, but on the nurturing of Christian character in the men and women of Canada. The Kingdom of God advanced as they asserted their high moral character over their lower nature and the environment so that the values of love, self-sacrifice, service, and social harmony became the guiding principles in all walks of Canadian life.

NOTES

1. See F. Landon, *Western Ontario and the American Frontier* (Toronto: McClelland and Stewart, 1967), pp. 267-268; and J.M.S. Careless, *Brown of the Globe, Vol. I* (Toronto: Macmillan, 1959), pp. 20-23 and 33-35.

2. C.W. Gordon, *Postscript to Adventure: The Autobiography of Ralph Connor* (Toronto: McClelland and Stewart, 1975), pp. 34 and 44.

3. R.T. Handy, *A History of the Churches in the United States and Canada* (Toronto: Oxford University Press, 1977), pp. 162-171.

4. S.D. Clark, *Church and Sect in Canada* (Toronto: University of Toronto Press, 1948), pp. 106-107.

5. See *Revivals of Religion: Addresses by Scottish Evangelical Leaders delivered in Glasgow in 1840* (Edinburgh: Banner of Truth, 1984). See also J.E. Orr, *The Second Evangelical Awakening in Britain* (London: Marshall, Morgan and Scott, 1949), pp. 58-77; Carwardine, *Trans-Atlantic Revivalism*, pp. 94-101 and 169-197; and A.L. Drummond and J. Bulloch, *The Church in Victorian Scotland: 1843-1874* (Edinburgh: St. Andrew Press, 1975), pp. 108 & 185.

6. Ruth Compton Brouwer, "Presbyterian Women and the Foreign Missionary Movement, 1876-1914: The Context of a Calling," *The Canadian Society of Presbyterian History Papers, 1984 & 1985*, pp. 9-10.

7. See McKillop, *Disciplined Intelligence*, pp. 56-57, 172-176, and 200-201; L. Armour and E. Trott, *The Faces of Reason: An Essay on Philosophy and Culture in English Canada, 1850-1950* (Waterloo: Wilfrid Laurier University Press, 1981), pp. 85-104; and R.D. Gidney, "Young, George Paxton," in *Canadian Dictionary of Biography, Vol. XI* (Toronto: University of Toronto Press, 1982), pp. 942-943.

8. J.H. MacVicar, *Life and Work of Donald Harvey MacVicar, D.D., L.L.D.* (Toronto: Westminster, 1904),. p. 67. On Young from the point of view of the ministers who studied under him and worked with him, see J.G. Hume, "Foreword," in G.P. Young, *The Ethics of Freedom* (Toronto: University of Toronto Press, 1911), pp. 1-7; J. Campbell, "Professor George Paxton Young," *The Varsity (*Toronto), Mar. 28, 1889; J.F. McCurdy (ed.), *Life and Work of D.J. Macdonnell* (Toronto: William Briggs, 1897), pp. 247-253; D.H. MacVicar, "George Paxton Young," *The Westminster* (Toronto), Mar. 3, 1900; W. Caven, "George Paxton Young," *Knox College Monthly* 9, no.5 (Mar, 1889):265-268; and *The Presbyterian* (Toronto), May 10, 1906.

9. Hume, "Foreword," p. 4.

10. On Hutton, see S.E.D. Shortt, *The Search for an Ideal: Six Canadian Intellectuals and their Convictions in an Age of Transition, 1890-1930* (Toronto: University of Toronto Press, 1976), pp. 77-113.

11. For a summary of MacLaren's thought, see William MacLaren, *Sixty Years' Retrospect: A Lecture Delivered at the Opening of Knox College on the 8th October, 1907* (Toronto: Armac Press, 1907).

12. W. Caven, "Clerical Conservatism and Scientific Radicalism," *Knox College Monthly* 14, no.6 (Oct. 1891):286.

13. J.A. Macdonald, "A Biographical Sketch," in W. Caven, *Christ's Teaching Concerning the Last Things and Other Papers* (Toronto: Westminster, 1904), pp. xxiv-xxv.

14. Gordon, *Postscript*, pp. 75-79.

15. Clark, *Church and Sect*, p. 70.

16. J.S. Moir, "James Frederick McCurdy: Christian Humanist," *The Canadian Society of Presbyterian History Papers, 1981*, p. 3.

17. McKillop, *Disciplined Intelligence*, pp. 176-181; and Armour and Trott, *Faces of Reason*, pp. 105-175.

18. MacVicar, *Life*, pp. 53-54.

19. G.C. Pidgeon, "Principal MacVicar," *Presbyterian College Journal*, 12, no.4 (1892-1893):471-472.

20. J.S. Moir, *Enduring Witness* (Toronto: Presbyterian Publications, 1975), p. 174.

21. Moir, *Sense of Proportion*, p. 19.

22. Kilpatrick's inaugural lecture discussed his views on the teaching of theology. See *The Westminster* (Toronto), Sept. 30, 1899.

23. On Patrick, see Kilpatrick's obituary in *The Presbyterian* (Toronto), Oct. 5, 1911.

24. Sir C.G.D. Roberts and A.L. Tunnell (eds.), "Kilpatrick, Thomas Buchanan," *A Standard Dictionary of Canadian Biography* (Toronto: Trans-Canada Press, 1938), p. 219.

25. Edward Caird, "Preface." in A. Seth and R.B. Haldane (eds.), *Essays in Philosophical Criticism* (Glasgow: James Maclehose, 1883), p. 3.

26. T.B. Kilpatrick, "Pessimism and the Religious Consciousness," in Seth and Haldane, *Essays*, pp. 246-277.

27. T.B. Kilpatrick, "Philosophy," in J. Hastings (ed.), *A Dictionary of the Bible* (New York: Charles Scribner's Sons, 1906), p. 848.

28. *Ibid.*, p. 848.

29. *Ibid.*, p. 849.

30. *Ibid.*, p. 851.

31. *Ibid.*, p. 851.

32. *Ibid.*, p. 851.

33. T.B. Kilpatrick, "Conscience," in Hastings, *Dictionary of the Bible*, pp. 469-470.

34. T.B. Kilpatrick, "Introduction," in *Bishop Butler's Three Sermons* (Edinburgh: T. & T. Clark, 1888), pp. 11-50.

35. *Ibid.*, p. 470.

36. *Ibid.*, p. 471.

37. *Ibid.*, p. 471.

38. *Ibid.*, p. 473.

39. *The Presbyterian* (Toronto), Aug. 27, 1914.

40. T.B. Kilpatrick, *New Testament Evangelism* (Toronto: Westminster, 1911), pp. 114-115.

41. Minutes, Executive of the Senate of Knox College, Mar. 15, 1909, Knox College Archives.

42. Minutes, Senate of Knox College, Apr. 5, 1911, Knox College Archives.

43. Acts and Proceedings of the General Assembly, Presbyterian Church in Canada (hereafter, *A&P*), 1908, Minutes, pp. 62-63. See also *The Presbyterian* (Toronto), Nov. 7, 1907.

44. T.B. Kilpatrick and J.G. Shearer, *The Kootenay Campaign: Evangelism and Moral Reform* (Toronto: Committee on Evangelism, Presbyterian Church in Canada, 1909).

45. Kilpatrick, *Evangelism*, pp. vii-viii.

46. *Ibid.*, p. 8.

47. *Ibid.*, p. 11.

48. *Ibid.*, pp. 56-59.

49. *Ibid.*, pp. 37-38.

50. *Ibid.*, pp. 36-37.

51. *Ibid.*, p. 193.

52. *Calendar of Knox College, Toronto, 1909-1910*, pp. 14-15.

53. T.B. Kilpatrick, *Christian Character: A Study in New Testament Morality* (Edinburgh: T. & T. Clark, 1904), p. 3.

54. *Ibid.*, p. 5. See also T.B. Kilpatrick, "The Character of Christ," in J. Hastings, *Dictionary of Christ*, pp. 281-297.

55. Kilpatrick, *Christian Character*, p. 4.

56. *Ibid.*, p. 34.

57. *Ibid.*, p. 88.

58. *Ibid.*, p. 113.

59. *Ibid.*, pp. 256-261.

60. *Ibid.*, pp. 114-115.

61. *Ibid.*, p. 269.

62. *Ibid.*, pp. 62-67.

63. *Ibid.*, pp. 190-191.

64. Kilpatrick and Shearer, *Kootenay Campaign*, p. 16.

65. *Ibid.*, p. 23.

66. Kilpatrick, *Christian Character*, p. 199.

67. *Ibid.*, pp. 245.251.

68. *Ibid.*, p. 180.

69. *Ibid.*, pp. 181-182.

70. Hutchinson, *Modernist Impulse*, p. 2.

71. *Ibid.*, pp. 164-174.

CHAPTER 3

THE INSTITUTIONAL FRAMEWORK:

THE GROWTH OF A CANADIAN DENOMINATION

The six protagonists of social Christianity who were to alter Canadian Presbyterianism so significantly began their work within the institutional framework of the Presbyterian Church in Canada in the 1890s. John G. Shearer went straight from Knox College to a pastorate in Caledonia, Ontario, where he served from 1888 until 1891. He moved to Erskine Church in Hamilton and ministered there until 1900, when he became full-time secretary for the Lord's Day Alliance, based in Toronto. Charles W. Gordon returned from Scotland and worked for a time with his ailing father in Zorra before accepting an appointment to a mission field in Banff, Alberta. He stayed there from 1890 until 1893, ministering to a mixture of miners, lumbermen, and tourists. Following a year in Scotland promoting the cause of mission work in the Canadian West, he returned to a new suburban congregation in Winnipeg, St. Stephen's. James A. Macdonald was minister at Knox Church, St. Thomas, Ontario, from 1890 until 1895. He then returned to Toronto where he was instrumental in founding a new Presbyterian publishing house, the Westminster Company. George Pidgeon began his ministry in the suburban parish of Montreal West in 1894. In 1898 he moved to Streetsville, near Toronto, and while there completed the requirements for a Doctor of Divinity degree from Presbyterian College in Montreal. In 1903, he was called to the Victoria Presbyterian Church in the Toronto suburb of Toronto Junction. Robert Falconer spent the last decade of the century teaching New Testament at Presbyterian College in Halifax. In 1904 he became principal of the college. T.B. Kilpatrick arrived in Winnipeg and taught at Manitoba College until he moved to Knox College in 1905. By the beginning of the twentieth century, all had risen to positions of influence and respect within the Presbyterian Church in Canada. But within what kind of institution had they chosen to work? Why did they consider it an appropriate base for their aggressive propagation of their religious and cultural ideals? To answer these questions, we must briefly review the institutional developments within Canadian Presbyterianism during the nineteenth century.

A National Denomination

On June 15, 1875, six thousand Presbyterians from all of the settled regions of Canada — the Maritimes, Ontario, and Quebec, along with a handful from Manitoba — gathered in Montreal's Victoria Hall Skating Rink to celebrate the unification of Presbyterianism in Canada. The union marked the culmination of a series of amalgamations among what had been ten separate groups of Presbyterians in British North America in 1844.[1] Regionalism remained a powerful factor in the life of the new church, with Home Missions, Foreign Missions, and other schemes divided into an eastern section for the Maritimes and a western section for the rest of Canada for fund-raising and administrative purposes. But the supporters of union felt that their common Presbyterianism and Canadianism, especially following the political federation of 1867, were more important than the social, economic, and religious factors that had divided them in Scotland and in Canada for years. The task of shaping the morals, culture, and spirituality of the new nation with which they were convinced God had entrusted them helped create a common bond and focused attention on the future of the young Dominion rather than on a past of religious controversy, factionalism, and colonial ties with the divided churches of Scotland.

J.L. Morris, a Montreal lawyer who acted as counsel for the Presbyterian Church in Canada for many years following union, expressed the mixture of patriotic and religious enthusiasm that lay behind the movement for union and would continue as a characteristic of the emerging social Christianity among Presbyterians in Canada. "We have an independent nation," he wrote, "a Dominion, which for the extent of its territory, fertility of its resources and prospects for the future, is unsurpassed by any in the world. Naturally and necessarily, therefore, a change must come over our church organization, and it is part equally of true patriotism and sound wisdom to acknowledge this and act upon it."[2] Morris saw that the development of church and state in Canada were interdependent, natural in a world God had created and necessary in a world God governed. As the nation was providentially transformed by the progressive movements of the nineteenth century — the growth of democratic institutions, commercial expansion, immigration, industrialization and urbanization — the institutions of the church must respond with parallel changes. The creation of an aggressive and centralized national denomination was an essential step in assuring that the new nation would mature under the watchful eye of evangelical Protestantism.

As with most things in Canada in the 1870s that claimed to be national, the Presbyterian Church in Canada in actual fact represented the regional viewpoint and interests of central Canada, especially Ontario. The "Ontario nationalism" of Newton Wesley Rowell and his fellow Methodists was shared by Presbyterians, reflected in the religious and political views of earlier Liberal politicians such as George Brown and Oliver Mowat.[3] In addition to the regional bias, a class bias was evident in the new church. H. Richard Niebuhr suggested that Calvinist denominations in general were representative middle-class churches, whose rise and development were influenced by the economic interests of the aspiring middle classes who, in turn, were influenced by "the faith of Geneva."[4] Detailed examination of documents to ascertain the occupational and class characteristics of Canadian Presbyterians has yet to be done. But the Scottish ethnic base of the denomination in Canada[5] and the predominance of Scots in the Canadian business elite[6] would lend support to a working hypothesis that Canadian Presbyterianism arose out of and served a central Canadian commercial middle class. In his history of the Presbyterian Church in Canada, John Moir added strong support to this hypothesis when he found evidence that the new church formed by the union of 1875 "represented the aggressive Presbyterianism of urbanized, industrialized, expansionist central Canada."[7] The regional, ethnic and class limitations of the body, as well as the aggressive expansionist attitudes it held, made the Presbyterian Church in Canada in the last quarter of the nineteenth century a good example of what sociologists of religion have called a denomination.

Over the course of the history of Presbyterianism in Canada, two other models of religious organization postulated by sociologists were represented — the ecclesia and the sect — but by 1875 these types, embodied in the Kirk and the Secessionist bodies, respectively, had come to exhibit many of the characteristics of denominations. This gradual transformation in the direction of denominationalism, prompted by social conditions in Canada, made union with the Free Church branches, the most denominational of the Presbyterian churches, a relatively painless process. It also guaranteed that the spirit of the Free Church would dominate the life of the new united church. Among sociologists of religious institutions, Milton Yinger has developed the most extensive classification of models for religious organizations. His descriptions of the ecclesia, the denomination, and the sect help in understanding the various strains of Presbyterianism in Canada in 1875.

The ecclesia, according to Yinger, was best exemplified by the established national churches of Europe. It was a predominantly conservative body, existing in harmony with the secular aspects of social life and universal in its purpose. It attempted to amalgamate with the state and the dominant classes and aspired to exercise control over the entire population. "The ecclesia," Yinger wrote, "as an inclusive social structure is closely allied with national and economic interests; as a plurality pattern its very nature commits it to adjustment of its ethics to the ethics of the secular world; it must represent the morality of the respectable majority."[8] Within Presbyterianism, this model was represented by the Church of Scotland. As the established church of the northern kingdom in Great Britain, it accepted the principle of Erastianism, or state funding and control, exercised largely through the local patron who was normally the major landowner in the district. In theology and social ethics, the Church of Scotland came to be dominated in the eighteenth and early nineteenth centuries by the Moderates, a religious party that accepted the social, cultural and political norms of the secular powers.[9]

Because it identified with the dominant interests in the society, the Church of Scotland was susceptible to sectarian protest from those elements that were disaffected with the established powers and whose personal religious needs were not met by the moderation of the religious establishment. The sect, as Yinger described it, was a group that repudiated the compromise of the ecclesia with the dominant social groups. It was either hostile or indifferent to the state and gained its membership through voluntary association. It was a movement in which the primary emphasis was the attempt to satisfy various individual needs, religious in essence but generated by social, economic, or psychological circumstances different from those that produced the dominant religious system. Such a movement would thus be a revolt against a religious system that did not meet those needs. Within Christianity, sects have characteristically held strict doctrinal and ethical codes rigidly enforced by community discipline.[10]

For the Scottish sectarian movements, the central issue over which they broke away from the established church was the control of the church exercised by the state through the patronage system. Taking their stand on the voluntarist position of complete separation of church and state, secessionists from the Church of Scotland established the Associate Synod in 1733 and the Presbytery of the Relief Church in 1761. Both bodies espoused the conservative theology and strict discipline of the Covenanting tradition of Andrew Melville, successor to John Knox in Scotland and leading opponent of the Stuart kings.[11] These secessionist movements were also influenced by the evangelical revivals of the eighteenth century that saw the moderate stand of the establishment as religious indifferentism and impersonal faith.[12]

By the beginning of the nineteenth century, the evangelical movement was making inroads into the Church of Scotland, creating two parties, the Evangelicals and the Moderates. At the same time, changes in the social and economic structures of Scotland created a commercial middle class whose interests often came in conflict with the landed interests of the ecclesiastical patrons. Further, their social and religious needs were not met by the moderation and apparent complacency of the established church. This group formed the next secessionist body opposing the establishment.

As with the eighteenth-century schisms, the central issue in these conflicts was the relationship between church and state, specifically the right of lay patrons to force their ministerial nominees on particular parishes. In 1843, 102 commissioners left the General Assembly of the Church of Scotland to form the Free Church of Scotland on the principle of non-intrusion, which asserted that, even though the church had spiritual independence in governing its own affairs, the state was still obligated to provide financial support. Theologically conservative, politically liberal or radical, socially active in missions and moral reform movements, the Free Church represented the emergence of the denomination in Scotland.[13]

Yinger describes the denomination as a class church. Its formation did not involve a rejection of the wider society, as did the rise of a sect, but rather represented the orientation of its particular constituency. Less rigid in its demands for religious commitment than the sect, the denomination was more capable of performing socially integrative functions for particular groups. Toleration of other religious groups made the denomination better adapted to a society in which there was a plurality of legitimate institutional alternatives. The pluralistic situation created competition among groups having essentially the same purpose, and the competition gave rise to integrated, professionalized, and bureaucratized forms of organization.[14]

When Presbyterianism arrived in the British North American colonies, largely via Scottish and Scotch-Irish settlers,[15] it encountered just such a pluralistic environment and, indeed, added to it with the divisions imported from Scotland. Roman Catholics, Anglicans, Congregationalists, Baptists, Methodists, and a variety of smaller sects vied for the allegiance of the colonists and for the favour and funding of the imperial and colonial governments.[16] How, then, did the ecclesial, sectarian, and denominational trends within Scottish Presbyterianism adapt to the marketplace competitiveness of the British North American colonies?

The ecclesial structures and attitudes of the Church of Scotland were poorly suited to the missionary efforts needed to provide Presbyterianism for a pioneer population in British North America. It was not until the formation of the Glasgow Colonial Society in the 1820s by the evangelical wing of the established church that serious missionary work was undertaken.[17] Even then, Church of Scotland congregations were concentrated in the towns and cities of Canada and composed largely of the upper levels of local society with Scottish backgrounds. Clergy were reluctant to venture to the backwoods of Canada because the preferments and endowments of Scottish congregations were much more attractive than might be found in small congregations that could only offer the colonial hardships of British North America.

Most of the Presbyterian clergy in the colonies in the pioneering days were drawn from Secessionist backgrounds. The evangelical zeal of that branch of the tradition generated considerable missionary effort. These ministers were more likely to go to rural areas and adopt an informal style of ministry which included some itinerancy. By comparison with the socially prestigious membership of the Church of Scotland congregations, drawn from the military, governmental, and business elites, the membership of the Secessionist bodies was drawn from the lower classes.[18] Even the sectarian forms of Presbyterianism, however, because of their continuing commitment to congregational structures and an educated ministry, were much less successful than the more flexible Methodists in serving the rural segment of the colonial population.[19]

If neither of the Presbyterian traditions represented in British North America prior to the 1840s was particularly successful in competing with other religious alternatives, the more settled social conditions that accompanied the emergence of an increasingly mature agricultural and commercial economy following the 1840s provided fertile ground for the growth of an aggressive evangelical denomination serving the religious needs of the emerging commercial classes, whether their base was primary products or secondary services. Such denominational bodies were created when the Free Church groups separated from the Church of Scotland in Canada and the Maritimes.

In 1843 and 1844, following the Disruption in Scotland, several deputations came to the colonies from the Free Church in Scotland. Evidence of their success was apparent when twenty-three of the sixty ministers in the Canadian Kirk Synod left to join the Free Church, leaving behind relatively comfortable livings. Fifteen of those who left had been sent by the Glasgow Colonial Society and its successor, while six others originally came from Secessionist backgrounds. The new Free Church was strongest in the western parts of Upper Canada where an expanding agricultural and commercial economy, together with the liberal political views fostered by the publishing empire of Free Churchmen Peter and George Brown, created a favourable environment for denominational growth. Growth was rapid, with four presbyteries expanding to seven by 1846.[20]

On the question of church and state that divided Presbyterians in Scotland, the Free Churches in British North America initially adopted the non-intrusionist stance of their sister body in the old country, but the debates over the secularization of the Clergy Reserves in Upper Canada and the general lack of state support for religion in the colonies led to a *de facto* voluntarist position by the early 1850s. What remained of the original Free Church stance, however, was the insistence on God's universal sovereignty over both church and state. The Free Churches adopted an aggressive attitude in matters of social policy, such as temperance, Sabbath observance, and anti-slavery, as well as an openness to co-operate with other groups in support of these movements for moral and social reform.[21] Further, that belief gave impetus to the competitive drive against the challenges of the papal aggression of the Roman Catholics, both French and Irish, and the enthusiasm of the Methodists, both of which were seen as threats to the ordered evolution of democratic institutions within the British system favoured by the rising middle classes.

The process of religious-cultural and organizational development from sect to denomination has been a common theme in the sociology of religion.[22] By the time Secessionist congregations were established in the colonies, that tradition had been in existence for at least a generation and many of the sectarian characteristics had softened. Further, on the frontier in Canada, Methodists and Baptists appealed much more to the sectarian constituency than did the Presbyterian theology and structures of the Secessionists. Finally, the increased prosperity of the 1840s and 1850s benefited those who had been established in the colonies for some years, adding to the wealth and social positions of many Secessionists. All these factors contributed to their willingness to unite with the Free Church to strengthen the competitive positions of Presbyterianism. In the Maritimes, the Free and Secessionist churches united in 1860 to form the Presbyterian Church of the Lower Provinces, while in Canada the union was achieved in 1861, creating the Canada Presbyterian Church. Both bodies adhered closely to the conservative theology of the Westminster standards, while traditional differences over church-state relations were made a matter of forbearance. The new body in the Maritimes had 82 ministers and some 15,000 adherents, while the Canada Presbyterian Church had 232 ministers and about 35,000 adherents.[23]

Less noted by sociologists of religion was the movement from ecclesia to denomination in the early part of the nineteenth century, but historian A.D. Gilbert made this the major thesis of his study of the relations between church and chapel in Victorian England. He noted that the ecclesiastical reforms that occurred in the Church of England between 1830 and the end of the Victorian era represented a gradual disestablishment.[24] A similar process affected the

Church of Scotland, though in the colonies the full support structures of establishment had never been available to the Kirk. With the settlement of the Clergy Reserves question in Canada in 1848, the last vestiges of co-establishment with the Church of England in the Canadas disappeared. The history of the Church of Scotland in Canada in subsequent years was one of stagnation and loss of clergy, many of whom went to Scotland where the Free Church exodus had left attractive congregations open. It was also a time of frustration for a younger generation of leaders, such as George Munro Grant, D.J. Macdonnell, and D.M. Gordon. Influenced by leaders of the revival in the Church of Scotland such as Norman MacLeod and John Caird,[25] these young ministers recognized the new competitive conditions and advocated more aggressive policies to ensure the growth and influence of the Kirk. It is not surprising to find these men leading the support for Presbyterian union in 1875 and emerging as leaders in the new united church.[26]

By the time Presbyterians from the Canadian provinces gathered in the skating rink in Montreal on that June evening in 1875, the strength and success of Free Church denominationalism was apparent to most. Seventy-five per cent of the 89,000 communicant members of the new Presbyterian Church in Canada came from that tradition (see Table 1). "By a Darwinian law of survival by selection," John Moir concludes, "the new church rapidly assumed the attitudes and interests of its most dynamic and majority element — the Free Church of Canada."[27] What Darwin also might have noticed, had he been interested in the natural history of the Presbyterian Church in Canada, was that the dynamic, competitive spirit of the Free Church was best suited to survival and growth in the pluralistic and expansionist environment of the new Dominion.

A New Metropolitan Centre

In the latter part of the nineteenth century, expansionist sentiment and activity in Canada was centred in Toronto and focused largely on the West as a new agricultural hinterland once the arable land in Ontario was occupied. It was hoped that the West would continue to fuel the commercial growth of Toronto and the St. Lawrence system.[28] While leaders of the expansionist movement in Toronto such as George Brown, editor of the *Globe*, made no apologies for the commercial advantages sought by western expansion, they also pointed to the humanitarian influences of culture and religion needed in the new territories. Indeed, Brown's enthusiastic support for the Presbyterian union of 1875 had much to do with his views on the future of the Canadian West.[29] As the Presbyterian Church in Canada grew during the last quarter of the nineteenth century, Toronto replaced Montreal as the metropolitan centre for

Canadian Presbyterianism. Statistically, it became the largest centre and, as the growth of the church demanded specialized functions and bureaucratic structures, it became the administrative hub.

Table 1
Statistics of the Uniting Presbyterian Churches[30]

	Ministers	Charges	Members
Canada Presbyterian Church	344	645	49,315
Church of Scotland in Canada	141	179	17,247
Presbyterian Church in the Lower Provinces	124	138	18,082
Church of Scotland in the Maritimes	31	41	4,622

An important, though largely neglected, feature of the theory of metropolitan dominance, outlined by J.M.S. Careless in his seminal article, "Frontierism, Metropolitanism and Canadian History," was the religious and cultural domination that accompanied the economic and political influence exerted by the metropolitan centre. In many ways, the story of the shifts in metropolitan dominance within the Presbyterian Church in Canada followed similiar patterns to those noted in secular life by historians and geographers.[31] It was a tale of four cities — Halifax, Montreal, Toronto, and Winnipeg. Toronto rose to rival and surpass Montreal,[32] Halifax remained relatively stagnant and declined in influence,[33] and Winnipeg boomed as an outpost of Toronto and the gateway to the West.[34]

In 1875, Montreal was the foremost metropolitan centre for Canadian Presbyterianism.[35] With 12 churches and almost 3,000 communicant members who contributed $94,237 annually, it accounted for 3.4 per cent of the total membership of the church and generated almost 10 per cent of the total national revenue. Toronto, however, was not far behind. Its 7 churches had some 2,000 members and its total revenue was $76,200, 2.5 per cent of the national membership and 7.8 per cent of the national funds. Halifax, with 6 churches and 1,500 members, contributed $37,979, accounting for 1.6 per cent of the membership and 3.9 per cent of the revenue. Winnipeg was still in its infancy, with 1 church and 177 members who raised $3,940.

Perhaps a clearer indication of the national commitments of the respective urban centres was the amount raised for the national schemes of the church, including home missions, foreign missions, and the colleges. Montreal raised $13,907, 15 per cent of the national totals and 15 per cent of all revenues raised for all church purposes, local and national. Toronto's $4,995 was 5 per cent of the national total and 6 per cent of its figure for all purposes. Halifax raised $3,650, 4 per cent of the national figure and 10 per cent of its total revenue. Winnipeg's $322 only accounted for 0.3 per cent of the national total, but was 8 per cent of the revenue of the single Winnipeg church. At the inception of the Presbyterian Church in Canada in 1875, Montreal was clearly the dominant centre, especially in the realm of finances (see Table 2).

Table 2

Metropolitan Statistics for the
Presbyterian Church in Canada in 1875

	Churches	Members	$ for Schemes*	Total $
Halifax	6	1,436	3,650	37,979
Montreal	12	2,967	13,907	94,237
Toronto	7	2,161	4,995	76,200
Winnipeg	1	177	322	3,940
National	706	88,228	93,610	982,671

* In 1875, the Schemes of the church included: the Colleges, the Home Missions Fund, the Augmentation of Stipends, the French Evangelization Fund, the Foreign Missions Fund, the Aged and Infirm Ministers' Fund, the Widows' and Orphans' Fund, and the Assembly Expense Fund.

By 1913, Toronto had established a clear metropolitan dominance over the national church. The number of churches there had grown to 41 with more the 27,000 members, or 9 per cent of the national membership. Montreal had 18 churches with slightly less than 10,000 members, or 3 per cent of the national figure. A comparison of the total revenue raised for all purposes by the congregations of the two cities revealed a similiar difference. Toronto churches raised $520,858, or 9 per cent of the total national revenue, while Montreal contributed $201,030, or 3.5 per cent. Support for the national schemes of the church also showed Toronto's primacy. From Toronto came $112,098, representing 22 per cent of the total raised by Toronto churches for all purposes and 14 per cent of the national contributions to the schemes of the church. Montreal contributed $45,707, a respectable 23 per cent of its total givings, but only 6 per cent of the national total. Indeed, by 1913, Winnipeg had surpassed Montreal in members with 10,000 members and revenues of $223,686. In givings to national schemes, it came close to Montreal with $39,333. Halifax, on the other hand, had shown remarkably little growth and suffered a relative decline, with only 1 new church, 500 new members, and an increase of $13,000 in total revenues over the 38-year period (see Table 3).

Table 3

Metropolitan Statistics for the
Presbyterian Church in Canada in 1913

	Churches	Members	$ for Schemes*	Total $
Halifax	7	1,900	9,011	51,268
Montreal	18	9,721	45,707	201,030
Toronto	41	27,269	112,098	520,858
Winnipeg	16	9,962	39,333	223,686
National	4,314	314,832	827,274	5,637,099

* In 1913, the Schemes of the Church included: Home Missions, Foreign Missions, Ministers', Widows' and Orphans' Fund, Aged and Infirm Ministers' Fund, Assembly Fund, Colleges, Pointe-Aux-Trembles Schools, Social Service and Evangelism, Deaconess Training College, Sunday School Society, and Young People's Society.

In the course of Toronto's emergence as the Presbyterians' metropolitan centre, two periods of rapid expansion coincided with two major influxes of British immigration, in 1881-1891 and 1901-1911.[36] Montreal's growth in churches and members over the three ten-year intervals was much more steady. When compared with the general urban growth of the respective cities, Toronto Presbyterians grew at a faster rate than their city, while Montreal Presbyterians generally lagged behind. As a percentage of the total population of their cities, Presbyterians in Montreal made up a consistent 2 per cent of the population, while Toronto Presbyterians grew from 4 per cent in 1881 to 6 per cent in 1911 (see Tables 4 and 5).

The shift in metropolitan dominance reflected in these statistics was also evident in the development of national structures and administrative staff for the Presbyterian Church in Canada. As N.K. Clifford has noted, from its beginnings in Geneva, Presbyterianism has been primarily urban in character.

Table 4

Metropolitan Statistics for the
Presbyterian Church in Canada
1875 - 1881 - 1891 - 1901 - 1911 - 1913

Churches:	Halifax	Montreal	Toronto	Winnipeg
1875	6	12	7	1
1881	7	12	11	1
1891	7	12	21	4
1901	7	16	27	8
1911	7	17	39	15
1913	7	18	41	16

Members:	Halifax	Montreal	Toronto	Winnipeg
1875	1,436	2,967	2,161	177
1881	949	3,630	4,153	525
1891	1,389	5,026	9,444	1,928
1901	1,767	6,529	13,169	2,920
1911	1,890	7,911	24,306	7,848
1913	1,900	9,721	27,269	9,962

Table 4 (Cont'd)

$ for Schemes:	Halifax	Montreal	Toronto	Winnipeg
1875	3,650	13,907	4,995	322
1881	5,583	80,520*	10,108	4,671
1891	5,412	28,026	46,475	4,291
1901	9,129	34,996	30,856	8,715
1911	8,759	36,191	66,312	35,378
1913	9,011	45,707	112,098	39,333

Total $:	Halifax	Montreal	Toronto	Winnipeg
1875	37,979	108,726	76,200	3,940
1881	34,190	158,226**	88,112	14,779
1891	34,671	114,096	192,708	28,364
1901	51,450	198,935	231,745	50,633
1911	41,298	237,165	453,890	202,914
1913	51,268	201,030	520,858	223,686

* $75,061 of this total came from Crescent St. Presbyterian Church, $72,180 of which was raised for a special college fund that year.

** $94,288 of this total came from Crescent St. and includes the special college fund.

It emphasized the rationalism and discipline of the academy rather than the emotionalism and spontaneity of the camp meeting popular with Methodists in North America.[37] Writing of the Presbyterian reaction to the revivals of the early nineteenth century, S.D. Clark observed: "Scottish Presbyterianism set itself solidly against the use of revivalistic methods in gaining recruits for the Church. Reliance was placed entirely upon the ordinary means of religious propagation."[38] For Presbyterians, reliance upon the ordinary means of grace in the structures and life of the church continued into the late nineteenth century. Typical of the reports of the Committee on the State of Religion to the General Assembly was that of 1885. "At a time when adventitious methods of imparting religious instruction are in vogue in our own as well as other lands," the report stated, "it must afford the members of Assembly particular pleasure that all our Synods speak in terms so satisfactory and so hopeful respecting the ordinary means of grace."[39] The institutional structures through which

Presbyterianism survived and spread dated back to the Reformation in Geneva and Scotland, a religious revolution that succeeded in alliance with the "middling element in society, the burgesses of the town and the lairds."[40]

The Form of Church Government, one of the Westminster Standards to which Presbyterian ministers subscribed upon ordination, provided for a hierarchy of church courts, each appointing representatives to the court above. The lowest court was the Kirk Session, composed of lay elders elected by the members of the congregation and presided over by the minister. Each of the higher courts — Presbytery, Synod, and General Assembly — was made up of an equal number of clergy and laity appointed by the lower courts. This structure provided for considerable lay input to the affairs of the church and offered the potential for support in expertise and finances for expansion and

---

Table 5

Urban Growth in Canada and the Urban Growth of Presbyterianism

Urban Population:	1881	1891	1901	1911
Halifax	36,100	38,437	40,832	46,619
Montreal	155,238	219,616	267,730	470,480
Toronto	96,196	181,215	208,040	376,538
Winnipeg	7,985	25,639	42,340	136,035

Quantity and % of Urban Growth:				
Halifax		2,337	2,398	5,787
		6. 5%	6. 3%	14. 0%
Montreal		64,378	48,114	202,750
		41. 0%	22. 0%	75. 0%
Toronto		85,019	26,825	168,498
		88. 0%	15. 0%	80. 0%
Winnipeg		17,654	16,701	93,695
		221. 0%	65. 0%	221. 0%

Table 5 (Cont'd)

Quantity and % of Presbyterian Growth:

Halifax	440 46%	378 27%	123 7%
Montreal	1,396 38%	1,503 30%	1,382 21%
Toronto	5,291 127%	3,725 39%	11,137 85%
Winnipeg	1,403 267%	992 52%	4,928 169%

% of Presbyterians in Populations of the Four Cities:

Halifax	949 (3%)	1,389 (4%)	1,767 (4%)	1,890 (4%)
Montreal	3,630 (2%)	5,026 (2%)	6,529 (2%)	7,911 (2%)
Toronto	4,153 (4%)	9,444 (5%)	13,169 (6%)	24,306 (6%)
Winnipeg	525 (6%)	1,928 (7%)	2,920 (7%)	7,848 (6%)

missions. It also contained the seeds of centralization, with the populous and wealthy urban centres dominating the courts.[41]

Presbyterians understood the ordinary means of grace to consist of a congregation gathered around the preaching of the Word and the administration of the Sacraments, with great emphasis placed in preaching and teaching on the fundamental doctrines of the faith. Instruction in the essentials of the Reformed tradition and the duties of the Christian life was the responsibility not only of the minister, but also of the elders and the families of the congregation. Nineteenth-century Presbyterians, in all branches of the tradition, adhered formally to the Westminster Standards — the Westminster Confession of Faith, the Larger and Shorter Catechisms, the Common Order of Worship, and the Form of Church Government. This elaborate system of doctrine, piety, and polity, combined with an ethical stress on the lordship of Christ over all life, generated serious efforts to educate both clergy and laity through urban-based colleges and religious periodicals, as well as through the pulpit, Bible study and family worship.[42]

The complex organizational structure and government of the Presbyterian Church meant that it did not have to undergo serious structural changes in order to respond to the urbanization of Canada. Recent research on Methodism in Canada has traced the transformation of that body from a rural to an urban institution following the Methodist union of 1884.[43] Detailed studies of the demographic and structural factors affecting Presbyterians during the nineteenth century have yet to be done, but when Presbyterianism came to Canada it was already an urban-based institution and had an organizational structure readily adaptable to the needs of a national church after 1875. That organizational structure enabled the Presbyterian Church to face the magnitude of the task of providing Canadians with the ordinary means of grace, especially in the rapidly expanding West and the burgeoning cities. It also allowed the church to take up the increasing burden of defending the values of Anglo-Saxon Protestant culture. These tasks became central factors in the decisions that led to the emergence of a centralized bureaucracy based in Toronto.

The first signs of bureaucratic organization and specialization came in those areas where the Free Church tradition was most aggressive — French evangelization and missions. Co-ordinated efforts at the evangelization of the French Roman Catholic population of Quebec were first undertaken by an interdenominational society drawing considerable support from Montreal's Free Church community. In 1869, the Free Church decided to establish a denominational committee and appointed Daniel Coussirat, a French-born and French-trained Huguenot who had served French Protestants in the United States, to teach French missions at Presbyterian College, Montreal. By the 1880s, a full-time secretary for French Evangelization was appointed and the committee was spending almost one-quarter of the mission funds of the national church. In the 1883 report of the committee to the General Assembly, it argued that nowhere in the world did Roman Catholicism possess greater power and wealth than in Quebec and at no period in the history of that church had it "been more opposed to the dissemination of God's Word, or more zealous in keeping the people in ignorance and superstition than at present."[44] But the 1890s brought stagnation and decline in the efforts to convert Canada's French Roman Catholic population. By this time, attention had shifted to home missions in the West where the French issue remained an important but not controlling factor.[45]

In 1881, the General Assembly appointed James Robertson as Mission Superintendent for the Canadian West, with British Columbia added to his field of supervision in 1890. Although some felt that the powers of oversight given to Robertson bordered on episcopacy, none could argue with the results that he reported to the Fifth General Council of the Alliance of Reformed Churches in 1892. "Eight years ago," he told the delegates, "we had 1 Presbytery; now 2

Synods and 10 Presbyteries. Eleven years ago we had 2 congregations; now 73; then 28 ministers; now 141; in 1881, we held services at 116 points; now at 667. Our communicants have risen from 1,153 to over 14,000, and the revenue from $15,000 to $203,000."[46] The numbers of congregations, ministers, and preaching points reported by Robertson indicated that he had to resort to methods not common within the Presbyterian tradition, such as student missionaries and travelling ministers. He assumed much of the responsibility for recruiting and fund-raising himself. He sought young, robust, and practical missionaries with the qualities of muscular Christianity found in the novels of Ralph Connor, written by C.W. Gordon, minister of St. Stephen's Presbyterian Church in Winnipeg and himself one of Robertson's recruits.[47]

Like Gordon, most of Robertson's early ministers came from Knox College in Toronto. Manitoba College in Winnipeg, established in 1871, offered preparatory courses in arts and theological training, eventually on a part-time basis for students with mission fields. But the numbers required for the work could not be satisfied solely by the small Winnipeg college. The early staff of Manitoba College came from those parts of Ontario most interested in western expansion. George Bryce, John Mark King, John Black, and Robertson himself came from Toronto, while Thomas Hart, a Queen's graduate, came from Perth in the Ottawa valley.[48] From a Presbyterian perspective, at least, Winnipeg in the late nineteenth century was an outpost of the Free Church expansionism of Toronto.

James Robertson represented the first break in the pattern of adding national or regional administrative responsibilities to the parish duties of clergy, which was the rule within the Presbyterian Church in Canada until the 1890s. The second break in the pattern came in foreign missions. Problems in the fields and the amount of correspondence involved in oversight led to the appointment of the Rev. R.P. MacKay as full-time secretary for the Board of Foreign Missions, Western Division, in 1892.[49] As the church's growth demanded more specialized work and resources, a sizeable bureaucracy of secretaries, editors, and support staff filled the Presbyterian offices in the Confederation Life Building in Toronto. By 1911, R.P. MacKay had been joined by A.E. Armstrong in Foreign Missions. J.H. Edmison and A.S. Grant administered Home Missions, assisted by two full-time superintendents in the fields, J.A. Carmichael in Saskatchewan and Manitoba and J.C. Herdman in Alberta and British Columbia. J.C. Robertson was secretary for a rapidly growing Sunday School movement, with R.D. Fraser and J.M. Duncan editing and managing Presbyterian Sunday School Publications. J.G. Shearer directed the extensive work of the Board of Social Service and Evangelism.[50]

Toronto also became the centre for the Presbyterian press. The official publication of the national church remained in Montreal, edited by Ephriam

Scott. But the independent papers, more creative and extensive in their coverage of the affairs of the church and the nation, were consolidated in Toronto when James A. Macdonald left his pastorate in St. Thomas, Ontario,in 1896 and came to Toronto to found, with D.T. McAinsh, the Westminster Company. Within a year, *The Westminster*, their monthly magazine, was amalgamated with *The Canada Presbyterian*, published by C. Blackett Robinson, former editor and publisher of *The Week*. Robinson became president of the Westminster Company and Macdonald continued as editor of its paper. By 1902, the new publishing venture had absorbed several Ontario and western Presbyterian publications and incorporated them into two periodicals, a weekly newspaper, *The Presbyterian*, and a monthly literary magazine, *The Westminster*. These publications offered the church a wide range of reporting and commentary on religious and secular affairs in keeping with the Free Church tradition of the lordship of Christ over all human affairs. In 1903, Macdonald accepted an invitation to become editor of the *Globe* in Toronto, but remained active in church affairs. His place at the Westminster Company was taken by Robert Haddow, a former classmate at Knox College in the 1880s and a colleague on the staff of the *Knox College Monthly*, an alumni journal founded during that period. In addition to the religious newspapers and periodicals issued by the Westminster Company, the firm published popular novels with religious and ethical messages by writers such as Ralph Connor and Marion Keith.[51]

In response to the physical growth of Canada in the last quarter of the nineteenth century, Presbyterians created new administrative structures and staffed them with a professional bureaucracy which was initially intended to supplement the traditional courts of the church. The structures were centralized in Toronto, the largest and most aggressive of the expansionist cities of central Canada. Underlying these institutional changes was the conviction that Protestant Christianity was an essential component of national well-being and that the Presbyterian Church in Canada was best suited to defend the moral and social values of Anglo-Saxon Protestant culture. In the competitive religious market of the expanding Dominion, the evangelical expansionism of the Free Church spirit and the co-ordinating structures of the Presbyterian polity served the denomination well as it developed into the largest Protestant body in Canada.

New Frontiers

The two areas in which Presbyterians faced the greatest challenges and therefore found the most powerful incentives for institutional adaptation were the two frontiers of the 1880s — the West and the cities. Both were presenting new social conditions and posing new social problems for those concerned with the eventual character of the new nation. The emphasis on the need for the church's presence in the community led naturally to proposals for new structures — enlarged mission boards, committees on moral and social reform and evangelism, Sunday School and Young Peoples' boards, and a publishing branch — that would enable the church to adapt and relate to the new situations.

James Robertson, the man who came to personify the missionary aggressiveness of the Free Church spirit in western Canada, had no hesitation in adopting methods that worked on the edge of or around the traditional Presbyterian system. His final goal, however, was always the establishment of organized congregations, connected through the Presbyterian polity. Such congregations were the primary means of assuring the influence of morality and religion in the life of the nation. "It should be the duty of the Church," Robertson lectured the General Assembly of 1888, "to lay broad and deep foundations of piety, purity and probity in this new land." Missionaries in the West were among the most faithful of patriots, continued Robertson, for they were "laying the foundations of social and religious life for generations to come."[52]

Robertson expressed special concern for two groups in the Canadian West, young men released from the moral and social restraints of home and immigrants who came from non-Anglo-Saxon backgrounds. The forms of evil that sought to seduce young men were legion, Robertson warned. "With evil seducers, impure companions, infidel associates, foul and atheistic literature, escape from contamination seems impossible," he reported to the 1890 General Assembly. "Are not the souls of men in Canada as precious as those in any portion of the world? To go in now and possess the country in the name of Christ is to confer untold blessings upon society and to generations to come."[53] Of equal importance to Robertson was the assimilation of new immigrants, in which the church had a central role to play. The great work of both state and church, he asserted in his report of 1889, was "to grind up, assimilate and Christianize this heterogeneous mass. Schools and college powerfully help in this process; but no power is superior to the Gospel of Christ in this great work, and to give the Gospel to these people is, it must be repeated, the first duty of the Christian Church today."[54] Robertson's efforts in establishing a Church and Manse Building Fund for the West under the direction of the General Assembly was one concrete expression of his concern that the church be a central presence in the life of the new society forming there.[55]

No single personality dominated city missions the way Robertson dominated the West, but the same assumptions about the centrality of the church for social well-being were accepted. As more people moved in and as the influence of religion waned, church spokesmen insisted that the best way to guarantee the continuance of moral and spiritual influence was to establish churches. D. McTavish, recipient of a D.Sc. in political economy from Queen's University in 1885 and minister of Central Presbyterian Church in Toronto, described the importance of cities for the welfare of the nation for readers of the *Knox College Monthly* in 1891 and suggested methods of city evangelization that were new to most Canadian Presbyterians. His analysis of the problems posed by cities relied heavily on the work of Josiah Strong, an American Social Gospel leader.[56] Quoting Strong, McTavish asserted that cities were the "nerve centre and storm centre of our civilization . . . the battle-ground of civilization and religion."[57] His list of dangers to which residents of the city were exposed included the saloon and its accessories, the gathering of a large number of the depraved and vicious elements of the population, the feeling of irritation that arises from social differences, and a constantly widening gulf between the evangelical churches and the masses, especially the poorer people.[58]

The church's responsibility was clear to McTavish. "To allow thousands to lapse," he argued, "as far as the true Gospel of Christ is concerned, and to leave them to irreligion, atheism or Jesuitism is to allow a festering sore to grow that will cause trouble to the peace and harmony of the city."[59] When McTavish turned to the institutional changes he thought necessary to respond to the new urban situation, he showed a clear grasp of the efforts and thought of urban missionaries in the United States, England, and Scotland.[60] He emphasized that the work must be done by regularly organized evangelical churches that were able to share the moral and spiritual influence of their faith through sustained personal contact and influence. To foster these close ties, McTavish suggested the adoption of the parish system of oversight for missionary and evangelistic work used by Thomas Chalmers in Scotland.[61] He was also impressed by the synthesis of cultural and religious uplift offered by St. Andrew's Institute, sponsored by St. Andrew's Presbyterian Church, King Street, Toronto. It provided a place where those who were deprived of the advantages of the wealthy and lived in the cheerless surroundings of the downtown districts "could listen not only to simple earnest Gospel talks if they chose, but to discussions of current questions and such instruction as would contribute to their comfort and welfare."[62] Initiated as a Sunday School programme in 1877, the Institute had taken on many of the features of settlement work by the 1890s.[63] McTavish concluded his discussion of the methods of city evangelization by stressing that permanent congregations were preferable to missions because of the stability of their presence and influence.[64] Powerfully argued as McTavish's case was, attempts to organize city mission work on a national level, with support mechanisms similiar to those created for the West, failed. Urban work remained primarily the responsibility of city presbyteries and individual churches within their bounds.[65] However, the need for new organizational approaches had been voiced and was to be reiterated by others, such as C.W. Gordon.

Shortly after arriving in Winnipeg in 1894, Gordon expressed a growing consensus among the younger clergy and the laity when he pleaded for a more efficient organization of energies and resources at the national level of the church. He called for the creation of an Assembly Executive consisting of the heads of the various departments and charged with policy-making and efficient administration. "An Assembly Executive," Gordon argued, "would do much towards securing unity, harmony, and therefore greater efficiency in work, would place the whole effective force of the Church at the disposal of the Church and so would enable her to concentrate this force as occasion might demand upon any part of the work at Home or Abroad. So, too, would the administration of each Department, backed as it would be by the whole Church, be more vigorous and more authoritative."[66] Gordon's views represented the attitudes of his new parishioners in Winnipeg's West End, drawn from the city's commercial elite whose ideas were guided by the principles of growth and efficiency.[67] His pleas fell on deaf ears as far as the creation of an Assembly Executive was concerned, but there were signs of a gradual implementation of Gordon's idea of more vigorous and authoritative national activity in the late 1890s, especially in relation to matters of moral and social reform.

Over the two decades following the union of 1875, the moral and social concerns of lower courts and congregations were well documented in the reports of the Committee on the State of Religion. The committee did not initiate or organize action on a national level, but rather gathered information on the work and influence of local bodies. Its questionnaires covered the pastoral work of ministers and elders, Christian education efforts, the piety of congregations seen in prayer groups and family worship, outreach and benevolent works, and, finally, "causes which operate against the spiritual progress and the development of Christian character." Responses expressed concern for the health and influence of the Presbyterian Church in Canada, the well-being of the Christian family, the moral and social restraints characteristic of nineteenth-century evangelical Protestantism, and the moral purity of national and political life.[68]

Although all these issues were of major concern to the Presbyterian Church as a whole, they were not dealt with on the national level. The two social issues that were dealt with had been issues of longstanding importance to the Free Church activists. These were Sabbath observance and temperance, and they justified special committees at the national level shortly after 1875.

Throughout the 1880s and early 1890s, the Assembly committees on temperance and Sabbath observance did little more than endorse statements by other voluntary associations and urge lower courts and congregations to act in their own jurisdictions. In 1895, the Assembly's committees on the State of Religion, Systematic Beneficence, Sabbath Observance, and Temperance were amalgamated "as an attempt to simplify the method of collecting information on important topics, and prevent the overlapping of such subjects as are closely related to each."[69] This move to make the reporting process more efficient did not involve greater initiative or activity on the part of the committees. But the establishment of the Committee on Sabbath Observance and Legislation in 1899 did mark a new departure. Its membership included the principals of four theological colleges, five Members of Parliament, a Manitoba M. L. A. , a judge, and several prominent educators, lawyers, and businessmen. Among the clergy on the committee was J. G. Shearer, then at Erskine Church, Hamilton, where he spent considerable time reorganizing the Ontario branch of the Lord's Day Alliance. In 1900, Shearer left the parish and became General Secretary of the Dominion Lord's Day Alliance where he organized and co-ordinated the work of a wide variety of interest groups to gain passage of the Dominion Lord's Day Act of 1906.[70] The Assembly's committee played an integral role in that national campaign, initiating policy and propagating it throughout the church. Local and provincial efforts remained important, but through the national committee the church was better able to bring the weight of its national structures to bear on public opinion, legislators, and law enforcement agencies, as well as to educate and lobby within its own constituency. The success of the committee was a key factor in the establishment of a broader committee to deal with an increasing number of concerns coming before the national church in the areas of moral and social reform.

The General Assembly of 1907 received overtures from the Synods of the Maritime Provinces, Toronto and Kingston, Montreal and Ottawa, and British Columbia, as well as from the presbyteries of Halifax, Toronto, Winnipeg, and Westminster, calling for a new national structure to deal with moral and social reform.[71] They resulted in the establishment of a Standing Committee on Temperance and Other Moral and Social Reforms. "It shall be the duty of this Committee," directed the General Assembly, "to study the moral and social problems confronting the people in the different Provinces, such as the relation of the Church to labor, political and commercial corruption, gambling, the social evil, the liquor traffic; to establish a Bureau of Information on moral and social questions; and to indicate lines of action calculated to remove the existing abuses and improve conditions in these regards."[72] Synods and presbyteries were instructed to set up similiar standing committees and one Sunday a year was appointed for a collection across the national church in support of the work of all these committees. The Assembly also selected a Secretary of the Standing Committee who would "give his whole time to the effective prosecution of this work."[73] The Secretary was John G. Shearer.

Joining Shearer as charter members of the new committee were George Pidgeon, who became convener, James A. Macdonald, and C.W. Gordon. T.B. Kilpatrick was appointed in 1911 after the Assembly's Committee on Evangelism, chaired by Gordon, was amalgamated with the moral and social reform body. Robert Falconer was not a member of the committee, but did work closely with it, especially in efforts to provide professional training for social service workers. Membership on the committee numbered between thirty and forty until war time restraints forced its amalgamation with the Board of Home Missions in 1915. Those who served on the committee came from across the country and included businessmen, judges and lawyers, politicians and educators, as well as clergy, though most were drawn from the urban centres of Canada. Shearer, Pidgeon, Gordon, and Macdonald were the leading spokesmen for the concerns of the committee as it sought to apply the principles of the Presbyterian progressives to the moral and social problems of the country.

* * * * *

The desire to preserve the presence and influence of the Presbyterian Church in Canada led church leaders, clerical and lay, to modify the institutional structures of that body to respond to the social transformations taking place in the community around them. Building on the aggressive and expansionist Free Church spirit which set the tone for the union of 1875, Presbyterians gradually centralized much of their work in the last quarter of the nineteenth century. Toronto emerged not only as the largest centre of Presbyterianism in Canada, but also as the metropolitan centre for a group of bureaucrats, editors, and educators who assumed a much greater role in formulating policy and propagating positions than had earlier generations of leaders.

With the establishment of the Committee on Moral and Social Reform, leaders of Presbyterian progressivism gained an effective structure through which they could educate, organize, and act in defence of the moral and social values they considered essential for national righteousness and well-being. It was largely from Toronto, then, that centre of Anglo-Saxon Protestantism and Ontario nationalism, that the Presbyterian critique of Canadian conditions emanated.

NOTES

1. Moir, *Enduring Witness*, pp. 101-145.

2. Quoted in J.A. Johnson, "Factors in the Formation of the Presbyterian Church in Canada, 1875" (unpublished Ph.D. thesis, McGill University, 1955), p. 160.

3. See J.S. Moir, "George Brown," and A.M. Evans, "Oliver Mowat: Christian Statesman of Ontario," in W.S. Reid (ed.), *Called to Witness, Vol. II* (Toronto: Presbyterian Publications, 1978).

4. H.R. Niebuhr, *The Social Sources of Denominationalism* (New York: Henry Holt, 1929), p. 80.

5. W.S. Reid, "The Scottish Protestant Tradition," in W.S. Reid (ed.), *The Scottish Tradition in Canada* (Toronto: McClelland and Stewart, 1976), pp. 120-136.

6. D.S. MacMillan, "The Scot as Businessman," in Reid, *Scottish Tradition*, pp. 179-202.

7. Moir, *Enduring Witness*, p. 144.

8. J.M. Yinger, *The Scientific Study of Religion* (New York: Macmillan, 1970), p. 262.

9. A.L. Drummond and J. Bulloch, *The Scottish Church, 1688-1843* (Edinburgh: St. Andrew Press, 1973), pp. 64-81 and 103-108.

10. Yinger, *Study of Religion*, pp. 253-256.

11. Drummond and Bulloch, *Scottish Church*, pp. 257-258.

12. *Ibid.*, pp. 25-63.

13. *Ibid.*, pp. 220-265.

14. Yinger, *Study of Religion*, pp. 264-266.

15. Moir, *Enduring Witness*, pp. 143-144.

16. J.S. Moir, *The Churches in the British Era* (Toronto: McGraw-Hill Ryerson, 1972), pp. 110-126 and 143-161.

17. E.A. McDougall, "Early Settlement in Lanark County and the Glasgow Colonial Society," *The Canadian Society of Presbyterian History Papers, 1976*, pp. 31-47.

18. Clark, *Church and Sect*, pp. 140-142.

19. *Ibid.*, pp. 132-142.

20. Moir, *Enduring Witness*, pp. 101-106.

21. *Ibid.*, pp. 124-127; and W.H. Elgee, *The Social Teaching of the Canadian Churches, Protestant, The Early Period* (Toronto: Ryerson Press, 1964), pp. 148-151 and 173-175.

22. Yinger, *Study of Religion*, pp. 266-273.

23. Moir, *Enduring Witness*, pp. 128-131.

24. A.D. Gilbert, *Religion and Society in Industrial England: Church, Chapel and Social Change, 1740-1914* (London: Longman, 1976), p. 141.

25. Drummond and Bulloch, *Late Victorian Scotland*, p. 1. See also D. MacLeod, *Memoir of Norman MacLeod, D.D.* (Toronto: Belford Bros., 1876); and Edward Caird, "Memoir," in John Caird, *The Fundamental Ideas of Christianity, Vol I* (Glasgow: James Maclehose and Sons, 1899), pp. ix-cxli.

26. W.S. Grant and F. Hamilton, *George Munro Grant* (Toronto: Morang, 1905); McCurdy, *Macdonnell*; and W. Gordon, *Daniel M. Gordon: His Life* (Toronto: Ryerson Press, 1941).

27. Moir, *Enduring Witness*, p. 144..

28. D. Owram, *Promise of Eden: The Canadian Expansionist Movement and the Idea of the West* (Toronto: University of Toronto Press, 1980). p. 48.

29. *Ibid.*, pp. 38-58.

30. Johnson, "Factors," p. 517.

31. D.P. Kerr, "Metropolitan Dominance in Canada," in J. Warkentin (ed.), *Canada: A Geographical Interpretation* (Toronto: Methuen, 1968), pp. 531-555; L.D. McCann (ed.), *A Geography of Canada: Heartland and Hinterland* (Scarborough: Prentice-Hall, 1982); and G.A. Stelter and A.F.J. Artibise (ed.), *The Canadian City: Essays in Urban History* (Toronto: Macmillan, 1979).

32. D.C. Masters, *The Rise of Toronto, 1850-1890* (Toronto: University of Toronto Press, 1947); and J. Spelt, *Toronto* (Toronto: Collier Macmillan, 1973).

33. T.W. Acheson, "The National Policy and the Industrialization of the Maritimes, 1880-1910," in Stelter and Artibise, *Canadian City*, pp. 93-124.

34. A.F.J. Artibise, *Winnipeg: A Social History of Urban Growth, 1874-1914.* (Montreal: McGill-Queen's University Press, 1975).

35. A.D. Gilbert, *Religion and Society*, pp. 23-27, argues that the best indices of growth and decline in the study of religious institutions focused on what Glock and Stark, in *American Piety*, called the associational dimensions of religiosity, i.e., the observed social behavior of individuals who participate in the religious practices, acts, and rituals. The social historian's task, Gilbert contends, was "to account for observed social behavior, however motivated, and to evaluate its importance within a wider societal context." For this purpose, church membership statistics are the most reliable data.

36. Spelt, *Toronto*, p. 85.

37. N.K. Clifford, "Urbanization and the Church Union Controversy," *Canadian Society of Presbyterian History Papers, 1979*, pp. 37-38.

38. Clark, *Church and Sect*, p. 136.

39. *A&P*, 1885, App., p. clxiii.

40. Reid, "Scottish Protestant Tradition," p. 118.

41. Clifford, "Urbanization," pp. 34-37.

42. Reid, "Scottish Protestant Tradition," pp. 119-120.

43. W. Magney, "The Methodist Church and the National Gospel," *The Bulletin* 20 (1968):3-95; and Semple, "The Impact of Urbanization on the Methodist Church."

44. *A&P*, 1883, App., p. 3.

45. Moir, *Enduring Witness*, pp. 154-156.

46. Quoted in *Ibid.*, p. 160.

47. J.L. and J.H. Thompson, "Ralph Connor and the Canadian Identity," *Queen's Quarterly* 79, no.2 (Winter 1972):159-170.

48. Owram, *Promise of Eden*, p. 44; and A.G. Bedford, *The University of Winnipeg: A History of the Founding Colleges* (Toronto: University of Toronto Press, 1976), pp. 3-20.

49. A. Thompson, *Life and Letters of the Rev. R.P. MacKay* (Toronto: Ryerson Press, 1932), p. 66.

50. See the list of committee and board secretaries in *A&P*, 1911.

51. Lorne Pierce, *The Chronicle of a Century* (Toronto: Ryerson Press, 1929), pp. 176-191.

52. *A&P*, 1888, App. 1, pp. x and xv.

53. *A&P*, 1890, App. 1, p. xx.

54. *A&P*, 1889, App. 1, p. xiv.

55. C.W. Gordon, *The Life of James Robertson* (Toronto: Westminster, 1908), pp. 177-199.

56. On Strong, see D.R. Muller, "The Social Philosophy of Josiah Strong: Social Christianity and American Progressivism," *Church History* 28, no.2 (June 1959):183-201; and P.R. Meyer, "The Fear of Cultural Decline: Josiah Strong's Thought about Reform and Expansion," *Church History*, 42, no. 3 (September 1973):396-405.

57. D. McTavish, "Cities and their Evangelization," *Knox College Monthly* 13, no.4 (Feb. 1891):178.

58. *Ibid.*, pp. 182-186.

59. *Ibid.*, p. 187.

60. For a discussion of the Americans upon whom McTavish drew, Josiah Strong, and S.L. Loomis, see H.F. May, *Protestant Churches and Industrial America* (New York: Harper Torchbooks, 1967), pp. 112-124.

61. On Chalmer's city work, see S.J. Brown, *Thomas Chalmers and the Godly Commonwealth in Scotland* (Oxford: Oxford University Press, 1982); and A.C. Cheyne (ed.), *The Practical and the Pious: Essays on Thomas Chalmers (1780-1847)*)Edinburgh: St. Andrew Press, 1985). Chalmer's work is set in its broader context of social attitudes and criticism within the Scottish churches in S. Mechie, *The Church and Scottish Social Development, 1780-1870* (London: Oxford University Press, 1960); and D.C. Smith, *Passive Obedience and Prophetic Protest: Social Criticism in the Scottish Church, 1830-1945* (New York: Peter Lang, 1987).

62. D. McTavish, "The Methods of City Evangelization," *Knox College Monthly* 13, no.5 (March 1891):246-247.

63. McCurdy, *Macdonnell*, pp. 287-309.

64. McTavish, "Methods," p. 247.

65. *A&P*, 1888, Minutes, p. 26. For a summary of what was being done in Toronto in the 1880s, see J.G. Shearer, "City Missions — The Work," *Knox College Monthly* 5, no.1 (Nov. 1886):35-38.

66. C.W. Gordon, "The New West and the New East," *Knox College Monthly* 18, no. 7 (Nov. 1894):286-287.

67. Artibise, *Winnipeg*, pp. 23-76 and 165-169.

68. For a summary of the concerns expressed in responses, see *A&P*, 1892, App. 19, pp. iii-iv.

69. *A&P*, 1896, App. 20, p. i.

70. A.M.C. Waterman, "The Lord's Day Act in a Secular Society: A Historical Comment on the Canadian Lord's Day Act of 1906," *Canadian Journal of Theology* 11, no. 2 (1965):108-123.

71. *A&P*, 1907, Minutes, pp. 23-24; and App., pp. 325-332.

72. *Ibid.*, Minutes, p. 56.

73. *Ibid.*, Minutes, p. 69. The committee had a penchant for changing names. In 1908, it reported as the Committee on Moral and Social Reform; in 1909 as the Board of Moral and Social Reform; in 1910 as the Board of Moral and Social Reform and Evangelism; and in 1912 as the Board of Social Service and Evangelism.

CHAPTER 4

THE SUBURBAN BASE:

THE PRESBYTERIAN CRITIQUE OF CANADIAN SOCIETY

The Presbyterian progressives' attitude towards the problems of moral and social reform was rooted in their social position as middle-class professionals who saw themselves as impartial arbiters of conflicts that threatened the harmony and welfare of the nation. Necessarily, their view was framed within the urban scene. By 1907, five of the six leaders considered in this study had come to live in Toronto, the exception being C.W. Gordon. Most lived in the new residential suburbs surrounding the University of Toronto: R.A. Falconer on St. George Street, J.A. Macdonald on Prince Arthur Avenue, T.B. Kilpatrick on Spadina Road, and J.G. Shearer on St. Vincent Street, now Bay Street between College and Bloor. These four were all members of Bloor Street Presbyterian Church, at the corner of Huron and Bloor, where George Pidgeon was called when he left teaching in Vancouver in 1915. Prior to his move West in 1909, Pidgeon had been at Victoria Presbyterian Church in Toronto Junction, an affluent suburb to the west of Toronto. Gordon served St. Stephen's in suburban Winnipeg, but maintained very close ties with Toronto, not only through his national church work but also through his publishers, the Westminster Company.

Because of the urban, professional middle-class bases of these leaders, the development of their thought and careers lacked a dimension that was of great importance to many of the most prominent Social Gospel leaders in Canada and the United States — and that was pastoral experience in urban slums in the early years of their ministry. J.S. Woodsworth, for example, was the director of All People's Mission in Winnipeg's North End;[1] Walter

Rauschenbusch spent his formative pastoral years in New York's Hell's Kitchen;[2] Charles Stelzle, head of the American Presbyterian Department of Church and Labor, was born in the New York slums and founded the Presbyterian Labor Temple, a working-class church in New York.[3] Through this experience, they gained a greater degree of identification with the cause of the working poor than the Presbyterian progressives ever had. The most prominent leaders of the Presbyterian Social Gospel moved directly from their university studies into middle-class parishes, professional occupations or teaching positions, and took up residence in the new uptown and suburban neighbourhoods.

From that vantage point, they observed what they considered to be a steady deterioration in conditions in Toronto and other Canadian cities and launched a sustained campaign in defence of the Christian morality and culture with which they had been raised. Their paradigm for understanding their role in society, compounded by an Idealist world-view and an evangelical Protestant fervour, led them to consider themselves neutral, though aggressive, referees in the various disputes that arose among groups or classes in modern society. In that identity they represented the interests of the whole social order. Their intellectual and organizational weapons were modernized to provide an efficient offensive against the immorality, conflict, and anarchy they saw threatening Canadian society. Their efforts were directed at equipping the middle-class professional and commercial community, of which they were a part, with the moral enthusiasm to undertake a crusade to protect and perfect the social, economic, and political system that had evolved in Ontario during the nineteenth century. They sought to legitimate the system and assimilate foreign elements into it, rather than transform its values and structures.

The Problem of the City

W.R. McIntosh, a member of Shearer's committee and convener of the Assembly's committee on Young People's Societies, issued a call to moral arms in *Social Service,* a textbook he compiled for young Canadians in 1911. "War, as the world has known it," he wrote, " is passing, but the virtues of war — its patriotism, courage and self-sacrifice — must continue, or civilization will become a spent force." Drawing from the words of William James, he argued that an aggressive Christian citizenship was the moral equivalent of war. "The war spirit," he continued, "must be enshrined in a new struggle. . . . And to this task — the overthrow of the many social and civic evils that afflict or threaten the life of the people — the young people are summoned to contribute of their moral courage and enthusiasm."[4] The fiercest battles for all Canadians, according to McIntosh's colleagues on the Presbyterian Board of

Moral and Social Reform, were in the cities of Canada, where social and civic evils were concentrated.

For the leaders of Presbyterian progressivism, Toronto became a laboratory in which they tested their tools of social analysis and their strategies for eliminating the problems of the city. Their response to the dramatic growth in population and the radical changes in the landscape of Toronto in the first decade of the twentieth century was shaped by the basic assumptions of their evangelical liberal Christianity. They sought to ensure that the Christian message of the love of God in Christ and the righteous character that resulted from the acceptance of that love would be the determining factor in the growth of Canada's largest city. As their fellow Presbyterians moved from the downtown core to the uptown sections of the city, north of College Street, taking their churches with them, the Presbyterian progressives decried the flight from the needs of the city. The irony, however, was that the reformers themselves were a part of this exodus, for they too lived and worshipped in the new residential areas north of the downtown core. The people whose uptown movement the progressives deplored were in fact their own neighbours.

John G. Shearer told the Pre-Assembly Congress, a gathering of some four thousand Presbyterians from across the country in Toronto in 1913, that the city was the citadel of the nation, manned by the country's most influential men, served by its most efficient organizations, and informed by its most important newspapers and journals. But the fortress of "piety, purity, and probity" was being infiltrated by a new and alien population which threatened the nation's strength and well-being. These people were not evangelical Christians, Shearer warned, a large number of them being "infidel in creed and pagan in life." The church was running away from the incoming tide of aliens, charged Shearer. He offered to show his audience at Massey Hall in downtown Toronto four evangelical churches, within blocks of where they sat, that had been closed in recent years. One became a vaudeville theatre, another a dance hall, and two became Jewish synagogues. If immediate action was not taken, Presbyterians would share responsibility for "permitting our cities to become hell!"[5]

Shearer's list of the issues at stake in the battle for the city stirred his audience to applause.

> At the peril of our national ideals, at the peril of our national rest day for all — the liberty of rest for each secured by the law of rest for all — at the peril of that human efficiency in industrial and commercial life that is only possible where people generally are sober, at the peril of our industrial and national freedom, at the peril of an honest ballot, at the peril of our institutions and liberties dearly bought, and that we do well to hold dear —

> I say at the peril of the Kingdom of Jesus Christ in Canada, at the peril of the very life of the Church in Canada, shall we neglect to redeem our cities?[6]

Shearer's speech, characteristic of the approach taken by his colleagues, called for a defence of the best of Canada. Reforms would perfect rather than transform the social order.

A favourite metaphor for the city used throughout the speeches and writings of the progressive leaders — the storm centre — was borrowed from Josiah Strong's *Our Country* (1885). James A. Macdonald, while editing *The Westminster* in Toronto, used the image to plead for church-wide support for those fighting the battle of the city. "The city is the strategic point in the warfare against evil;" he wrote, "the storm centre is there; there the fiercest battle wages." Those who stood "all the day long in the full front of the struggle for better manners, purer laws and a more wholesome public life" deserved the active encouragement and support of people across the nation.[7] Aggressive missionary work in the city called for a sinewy and "manly" Christianity that called for the highest quality of moral character and needed the support of all those concerned with the preservation of civilization. As the decade unfolded, the analysis of the city presented by the Presbyterian progressives became more sophisticated, but the fundamental evangelical concern with Christianizing and civilizing those alien to the moral and social values of Protestantism remained constant.

One of the most disturbing developments in Toronto for Macdonald and his associates was the growth of economic and ethnic ghettos in the city. The lines of separation between classes and races (although Toronto's non-Anglo-Saxon population remained small during this period) were hardening, making it increasingly difficult for the church to exercise its harmonizing influence. Among the ignorant and the immoral, who, according to the Presbyterian reformers, made up the majority of the population of Toronto's downtown, the process of moral infection and degradation was escalating continually and rapidly, especially as churches abandoned those parts of town.[8] By 1907, *The Presbyterian* was drawing attention to the dividing line between the suburban garrison and the urban battlefield. "The present situation," the editorial stated, "is that north of a line drawn east and west somewhere between Carlton and Queen Streets by far the largest amount of wealth and the greatest number of possible Christian workers is found, and south of that line there is the greatest field for effort. These frontier congregations must not be left to fight the battle alone."[9] The social divisions that became apparent as Toronto grew posed a threat to the vision of a homogeneous Protestant nation. This was a threat second only to the moral threat presented by the commercialization of vice that exploited the ignorance and weakness of the city's population. By 1911, Presbyterian progressives had strengthened their arguments for moral and social reforms with an historical and statistical analysis of the factors contributing to the physical growth and moral deterioration of the city. The most comprehensive statement of their assumptions and approaches to the problem of the city appeared in McIntosh's *Social Service* in an article by Queen's political scientist O.D. Skelton. Skelton was a member of Shearer's Board and author of an award-winning critique of socialism in 1911.[10]

During the nineteenth century, according to Skelton, populations in many countries drifted cityward. The foremost cause was "the invention of power-driven machinery which has led to the concentration of production in large establishments, and the consequent dying out of the old home industries."[11] On the one hand, the long hours of hard work that farm work called for seemed unbearable and drained the country of rural population. On the other, opportunities for education, wealth, and recreation pulled the population towards the city. The concentration of dwellings, industries, traffic, wealth, and the poverty that went with large concentrations of people created problems that even the new professionals — engineers, social planners, and social workers — found hard to resolve. The result, according to Skelton's analysis, was a drift from the traditional "moral moorings" in the burgeoning cities of Canada.

American and European cities, by Skelton's standards, had already lost the war against the forces of evil. The urban environment there suffered from corrupt politics, speculative greed, tenement slums, cramped streets, inadequate housing, and lack of parks or playgrounds, all of which contributed to a loss of health and decency among the population. Further, good citizenship suffered from "moral bankruptcy through exposure to the concentrated saloon and gambling interests, with little constructive attempt on anyone's part to provide alternative means of recreation for the working millions." Rapid urban growth, Skelton continued, "has meant a people precociously keen and quick, but lacking often in mental poise and spiritual insight, in the calm, steadfast strength that comes from quiet and from communion with elemental nature."[12]

Skelton favoured those movements for urban reform that promised efficiency, impartiality, and purity. Though he deplored the degenerate civic morals of American cities, he was especially impressed by the civic renaissance in the United States, "a new growth in pride in one's city, a new sense of the need of thinking, not in continents but in communities, a new realizing of neighbourhood responsibilities."[13] Political regeneration required not only an interested citizenry but also governmental structures that would register the general will faithfully. Skelton himself favoured commission regulation and public ownership of utilities. City planning, he noted with approval, was "primarily an endeavour to plan instead of drift, to put forethought for the common good in place of individual preoccupation with present gain."[14] The city health movement presented a vision of a purified and organized environment, "of cities districted into business and industrial and residential quarters, of tenements built with ample light and air and equipment to encourage rather than kill decency, of reforms in recreation and the provision of food and drink and in the training of the mothers of the future which will stay the slaughter of the innocents."[15] Progressive education sought to train the child in closer relation to the community, to instruct the foreigner in the language and the ideals of the nation, and to provide men and women in the city with "mental food and stimulus" through lectures, clubs, and the press. Finally, moral reform campaigns attempted to eliminate the saloon, the gambling den, and the brothel, and to provide constructive alternatives through organized charity. Skelton made special note of the influence of the Chicago urban reformers, Jane Addams and Graham Taylor, on the American civic renaissance.

The church had an essential role to play in urban reform, said Skelton, and was just beginning to recognize the need for a change in spirit. It had been hindered "by survivals of ultra-individualist theology and by the fact that the churches best able in men and means to share in the work of city upbuilding were usually isolated in residential districts away from the masses to be ministered to, and, unlike hospitals, were conducted as if meant for the healing of the subscribers rather than of those without the gate."[16] But Skelton warned against "committing the Church to hard and fast endorsation or condemnation of policies on which there is wide difference of opinion among honest men," such as the single tax, free trade, socialism, and other panaceas.[17] The church should aim rather at securing full and free discussion of such issues and ideas, at studying existing neighbourhood conditions, and at developing among its own members the social conscience and social enthusiasm needed to deal with the problem of the city. Acknowledging that the church was one of many agencies of social helpfulness, Skelton urged co-operation with the school, the press, voluntary organizations, and the government, either by initiating programmes of social service that would be assumed by some public agency once they were established or by lobbying for legislative action to implement reforms. Skelton's views on the appropriate means of church participation in Canada's civic renaissance exemplified the collectivist liberalism of the leaders of Presbyterian progressivism who sat with him on Shearer's Board.

If the problems themselves were new in both quantity and quality, the basic strategy favoured by Skelton was familiar. The church was seen to be best suited for work in which personal contact and sympathy were most needed. Agricultural settlement, commercial enterprise, and industrial expansion had conquered the continent. The new frontier was the urban neighbourhood and the new challenge was to create the environment that would nurture a moral community. The church was crucial to this task. It saved society by saving the individual, "creating a new man with the dynamic force needed to turn the wheels of whatever organization appeals to him as best fitted for the work of making the city 'the city of God.'"[18] Skelton's social philosophy, emphasizing the social nature of men and women, the importance of community, and the need for a greater commitment to organizational efficiency informed by the new insights of the social sciences, supplemented rather than supplanted the traditional evangelical concern with changed individuals and individual responsibility. Ultimately, Skelton and his colleagues believed that the moral and social purity of the nation depended on the character of the people who worked through its institutions. Any change in structures required a prior change in personal character. A city of God depended on a Christian citizenry.

The year Skelton's essay appeared also marked the conclusion of a two-year period of study and travel by members of the Board of Moral and Social Reform on the problem of the city. When it became apparent that the urban presbyteries were putting their money into suburban expansion, the Board turned its attention to the downtown problem. Facing the problem of the city, according to the report prepared, meant facing a variety of problems at once. "Besides being a problem of Evangelism," the document stated, "it is a problem of economics, of ethics, of philanthropy, of politics, of social and moral reform of every variety — temperance, gambling, Sabbath desecration, various forms of vice, of alien races and tongues, of housing, sanitation, education, recreation, etc."[19] The solution involved both the transformation of the environment and the regeneration of people with the Gospel of the Kingdom as the only sufficient instrument and the church as "the one agent that can hope to succeed in so great a work."[20] The report warned Canadian Presbyterians that the American experience of unassimilated immigrants would be repeated in Canada if the environment of the masses was not improved so that people could be Christianized and Canadianized.

Failure in this mission meant that "the mob will rule, which means the anarchy of ignorance, vice and crime, and therefore the doom of destruction and death." Canada stood in a privileged position among the nations of the world, "last in the procession of nations and because the whole heritage of history is ours and because we ought, in consequence, to be wiser, stronger, and better than any nation that has been, if we fail to measure up to our opportunity and responsibility, if we fail to solve the problem of the city we shall merit the condemnation of God, and the curse of the children of coming Canadian days and of the other nations yet to be."[21] The note of panic in the report's rhetoric was, in part, an attempt to arouse the church at large to greater efforts to ensure that the forces of moral purity and righteousness would rule the cities of Canada. But it was also a despairing apprehension that the battle had already been lost. The churches were deserting the congested areas of the city and abandoning the people there to the dangers described in the report.

The analysis of the urban problems Presbyterians developed during the first decade of the twentieth century drew upon the best data and strategies available in the North Atlantic world. At the heart of their concern was the moral decline they found among the majority of the urban population. They were convinced that the church was an essential, though not the only, agent dealing with the problem. In their ideal vision of city work, the members of Shearer's Board combined a concern with the basic necessities of life with a fear of losing a homogeneous society in which the church would shape the morals, religion, and culture of the nation.

The Pre-Assembly Congress, 1913

The Pre-Assembly Congress of 1913 was organized by the Toronto bureaucracy and marked the triumph of the liberal apologetic for evangelical Christianity among Canadian Presbyterians. In theology, the speakers sought to interpret Christianity in terms acceptable to modern thinkers, while in social policy they sought to articulate a collectivist liberalism suited to an industrial and urban society. Many of the speakers were members of the Board of Social Service and Evangelism and most came from urban centres. They offered a critique of Canadian society that touched on the major themes and assumptions of Presbyterian progressivism: the complementary nature of evangelism and social service, representing individual and social salvation; the identification of humanizing with Christianizing, and Christianizing with acceptance of Anglo-Saxon culture and institutions; and the conviction that a union of Canadian churches would bring together the best of denominational tradition in the common task of winning Canada for Christ.

The problems faced by Canada, noted R.P. MacKay, Congress chairman and General Secretary of the Board of Foreign Missions, were unprecedented.[22] Speakers at the Congress sketched a background of problems arising from non-Anglo-Saxon immigration, the erosion of family life, the organization and commercialization of prostitution and liquor, political corruption, bitter industrial relations, and the co-existence of wealth and poverty. Against this background speakers challenged their audience to respond to the need for moral regeneration. C.W. Gordon, whose reputation as novelist Ralph Connor made him a popular spokesman for Presbyterian progressivism, insisted that the future of Canada would be determined by the churches more than by any other factor in the nation's life. "Religion," he claimed

> is the soil out of which well-doing and well-being spring; and if Canada is ever going to be great and become one of the world powers, and is to bring light and leading to the nations, it will not be because of her great wheatfields, or her marvelous resources, but because of the character of the people, because of our relation to Almighty God. It is a righteous Canada that will endure, and no other; it is a Canada of brethren that will hold together, and no other; and it is a Canada in which peace is love and peace is sought that will be blessed by God.[23]

The nation was the bearer of the values of Christian civilization and the churches must defend and propagate those values throughout the social order.

The strategy most commonly suggested for dealing with these problems was moral persuasion. If, through such modern and scientific investigative techniques as social surveys, the facts about social problems were discovered, and if, through pulpit, press, and other educational channels, the Canadian public were informed of the social conditions in their nation, then, the speakers assumed, changes in attitudes and conduct would follow that would eliminate the causes. In some cases organization would be necessary to stimulate action and legislation to enforce the will of the community, but the key factor was the creation of an informed and enlightened public opinion.

The task of shaping a public conscience that would preserve the culture of evangelical Protestantism was frequently presented in the language of the military campaign. W.T. Herridge, minister at William Lyon Mackenzie King's congregation of St. Andrew's in Ottawa, issued an evangelical call to arms in the battle between "degrading self-indulgence and noble self-sacrifice for the sake of others." Of all forms of work, Herridge argued, "none will prove so lucrative as the manufacture of men who have wider purposes than mere personal aggrandizement, men who are prepared to live for their country, whether called upon to die for it or not, loyal and brave crusaders against everything that would mar its welfare, or degrade its ambitions, or imperil its good name before the world."[24] Herridge struck a common note of identification between the development of citizens of good character and the progress of the nation. Both were dependent on the spread of the Christian gospel.

The primacy of evangelism as a means of spreading the faith and building character was apparent in many of the Congress speeches. John G. Shearer spoke of the foundation laid for social Christianity by an evangelical conversion experience. Changing the environment and transforming social life was necessary, but not sufficient. "It is essential," he told his listeners, "that the heart be regenerated, that the people should be saved, that the character should be transformed; and that can be done to the full only by bringing people in contact with the living, life-giving, risen, glorious and glorified Son of Man."[25] The only base on which lasting social reform could be founded was thought to be a population of men and women whose lives were dedicated to the person and spirit of Jesus. James A. Macdonald, by this time editor of the *Globe*, defined the spirit of Jesus as "the pregnant idea of a kingdom in which they were the greatest who serve and they were the kingliest who love." The central power of the gospel for Macdonald was the power of ideas. The release of the idea of the kingdom of love and service from the mind of Jesus was "the most revolutionary thing in all history."[26]

Images of the kingdom of love and the ideas of love and service provided the necessary connections between the personal and social dimensions of faith. Murdoch MacKinnon, a gold medallist and tutor in mental and moral philosophy under John Watson, posited that the Gospel not only was capable of social application but was by its very nature social from centre to circumference. "The Kingdom is a distinctively social concept," he said,

> whose roots are set in the Messianic hopes of Israel, and when the Son of Man made repentance and personal regeneration the condition for participating in the privileges and responsibilities of the Kingdom, he combined two aspects which are essential to a universal religion and place a social Gospel in the forefront of his divine ministry.[27]

The holism of personal and social salvation led to a corresponding wholeness in the church's organized efforts at evangelism and social service.

However, it was recognized that the church on its own was unequal to the task of Christianizing civilization. It had to make its influence felt throughout the various social institutions that shaped the life of Canada. Robert Law, Professor of New Testament at Knox College, reminded the Congress that much of the church's work had to be done indirectly, through the whole organization of society. "The Church is to make itself the conscience of society," he urged, "the leavening principle at work in its life; it is to be Christ's eyes looking at the facts of the modern world, Christ's brain thinking out the problems these present, Christ's voice appealing to the conscience of the community, Christianizing public opinion and public policy."[28] Church members were Christ's instruments of self-expression not only in religious and evangelistic activities at home and abroad, but also in Parliament, in local legislatures, and in all spheres of civic administration and influence. When

Congress speakers mentioned the chief allies of the church in defending Christian civilization, they referred to those that shaped character rather than those that wielded power — the college, the press, and, above all, the family. Through these institutions the Christian faith would mould public opinion and determine social policy.

In outlining the training for service provided by the universities and theological colleges of Canada, Robert Falconer, President of the University of Toronto and formerly Professor of New Testament at Presbyterian College in Halifax, reminded his listeners of the Presbyterian commitment over the years to a learned and practical faith. He stressed the importance of having students for the ministry complete a liberal arts degree before studying theology, since this would give them a broader understanding of the environment within which they lived and the way thought had shaped and changed that environment."The wise guide," Falconer advised, "is he who, with wide experience of human ways and concrete knowledge of the world of men, is able to discern what is good from evil, and to set forth and adorn a method of life which is reasonable and of true godliness."[29] Falconer welcomed the contributions that the intellectual awakening of the nineteenth century had made to the faith and work of the church. But he pointed out that the application of new scientific knowledge to raw materials and industry had created new social problems as well as bringing many social benefits. Further, new movements of thought had disturbed many within the church who "at first drew around them more tightly the garments of their comfortable doctrines, but soon in setting about the remedying of conditions, they loosened them, and found a new glow."[30] The liberalization of Christian thought evident in Canada's universities and colleges made an important contribution, in Falconer's opinion, to the efforts at applying the permanent truths of Christianity to the manifold problems of modern life.

If the universities and colleges provided the prime means of shaping the character of those who would assume roles of moral and intellectual leadership in Canadian society, the press provided a means of access to a much broader, but no less important, audience. R.D. Fraser, editor and business manager of Sunday School publications for the Presbyterian Church in Canada, stated that both church and press were first and foremost educators. Describing the impressions of an imaginary visitor from some unknown corner of the earth, Fraser ventured that he would not have to be told from what latitude his listeners were gathered, for he would readily see that they had spent their lives "in the tonic atmosphere of this northern clime" and thereby developed characters of vigour and ruggedness. "And the newspapers," he continued,

> do largely for the intellectual life of the people, and for their social life, what the atmosphere does for the physical life. They are a great formative

> and molding influence. . . . They go where the voice of the preacher does not go; they go even where the work of the teacher does not go. . . . they are everywhere, and always with us, and they create an atmosphere; thus it is of great interest to the newspapers themselves that they shall have a proper standard.[31]

Fraser was gentle in his criticism of Canadian papers, noting that many had not yet learned to discuss politics with fairness or give the place they ought to the serious things of life. He concluded by reminding the audience that papers generally printed what their readers wanted, thus placing the blame for the quality of the Canadian press on his listeners. The effectiveness of the press as a vehicle for Christianizing civilization would increase only as Christians demanded it.

The home, however, held first place in the hearts of those Presbyterians gathered in Massey Hall. J.W.A. Nicholson estimated that there were roughly 200,000 Presbyterian homes in Canada in 1913. From those homes came the future citizens of the country, making the family a primary and potent influence in shaping the national life. The home occupied a unique and strategic position. "The home is the first temple," he said, "the first school, the first workshop, and the first medium of intercourse with the larger community. It is well that the church should always remember that the mother is often the first priestess, her bosom the earliest confessional, and her lips the earliest oracle of God for her child."[32] Nicholson went on to discuss the ways in which the Christian family should foster brotherhood and service sanctioned by a living faith in the fatherhood of God. Bruce Taylor of Montreal, a Glasgow graduate and a successor to T.B. Kilpatrick at Ferryhill Free Church in Aberdeen, described the elements of family life he felt important to the exercise of its proper influence on the life of the nation. High on his list were: a pious attitude towards God and towards life, the maintenance of an active interest in literature and public affairs, and a parental commitment to instill uprightness, honour, and purity.[33] Throughout the discussions of social problems and their remedies at the Congress ran the theme of providing or supplementing the influences of the Christian home where they were lacking.

Both the hopes and the fears of those Presbyterians at the Congress became clearest in their consideration of the problem of the foreigner. Non-Anglo-Saxon immigration, stimulated by the policies of the Laurier government and the economic boom that coincided with the Laurier years, posed the most visible threat to the national vision of Presbyterian leaders. Frequent references were made to the liberty and opportunities provided by British-based institutions and to the enlightenment and moral uplift offered by Anglo-Saxon culture. The key to success in assimilating the foreigners was

Christianization. The intent of assimilation was thinly veiled by a rhetoric of mixing or blending. W.D. Reid of Montreal, formerly Superintendent of Missions for Alberta, combined the vision of a mixed race with the assumed dominance of the northern races to create an ideal character type remarkably Anglo-Saxon in its final form. "Woven into the texture of the life of this great nation," he speculated, "shall be the impulse of the Celt, the endurance of the German, the patience of the Slav, the daring of the Northman, the romance of Italy, the suavity of France, the buoyancy of Ireland, the shrewdness of Scotland, and the enterprise and leadership of England. What a nation it should be."[34] Ethnology had convinced Reid that the mixing of races produced the strongest type of people and he was convinced that immigration brought the most vigorous, enterprising, and ambitious of the various races to Canada's shores. Reid's vision of the future of Canada bore the stamp of the view of historical evolution held by those influenced by the Idealists. Briefly, the theory was that certain ideas and character traits came to their highest expression in different traditions and races. As history progressed, these qualities were synthesized as they encountered one another. For Reid and his colleagues, the chief agent of synthesis was liberal Anglo-Saxon Protestant culture.

A similar vision of unity played an important role in supporting the movement for church union in Canada among the evangelical Protestant denominations. Almost to a man, leaders of Presbyterian progressivism saw church union as a necessary step in defending and spreading Christian civilization. Following the congregational vote of 1912, the controversy among Presbyterians over the proposed union with the Methodists and the Congregationalists was on the increase. At the 1913 Congress little open discussion of the matter took place. Robert Falconer, however, a leading proponent of union, could not resist some mention of its importance and motivation. "One of the reasons of our denomination divisions," Falconer suggested, "is that in former days, when the knowledge of history and of the processes of human thought was less than it is now, even the most learned theologians often confounded the non-essential with the essential."[35] In recent years, however, a growing unanimity among scholars as to the essentials of Christianity had laid a firm foundation upon which to build a united church. For Falconer and his fellow speakers at the 1913 Congress, what was essential was a practical and public Gospel that would speak to the needs and opportunities of a young and expanding country where the prestige and power of the church were being threatened by a variety of social transformations.

Congress participants heard clearly the central message of the Presbyterian progressives — a blending of personal and social redemption; moral and social leadership provided by the church and its institutional allies;

the opportunity for elevation and enlightenment offered only by liberal Anglo-Saxon Protestant culture; and the need for co-operative efforts to build the Kingdom of God in Canada. In the context of these ideals, progressive Presbyterians articulated a critique of Canadian society that emphasized the failure to realize moral ideals and the fear of social disintegration under the pressure of developing conditions. The Toronto-based bureaucrats, educators, and journalists who organized the Congress as a vehicle for Presbyterian progressivism sought to mobilize the members of the Presbyterian Church in Canada behind their vision of the church as the guardian and the nation as the bearer of the best in Anglo-Saxon Protestant civilization.

The Urban Core and Settlement Work

Delegates to the 1913 Pre-Assembly Congress were encouraged to visit the new showplace of urban mission work sponsored by the Board of Social Service and Evangelism — St. Christopher House. Located just northeast of the corner of Bathurst and Dundas in downtown Toronto, the settlement was the mother house of a chain of social settlements Shearer's Board began establishing in Canada's major cities in 1912. St. Christopher and its daughter houses symbolized both the success and the failure of the Presbyterian progressive leaders, based in suburban churches and living in spacious residential neighbourhoods. Settlement work promised the triumph of scientific methods of social research and analysis, efficient civic planning, and organized social work. It relied, to a large extent, on the work of university-trained professionals who made extensive use of the new social sciences in approaching the problems of the city. But settlement work of this kind was not quite within the scheme of social regeneration envisaged by the Presbyterian progressives. Accepting it involved an admission of defeat on their part, for their original dreams of full-fledged churches serving downtown neighbourhoods and backed by the enthusiastic support of the rest of the country did not materialize.[36]

The origins of that unrealized ideal of city work in the minds of the Social Gospel leaders can be traced back to their initial exposure to the city as students. Writing in the *Knox College Monthly* in 1886, John G. Shearer and a fellow student, P. Nicol, described their impressions of and hopes for mission work in Toronto. Nicol was convinced that the only reason for the lack of support for city missions was ignorance of the need. He was confident that this problem would be solved quickly now that the Presbyterian Ministerial Association of Toronto had divided the city into mission districts, each one the responsibility of an established city congregation. The most important work of the city mission, according to Nicol, was the persistent personal contact of

Christian workers with the neighbourhoods, especially with mothers and children of homes he saw poisoned by overwork and alcohol.[37] Shearer described the work done at the Elizabeth Street Mission, supported by Daniel McTavish's Central Presbyterian Church. It was one of eight missions then operating in Toronto, each under a different congregation and each doing similar work. The programmes included a Sabbath School, a Band of Hope (to promote temperance among children), a Penny Savings Bank (to promote thrift among children), girls' sewing classes, mothers' meetings, cottage prayer meetings, a medical dispensary, tract distribution, and worship services. Of equal importance to evangelization was the promotion of the health and welfare of the family, accomplished largely through work with mothers and children on a personal basis. The hope was that the missions would grow eventually into self-supporting churches.[38]

The guiding principles Shearer and Nicol expressed as students remained the operative goals for Presbyterian city work until World War I — spiritual and moral regeneration stimulated by personal contact and support for a wholesome family life. But their dreams of self-supporting churches as the means of accomplishing these goals were frustrated by a dramatic change in the geography of the city and an unwillingness on the part of most Toronto Presbyterians to respond as the progressives proposed.

By the end of the nineteenth century, the downtown district of Toronto had been completely transformed by commercial expansion and residential crowding. In the wake of these developments, established downtown churches were moving to new uptown locations, in the midst of the residential neighbourhoods that housed the traditional church-going middle classes. The major controversy among Toronto Presbyterians on this issue arose when Knox Presbyterian Church proposed in 1899 to move from the corner of Queen and Bay to Spadina Avenue, just below Harbord and close to the University of Toronto. In the ensuing debate, James A. Macdonald noted that the well-to-do had moved uptown to more desirable residential areas and their places had been taken by a less stable population of less ample means."The district has been changed in character, but its population has increased, is rapidly increasing, crowding into rooms over shops, into lodging housing, and into narrow quarters where family life is with difficulty maintained." Macdonald was convinced that social stability was threatened if Presbyterians withdrew from "the thickening fight in downtown Toronto."[39]

Macdonald argued that Knox's promise to continue to support mission work in the downtown area was not enough and amounted to a policy of "Here I am, send him." This approach, he observed, had characterized European and American churches in the nineteenth century and the cities had been lost. The attitude that led to such moves was the worst heresy troubling the modern church. "The argument for removal," Macdonald wrote in *The Westminster,*

> is based on the notion that the Church is in the world to be ministered unto, not to minister; that it is a religious club, not a missionary force; that it may seek places where people are nicest, not where they are neediest; that the most cultured and most highly-favoured church members are exempt from self-sacrificing service to the unfit and the unfortunate, and may do their religious duties by proxy — by contributing for the erection of a mission building and the payment of a Bible-woman.[40]

The aggressive missionary spirit of the Free Church tradition in which Macdonald had been raised came through in full force when he wrote of the city. So too did his assumption that once people understood the need, they would act in the appropriate way.

But William Mortimer Clark, a prominent Toronto lawyer who was chairman of the Board of Management of Knox College and a former vice-president of the Equal Rights Association, had a more realistic view of the impact of the changes in the downtown area on his congregation and their probable response. Knox Church, he claimed in a letter to *The Westminster*, had lost eight hundred members to uptown and suburban churches. The poorer classes of people that had moved into the neighbourhood surrounding Knox would not associate themselves with the affluent congregation assembled at Knox. Numbering Macdonald among "a cloud of volunteer and somewhat impertinent advisers," Clark responded to the charges of abandoning the city by listing twelve churches and missions still serving the core. The issue, for Clark, was simple. If Knox was to survive as a strong congregation, it had to follow its members to the new residential sections of the city. The social and economic divisions that increasingly characterized life in Toronto were accepted and would not be overcome by Macdonald's idealism and rhetoric. As the first decade of the century unfolded, developments proved Clark to be right.[41]

In 1903, a new effort to meet the religious needs of the city through more efficient and business-like management was undertaken with the establishment of the Toronto Presbyterian Union. The guiding principle was that the stronger churches would help the weaker churches. Leadership came from prominent Toronto businessmen — Robert S. Gourlay and P.H. Burton, both councillors of the Canadian Manufacturers' Association, G. Tower Fergusson, a past president of the Toronto Stock Exchange, John Wanless, Jr. , R.C. Steele, Major John A. Carlaw, and R.A. Gray.[42] The progressives had high hopes that the new organization would bring money and men to those downtown areas that suffered social exclusion and posed a threat to social well-being. "Among the ignorant and the immoral classes the process of moral infection and degeneration goes steadily and rapidly on until in many large cities the sweltering mass of moral corruption is simply appalling." With these words of warning, *The Presbyterian* welcomed the establishment of the Union and urged Toronto Presbyterians to take immediate and collective action in order not to "surrender the forts and to leave the field to the control of the forces of evil." The Union had the opportunity to make a major contribution to the moral crusade to preserve the religious life of Canada where it was most threatened.[43]

But they failed. A detailed report on the work of the Union in 1906 described extensive efforts to establish and finance churches in the newer residential districts, but little strengthening of downtown work.[44] By 1907, the Union was concerned exclusively with the construction of new churches to keep pace with the residential expansion of the city.[45] Church extension gained widespread support, but the moral equivalent of war in the inner city did not.

Yet even from this apparent failure the progressives reaped an eventual benefit. The establishment of what became the Board of Social Service and Evangelism in 1907 gave the progressives a better base of operation for their assault on the problems of downtown Toronto. They now controlled a national agency, had national exposure through the Assembly, and could bring the prestige and resources of the national church to their campaign for the purification of Toronto and other Canadian cities. By 1909, members of the Board were travelling and gathering information from British and American cities on downtown work.[46] Their studies and experience contributed to the report on the problem of the city submitted to the 1911 Assembly and coincided with overtures from the presbyteries of Montreal, Toronto, Winnipeg, and Westminster asking that city work be placed under the Board.[47] This mandate enabled the progressives to work around presbyteries and local organizations to establish the kind of city work they felt best suited to the needs of the downtown districts. The most attractive form of city work was carried out through the social settlement, an institution Presbyterian progressives had followed with considerable interest since the 1880s.[48]

A special committee of the Board had recommended the adoption of settlement work in 1910, arguing that social settlement was designed to humanize, civilize, and Christianize. The evangelical motivation of the work was paramount. "We are going into this work," the committee stressed, "not merely inspired by a thin, sentimental humanism, but because we are Christian people who seek the advancement of Christ's Kingdom and the saving of men's lives."[49] *The Presbyterian* welcomed the evangelical settlement idea as the best means of reaching "those who have been more sternly buffeted by adversity and sin, whose lives are wrecked or almost so."[50] St. Christopher

House in Toronto was the first of a chain that eventually numbered five across the country. In addition to the evangelical outreach made possible by these outposts in Canada's cities, they provided research and training for specialized city work.

One must note, however, that settlement work was not an altogether new sphere of service. Although informed by a more sophisticated analysis of the city and its problems, and backed by a better organized network of service agencies, the work of the evangelical settlements was in its scope and purpose much the same as that of the city missions Shearer had worked with in his years at Knox College. The focus remained the preservation of religious influences that would guarantee social stability, with a special emphasis on the strengthening of the Christian family.

Moreover, settlement work did not prove to be quite the rallying point in the war for the inner city that its planners had envisaged. The low level of voluntary support for St. Christopher House from Toronto churches, however, indicated that Macdonald's fears of the "Here I am, send him" policy had been well-founded. Twenty volunteers from a Presbyterian population of 25,000 communicant members in Toronto in 1913 did not represent enthusiastic support. Further, much of this support came from Bloor Street Presbyterian Church, where Shearer and Macdonald were members.

In the final analysis, settlement work as a response to the problem of the city did more to satisfy the desire of suburban churchmen to defend their vision of national virtue than to meet the needs of a downtown population. None of the Presbyterian progressives had first-hand experience with working-class congregations or immigrant populations. Because of their lack of experience, they seized upon settlement work as the best strategy available to them.

* * * * *

The history of inner city work by the Presbyterians shows some of the major weaknesses in their social vision. Yet, paradoxically, it also shows the force of that vision which, notwithstanding problems of tactics, gradually reshaped the social policies of the Presbyterian Church in Canada. Working within the church, and also through allied institutions such as the press, schools, and universities, Presbyterian progressives sought to create a responsible Christian citizenry in Canada, guided by the best that Anglo-Saxon Protestant culture had to offer. Church structures changed in response to new circumstances and needs and in the light of new insights from the social sciences. The social critique presented by these leaders changed with the transformations brought about by the impact of industrialization and urbanization on Canadian society and was shaped by collectivist liberalism in its social analysis and strategies for reform. But it is important to note that these leaders were by no means revolutionaries either in principle or in purpose. Their fundamental religious and cultural loyalties remained rooted in the Ontario Presbyterianism in which they had been raised or had adopted. Their personal journeys took them from prosperous, middle-class farms and towns to prosperous, middle-class suburbs. What they strove to do was to reconfirm the commitment of Christianity to establish the Kingdom of God as a functioning reality. Given their personal backgrounds, the goal became one of seeking moral and social reforms in Canada designed to defend and propagate the culture and institutions that maintained the liberal values they had come to value.

NOTES

1. On Woodsworth, see K. McNaught, *A Prophet in Politics* (Toronto: University of Toronto Press, 1959); and Smillie, "The Woodsworths;" on All People's, see G.N. Emery, "The Methodist Church and the 'European Foreigners' of Winnipeg: the All People's Mission, 1889-1914," *Historical and Scientific Society of Manitoba Transactions* (1971-1972), pp. 85-100.

2. On Rauschenbusch, see D.R. Sharpe, *Walter Rauschenbusch* (New York: Macmillan, 1942); and C.H. Hopkins, *The Rise of the Social Gospel in American Protestantism, 1865-1915* (New Haven: Yale University Press, 1967), pp. 215-232.

3. On Stelzle, see G.H. Nash, III, "Charles Stelzle: Social Gospel Pioneer," *Journal of Presbyterian History* 50, no.3 (1972):206-228.

4. W.R. McIntosh (ed.), *Social Service* (Toronto: Presbyterian Publications, 1911), p. 3.

5. J.G. Shearer, "Redemption of the City," in *Pre-Assembly Congress* (Toronto: Board of Foreign Missions, Presbyterian Church in Canada, 1913), p. 171.

6. *Ibid.*, p. 171.

7. *The Westminster* (Toronto), Sept. 15, 1900.

8. *The Presbyterian* (Toronto), Nov. 14, 1903.

9. *The Presbyterian* (Toronto), Mar. 7, 1907.

10. O.D. Skelton, *Socialism: A Critical Analysis* (New York: Houghton Mifflin, 1911).

11. O.D. Skelton, "The Problem of the City," in McIntosh, *Social Service*, pp. 34-35.

12. *Ibid.*, pp. 37-38.

13. *Ibid.*, p. 38.

14. *Ibid.*, p. 39.

15. *Ibid.*, p. 40.

16. *Ibid.*, p. 41.

17. *Ibid.*, p. 42.

18. *Ibid.*, p. 42.

19. *A&P*, 1911, App., p. 267.

20. *Ibid.*, p. 268.

21. *Ibid.*, pp. 269-270.

22. R.P. MacKay, "Introduction," *Pre-Assembly Congress*, p. v.

23. C.W. Gordon, "The Canadian Situation," *Pre-Assembly Congress*, p. 88.

24. W.T. Herridge, "The Message," *Pre-Assembly Congress*, pp. 30-31.

25. J.G. Shearer, "The Redemption of the City," *Pre-Assembly Congress*, p. 172.

26. J.A. Macdonald, "The Relation of the Church to the Social and Industrial Situation," *Pre-Assembly Congress*, pp. 214-215.

27. M. MacKinnon, "The Church and the New Patriotism," *Pre-Assembly Congress*, p. 209.

28. R. Law, "The Church," *Pre-Assembly Congress*, pp. 45-46.

29. R. Falconer, "Training for Service — By the College," *Pre-Assembly Congress*, p. 75.

30. *Ibid.*, p. 30.

31. R.D. Fraser, "Training for Service — By the Press," *Pre-Assembly Congress*, p. 78.

32. J.W.A. Nicholson, "Training for Service — By the Home," *Pre-Assembly Congress*, p. 56.

33. B. Taylor, "Training for Service — By the Home," *Pre-Assembly Congress*, pp. 50-53.

34. W.D. Reid, "The Non-Anglo-Saxons in Canada — Their Christianization and Nationalization," *Pre-Assembly Congress*, p. 125.

35. Falconer, "College," p. 74.

36. For details on the founding and operation of St. Christopher House, see B.J. Fraser, "Education for Neighbourhood and Nation: The Educational Work of St. Christopher House, Toronto, 1912-1918" (unpublished M.A. thesis, University of Toronto, 1975).

37. P. Nicol, "City Missions — Their Object," *Knox College Monthly*, 5, no.1 (Nov. 1886):33-34.

38. Shearer, "City Missions," pp. 35-38.

39. *The Westminster*, (Toronto), Apr. 29, 1899.

40. *The Westminster*, (Toronto), Apr. 29, 1899.

41. *The Westminster*, (Toronto), May 27, 1899.

42. *The Presbyterian*, (Toronto), Feb. 15, 1906.

43. *The Presbyterian*, (Toronto), Nov. 14, 1903.

44. *The Presbyterian*, (Toronto), Feb. 15, 1906.

45. *The Presbyterian*, (Toronto), Oct. 17, 1907..

46. Minutes, Executive of the Board of Moral and Social Reform and Evangelism, Presbyterian Church in Canada, United Church Archives.

47. *A&P*, 1911, Minutes, p. 50, and App., p. 301.

48. See B.J. Fraser, "Theology and the social gospel among Canadian Presbyterians: a case study," *Studies in Religion/Sciences Religieuse* 8, no.1 (1979):36-38.

49. Minutes, Executive of the Board of Moral and Social Reform and Evangelism, Presbyterian Church in Canada, Nov. 16, 1910, United Church Archives.

50. *A&P*, 1912, App., p. 321.

CHAPTER 5

THE STRATEGY :

CREATING A CHRISTIAN COLLECTIVE CONSCIENCE

The character of a nation, Kilpatrick argued throughout *Christian Character*, was formed by the collective conscience of its citizens. His emphasis on the public conscience provided the basis of the fundamental strategy of the leaders of the Presbyterian progressive forces. Trusting in the inherent morality and rationality of men and women, and confident that British democratic institutions provided the best opportunity for righteousness to shape the life of Canada, they focused their attention on creating a Christian collective conscience through moral persuasion. J.G. Shearer expressed their basic assumptions and hopes shortly after his appointment as General Secretary of the Dominion Lord's Day Alliance in 1901. While public opinion had come into its own in the nineteenth century as a significant power in political decision-making, the question of whether the *vox populi* was always the *vox Dei* remained. "Too often," warned Shearer, "it is the opinion of the profane, the immoral, the irreligious, that governs. Why? Because the reverent, the pure, the religious, do not speak, and it is only expressed opinion that exerts its legitimate influence."[1] The assumption, a somewhat naive one, that an enlightened public opinion, expressed through the social and political institutions already in place in Canada, would solve the problems of Canada and bring about the Kingdom of God was characteristic of all the work undertaken by the leaders of the Presbyterian progressive element.

The pulpit and evangelistic campaigns were the most direct means available to the church in educating the Canadian collective conscience. Church leaders also developed a modern and extensive Sunday School programme for the children and youth of their congregations. They realized, however, the congregation and the crusade could not stand alone as avenues of influence on public opinion. The press, both religious and secular, was a powerful instrument in creating public opinion. They also recognized that the public schools and universities of Canada had a great impact on the moral character of the nation. They expressed little regret that the church had given up the task of non-theological education, but kept a careful eye on educational affairs to ensure that Christian values were preserved at the centre of the curricula. But the institution that stood first in the minds and hearts of the Presbyterian progressives as a moulder of righteous character was the Christian home. Throughout their writings the home emerges as the most efficient and effective means of creating a Christian public conscience. Indeed, much of the programme of the Social Gospel among Presbyterians was aimed at preserving and strengthening the influence they thought had been traditionally provided by the Christian home in the life of the nation.

The Christian Home

Several speakers at the Pre-Assembly Congress of 1913 extolled the virtues of the Christian home as the most basic and effective means of nurturing Christian character and moulding a Christian public opinion. A.G. Sinclair, a member of Shearer's Board from Winnipeg, opened his speech entitled "The Family at Home" with a ringing affirmation of the central importance of the home in the thought of these churchmen. Modern science, Sinclair declared, agreed with the Bible in making the family the basic unit of society. "The condition of home-life," he continued, "is the test of all civilization and all progress. You can estimate the danger to the nation of any one of the great social evils of our day by its destructive effect on the home. And family welfare is the final test of every proposed step of social amelioration."[2] The sentiments that Sinclair expressed were not new to his listeners. The centrality of the home and the health of the Christian family had long been the nucleus of Presbyterian piety and social thought.

For J. Thompson of Sarnia, writing in the *Knox College Monthly* in 1892, the wisdom of his Presbyterian forebears was exhibited in their stress on family religion which produced a solidity of character, a sturdy independence, a shrewd sagacity, an indomitable will, an integrity, and a fear of the Lord that made Presbyterians leaders in society wherever they might be. The Christian home was the root of moral and social order. "But in order to conserve the moral forces we possess and gain others," Thompson warned, "we must return to the good old paths and anchor the hearts of our people around the home, for this is the foundation of all moral stability, and we touch the root of the social tree when we touch family life."[3] Six years later James A. Macdonald echoed Thompson's views in *The Westminster*. "The root of the social order is in the home," he wrote, "and we must not allow our discussions of politics or our criticisms of educational systems to hide that fact....The Christian ideal is to prepare for larger freedom by a deeper education, and by a fuller appropriation of those spiritual forces which come from the Church and the Christian home, forces which act from within outward, and build up a character which has true beauty and abiding strength."[4] As Macdonald noted elsewhere, the work of the home was the primary means in the hands of humanity to redeem its fallen race. "The hand that rocks the cradle rules the world."[5]

In his handbook on Christian character, Kilpatrick also affirmed the centrality of the family in shaping the social order, especially through its influence on the moral character of the children. "Here individual character is cradled and nourished," Kilpatrick stated. "Here disposition gets a bias which it will scarcely afterwards lose. Here habits are formed which become a second nature, and are the very stuff of which our character is made. Here ideas are fixed in the mind, and convictions are rooted in the heart, which will determine the whole subsequent career." The vigour or the decay of a nation could be traced directly to the homes from which its citizens had come, a fact that Kilpatrick insisted be fully recognized in all political, educational, or economic schemes for improvement.[6] The most important hand that cradled and nourished the character of Canadian citizens was that of the mother and the views expressed by Presbyterian progressive leaders on the role of women in society arose largely from their perceptions of the importance of family life.

C.W. Gordon, describing the conserving influence of the Women's Foreign Missionary Society in 1889, noted that, since women are supreme in the home, the spirit ruling their minds would shape the home environment and its fruits." If she is a woman devoted to Jesus Christ, the presence of her Master will hallow her home, and those who dwell with her in it cannot but be influenced by that gracious presence. Religion will not be laid aside with Sunday clothes, but will become a part of the everyday life." Christian mothers, Gordon concluded, meant a Christian nation.[7] Gordon's view of the ideal woman was epitomized by his fictional character Mrs. Murray, the heroine of *The Man From Glengarry* fashioned after his mother. Her practical and evangelical faith, radiating from her home to the church and the community, provided the steadying influences that formed Ranald MacDonald, the hero in the novel, into a model Canadian citizen.[8]

For James A. Macdonald, the womanly standard was set also by her role in the home. Warning of the dangers of girls leaving their homes for careers in business, he asserted that it was "in the privacy and relaxation of home that all their finer parts are exercised and grow, faith, self-sacrifice, reverence, humility."[9] In an address to the Women's Home Missionary Society in 1909, his comments showed that little had changed in the perception of Presbyterian progressives since Gordon's *Knox College Monthly* article some twenty years earlier. The hope of the nation, Macdonald told his audience, was in the homes of the people. "The impulse given to the best elements in home life, the words of cheer, the higher ideal, the new inspiration, which go out through the framework of this Society to the remotest bounds of Canada tell very directly and very powerfully on Canada's national character," he said. "Every work of love blesses those who give and those who take; and in the great days of testing which are sure to come, the quality of the Canadian nation, its strength and steadiness and endurance, will be to the praise of those who through the churches and in the homes of the people ministered in patience and love the truth that makes all men free."[10]

In stressing these feminine virtues, Macdonald was also attempting to counter the modern movement of women into non-traditional roles. While his own views of women and their role in society had changed little, Macdonald was aware that the expectation of some women in Canada had shifted from the home to wider spheres of activity and influence. He tried to convince his listeners, however, that the notion that women could best participate in national life by taking an active role in politics through the franchise and Parliament was mistaken. As the life of the people became more complex, the political process lost its pre-eminence as the organ of public opinion and the master of public life. "The really dominant forces," Macdonald advised, "are far back in the everyday life of the people, and are developed and organized and directed by the many voluntary societies that create opinion and inspire to higher ideals of life and service." He insisted that women who really cared for the betterment of conditions and the regeneration of life in Canada could find doors open that would lead to fields of usefulness and influence far greater than politics, and none more powerful in the Christianization of their civilization than the home.

For the progressives, rooted as they were in the piety of mid-nineteenth-century Presbyterianism, the ideal home they sought to preserve was ruled by the kingly and priestly authority of the father, was maintained and guided by the self-sacrificing love and devotion of the mother, and included a regular diet of family worship, Bible study, and religious training.[11] But this pattern of family life was in crisis by the end of the nineteenth century. The fears expressed by Thompson in the *Knox College Monthly* of the waning influence of the Christian family were common in Presbyterian publications and reports during the 1890s and the 1900s. In 1909 a questionnaire sent out by the General Assembly's Committee on Church Life and Work dealt exclusively with the health of the Christian home in Canada. The returns expressed a unanimous desire for its preservation. "Inasmuch as the home is the corner-stone of Church and State," the report said, "and as it is essential to the well-being of both that it should breathe the atmosphere and be filled with the fragrance of that presence that rendered the Nazareth home so ideal, let us seek more and more to unite our forces against the evils that threaten them and keep before our people as pastors and elders the great truth that the home, not the individual, is the unit of society."[12] But the committee's report reluctantly recorded the recognition that the structures and influence of the Christian home were rapidly deteriorating, in spite of repeated efforts to revive and restore its power.

Much of the work of the Presbyterian reformers in the early years of the twentieth century was designed to compensate for the failure of the home, especially on the Western and urban frontiers, by supplying the discipline and training once provided by the Christian family. Josiah Strong, the American Social Gospel leader whose writings were frequently cited by Presbyterian progressives, pointed out in an article published in *The Westminster* in 1897 that, when the home failed to provide a suitable environment for the development of body and soul and a proper training in the duties of citizenship, other institutions had to take over. "In the human organism," he pointed out, "when some organ refuses for any reason to perform its proper function, that function is often performed more or less imperfectly by some other organ or organs. Thus, in the larger organism of society, when some function essential to its health is neglected by its proper organ, it is sometimes more or less imperfectly undertaken by some other, an instance of which is afforded when the church undertakes the neglected functions of the home."[13] Through the support for voluntary bodies, such as the missionary societies, temperance organizations, and Sabbatarian groups, as well as in many of the internal changes in the structures and programmes of the church, progressive leaders sought to preserve and propagate the domestic ideals of their youth. Of the various reforms and programmes promoted and supported by the church, none embodied better the intention of recreating a proper Christian family environment than the chain of evangelical settlement houses in the slums of Canada's major cities.

Members of Shearer's Board of Moral and Social Reform had been observing and commenting on the effect of social settlement work on urban family life since James A. Macdonald's visit to Toynbee Hall in the East End of London in 1889. Settlement work offered particularly attractive opportunities for taking the ideals of moral righteousness and social harmony to the broken families of urban tenements. William Lyon Mackenzie King, for example, reported on Hull House in Chicago for *The Westminster* during his student days there. "Hull House," he reported, "is the home of ladies and gentlemen of culture and refinement of a high order; but it is something more — it is a common meeting place of rich and poor, of the schooled and the uneducated, of those favoured by fortune and of those have fared ill in the lot of life. It is, in a sense, a *place de la concorde*, where mutual love and sympathy are created and fostered amongst all sorts and conditions of people, a potent agency for good will and good works."[14] Much of the day-to-day work of settlements centred on children's programmes and mothercraft, with the express purpose of preserving the influence of the Christian family and providing the missing elements in a healthy home life. Representative of this kind of effort was the White Shield Mothers' Club at St. Christopher, the mother house of the Presbyterian chain. It brought the mothers of the neighbourhood into close personal contact with the settlement workers "to be the 'Shield' to protect and keep clean and pure the best things of life for themselves and their neighborhood."[15] Settlement workers, professional and volunteer alike, were encouraged to see themselves as one family among many in their neighbourhood, albeit a family with specialized skills and training that would enable them to bring more effectively the uplifting influences of morality and religion to their neighbours.[16]

The social cost of the failure of the home to mould Christian character was high in the minds of Presbyterian reformers. The worst and most expensive class of people, an editorial in *The Presbyterian* argued in 1903, were those who had not learned "the science of living in harmonious relations with their fellow men."[17] The best nursery of social harmony was the Christian home, but parents were not assuming their responsibilities for exercising authority and teaching the moral and spiritual values necessary to social stability and harmony. That, in essence, was the principal reason the Presbyterian progressives gave for the decline of the Christian home. As early as 1898, James A. Macdonald admitted that the failure of parents to realize their responsibilities was a commonplace statement among social critics, religious and secular alike. "When we call in the curfew bell and the policeman," he wrote, "we are making a confession of failure, and the failure will become all the more bitter and complete if we look too much to Egypt and place too great reliance upon external restraints. The bit and the bridle can never take the place of the loving eye."[18]

The emphasis of Macdonald and his progressive colleagues throughout their careers was on the cultivation of moral character that would provide the qualities of citizenship needed to make Canada a Christian nation. The home did not stand alone as an agency "by which the raw material of childhood is moulded into the finished product of citizenship," but it was the first in point of time and importance in their minds.[19] All moral and social reform found its starting point and its continual guide in the family. Yet, it was also the experience of the progressives that the family was proving incapable of providing the necessary moral and religious nourishment. What instruments, then, could the church use to ensure the development of Christian virtues in Canada? Standing with the home and helping to shape a Christian collective conscience in Canada were the church, the press, and the school. All exercised an important influence on the minds and hearts of Canadians and were important elements in the strategy of the Presbyterian progressives.

The Pulpit and the Platform

The primary means by which Presbyterian divines tried to shape the minds and hearts of their parishioners was preaching. The sermon interpreted and applied the message of the Bible and occupied the most important place in the Presbyterian order of worship. Sunday afternoons in Presbyterian homes ideally were spent in discussion of the morning's sermon and religious instruction. Family legend held that the foundations of George Pidgeon's reputation as Canada's greatest preacher were laid behind the family home in Quebec's Eastern Townships where the Pidgeon children played church, with George atop the woodpile preaching. As he remembered it, the religious atmosphere of the Pidgeon home was a model of Presbyterian domestic piety, where questions of doctrine, piety, and the religious life were often discussed.[20] It was Pidgeon's ability in the pulpit, rooted in the fertile soil of family religion, that, combined with his work in moral and social reform, gained him the new teaching post in Practical Theology at Westminster Hall in Vancouver in 1909.

The theological shift to an evangelical liberal apologetic, of which Pidgeon was a part, changed the traditional doctrinal emphasis of much Presbyterian preaching, but it did not alter its centrality in Presbyterian piety and worship. The minister was still primarily a preacher of the Word and expected to make an intelligent appeal to the mind as well as an emotional appeal to the heart. For evangelical liberals, this meant preaching based on a Christian apologetic adapted to the intellectual and social climate of their age. Pidgeon began his courses in preaching with "a study of some of the great preachers of the Christian era and of the way they adapted their messages to their times."[21] In the early twentieth century, Pidgeon argued, the essence of the gospel had to be reinterpreted in the categories of modern thought.

Modern ideas in natural science, historical investigation, sociology, economics, and psychology, according to Pidgeon, enriched the appeal of the old Gospel. They strengthened and deepened the Christian message. In order for the pulpit to retain its power in contemporary society, wrote Pidgeon, the preacher must offer solid food in spiritual truth seasoned with the best of modern scholarship. "The health of a man," he continued, "is determined by his ability to assimilate strong food, and the vigour of a religion lies in its power to assimilate the truths in the world around it, and take into its system the strength that is in them. To build up our people in grace and strength we must feed them with this substantial food."[22] In order to prepare this spiritual feast, the preacher needed a wide and current interest in the various dimensions of cultural life — social, political, economic, literary, and religious. A preacher's entire life, Pidgeon insisted, even his hobbies, were to be devoted to "the broadening and deepening of his thought, the refinement of his feelings, and the general culture that everyone must have who aspires to be a leader of men."[23]

In the wake of the evangelical revivals of the nineteenth century, the new generation of preachers was more conscious of the emotional appeal of preaching. C.W. Gordon argued that preaching was the noblest form of oratory because of the breadth and depth of its subject and its means. "It penetrates to the heart's most sacred shrine for its strongest impulse, the duty to right," he said to his fellow students at Knox College in 1886, "it sustains this impulse with the purest affection, calling forth love by a sight of love strange in human history; it presents of action the highest achievement, the perfecting of character into the likeness of the Son of God; it speaks of results weighty with eternity in joys ineffable, in sorrows of voiceless woe, and offers to desire the fullest of satisfaction in the infinite treasure of Almighty God."[24] For Gordon, emotion was the link between intellect and will and the effective stimulus to action. "Truth by statement and argument," he continued in his address, "may furnish engine, wood and water, but without the fire of Emotion the big wheel will not move."[25] Evangelical preaching was the fire that would move church and nation towards morality and righteousness.

T.B. Kilpatrick shared Gordon's views on the appeal and impact of evangelical preaching. The sermon appealed to the reason, he argued in *New Testament Evangelism*, for Christ was the incarnate truth; to the conscience, for it opened the profoundest problems of right and wrong and penetrated to the ultimate relations between humanity and God; to the imagination, so that humans might envisage the divine realities; and to the emotions, since the preacher must not be content until people react to the message with passion and conviction. Above all, Kilpatrick concluded, "Evangelistic Preaching aims dead at the Will. What it seeks is a Verdict, a judgement of value passed upon the Gospel, a decision absolutely, utterly, and conclusively, in its favour, an act of the man in which he passes from his sin to allegiance to Christ."[26] Kilpatrick's favourite preachers of the nineteenth century included some of its great liberal pulpiteers — F.W. Robertson, Phillips Brookes, Horace Bushnell and R.W. Dale, but he also expressed great admiration for conservatives, such as Charles Spurgeon and Dwight L. Moody, who could move the hearts of people in favour of a relationship with Christ.[27] For Kilpatrick, their appeal to men and women to commit themselves to Jesus Christ and to live out that decision in their daily lives was much more important than the matters of theological controversy that divided them. They all preached a practical Christianity rooted in the evangelical experience of God's saving love in Jesus Christ.

Preaching of this nature was seen by Presbyterian progressives as a key element in their strategy to shape a Christian collective conscience through moral persuasion. Its power lay in its impact on the internal process of character formation and was felt indirectly in society through the lives of those moved by its message and appeal. Pidgeon admitted that the pulpit alone could not reform the world. In times when the church exercised its most positive influence on the social order, such as the Reformation and the English Revolution, the principles laid down by the pulpit were carried into action by believers in every line of life. "The pulpit must now," he challenged, "emphasize more strongly than ever the principles that ought to regulate human life, but these principles must be applied by Christian statesmen to politics, by Christian merchants to commerce, by Christian professional men to the professions, by Christian workers everywhere to the peculiar conditions that meet them."[28] The difference between the evangelicalism of the nineteenth century and that of the twentieth, as Pidgeon saw it, was the difference between the politics of John Bright and those of Lloyd George. The former was based on individualism, while the latter recognized the social nature of men and women and sought a collective expression of the moral will of the nation. The church provided the internal dynamic in the life of the nation which shaped the individual components of the larger whole and set the standards for the collective conscience which preserved those moral values necessary for the purity and stability of the social organism.[29]

Pidgeon insisted that evangelical preaching was a necessary complement to the church's moral and social reform work. Every organism, he was convinced, had a double function, one for defence and the other for sustenance. The blood had white corpuscles which fought disease and red corpuscles which nourished the physical system. Similarly, "the church that would save men must overthrow the customs and forces that destroy them, as well as lift these men themselves to a higher plane of living."[30] The way in which these two facets of the church's work were linked together in the minds of the Presbyterian progressives was apparent in the report written by Shearer and Kilpatrick on the evangelistic campaign in the Kootenays in British Columbia in 1908.

Given the vital role of evangelical preaching, the progressive leaders needed a programme to put it into place. At the urging of C.W. Gordon, convener of the Committee on Evangelism, the Presbyterian General Assembly of 1908 adopted Wilbur Chapman's system of Simultaneous Evangelism. For Gordon, the programme had three advantages. The meetings were organized in a decentralized fashion, allowing local preachers to speak to local congregations. National and international evangelists had to conduct only one or two mass meetings to draw attention to the several local meetings. Further, the planning and work of the crusades were conducted co-operatively by a federation of local churches and voluntary organizations, guaranteeing that the campaign would be directed to the specific needs of the community. Finally, the co-operation among local agencies of moral and social uplift strengthened their work within the community and convinced them of the advantages of more unified efforts. The purpose of the programme was two-fold: to show people the power of Christian principles, and to convince them of the need for Christian character in defending the nation's virtue and purity against threats posed by Canada's growing social problems. These constituted the battleplan Gordon and his colleagues adopted in creating a Christian collective conscience.[31]

Gordon's committee published the Kootenays report of Shearer and Kilpatrick so that Simultaneous Evangelism might be promoted across the country. The report contained an extensive social analysis of the district, as well as an assessment of the reasons for the lack of success. In both analysis and assessment, Kilpatrick's proviso that the family be the standard and guiding principle of social reform was paramount. So too was the weakness of that institution on the frontier. Mining dominated the economy of the district, though there was some ranching and fruit farming. Sixty per cent of the population were foreigners, most employed in the mines. They came attracted by high wages and had no thought of establishing homes or families. The results threatened the social stability of the new province of British Columbia, producing "intense individualism and sectionalism, comparative absence of public opinion, weakened sense of social responsibility."[32]

Shearer and Kilpatrick had to admit that church work in the Kootenays had not been a success. The problems they listed all related to the absence of the restraints and obligations normally associated with family life. They cited religious indifference and lack of interest in the higher concerns of humanity's moral and spiritual life, "a kind of chill in which it was difficult to do earnest work." Disregard for the Lord's Day and the power of the liquor interests were added deterrents to the success of the church. Finally, "the presence of the brothel with its scarlet women and their ten times more numerous patrons, scarlet men, in some centres segregated and officially tolerated, and so institutionalized in the community life, with all its deadening and demoralizing influence on moral, social and religious conditions," worked against the uplifting influence of the forces of moral and social reform.[33] The problems identified had nothing to do, said the investigators, with the social or economic structures of the community that needed to be changed in order for the Kingdom of God to be realized more fully. Rather, the problems arose out of moral and religious conditions on the frontier, where the normal social restraints were weak. Consequently, the need was pressing to reinforce those restraints and elevate the moral and religious perceptions through the influence of the church in order that the system might gain stability and work harmoniously and efficiently.

One of the few notes of success in the lengthy report that did not sound exaggerated was the evidence of a "quickening of the social or civic conscience" of the communities where local branches of the Y.M.C.A., the Laymen's Missionary Movement, or the Moral and Social Reform Council of Canada were formed, "with influential men forming the membership."[34]

The Kootenay campaign of evangelism and moral reform found its most responsive audience among those middle-class community leaders already connected with the church who were seeking to legitimate and defend their moral, social, and religious values in a pioneer community.[35]

In 1910, the decision to amalgamate evangelism and moral and social reform under the same board was taken in the hope of "conserving the spiritual dynamic attendant upon a continuing revival of religious conviction" and bringing the whole church "great and permanent uplift" through the multiplication and co-ordination of evangelistic preaching and reform efforts.[36] Such activities were a necessary adjunct to or replacement for the influence of the Christian home and a most reliable way of creating a public opinion that would express the desires of those Shearer had called "the reverent, the pure, the religious."

The Press

Besides evangelical preaching, the written word was another weapon in the campaign of the progressives to instruct the Christian conscience of the nation. The press could always reach inside the private home and continue the education disseminating from the pulpit and the platform. "A Paper for the Home" was the masthead for the weekly journals founded by James A. Macdonald and the Westminster Company, *The Westminster* and *The Presbyterian.* Macdonald's views on how the religious press could support the home and the church were explained in an editorial in *The Westminster* in 1900. Its function was three-fold: to defend the fundamental principles of historic Christianity, to discuss the great moral issues of the day in a spirit of fearless adherence to truth and righteousness, and to keep the church informed on the great movements of the age so it would not fail in its task of prophetic leadership.[37] In a later speech, delivered while Macdonald was managing editor of the Toronto *Globe*, he described the secular press in similar terms, arguing that it was the university of the common people. "As no other institution or agency," he told the Religious Education Association in the United States, "the Press goes into the homes of the people, of all the people, and to a degree creates the atmosphere of their lives and influences the current of their opinions."[38] The press was an integral part of the nation's home life as a purveyor of news, a teacher of values, and a guide and leader in democracy. Religious or secular, the press had both the opportunity and the obligation, in Macdonald's mind, to rise above selfish or partisan motives and give ethical leadership through its positive contribution to the formation of a collective Christian conscience in Canada.

The foundations of Macdonald's career in journalism, as well as the basics of his understanding of the ethical obligations of public leaders, were formed during his student years at Knox College. In 1885 he joined the editorial staff of the *Knox College Monthly,* a journal established two years earlier as a student publication. Under Macdonald's entrepreneurial leadership, the magazine expanded in 1889 to become an alumni journal published by D.T. McAinsh, who was to become Macdonald's partner in the establishment of the Westminster Company in 1896. The *Monthly* quickly became a recognized medium for the spread of evangelical liberalism among its Ontario readership.[39]

Macdonald's perception of social responsibility was grounded in the "strong, positive, evangelical Christianity" of William Caven, Principal of Knox College from 1873 until his death in 1904. Caven had grown up in southwestern Ontario and brought with him to the college the political liberalism, the missionary enthusiasm, and religious insistence on the headship of Christ over church and state that characterized the Canada Presbyterian Church that dominated the district.[40] Caven had, in Macdonald's opinion, quickened the spiritual life of the church and lifted it to a higher level by his teachings and public activities.[41] The centre of Caven's theology was the

Atonement. Dissociating himself from orthodox dogmatists on the one side and "generous and genial" liberals on the other, Caven believed that Christ's propitiation for the sin of humankind on the Cross was at the heart of the gospel.[42] Paul's theology of the great doctrines of grace, centred on sin, atonement, redemption, faith, and righteousness, were what Macdonald remembered of Caven's teaching. "The great doctrines of Paul's theology," Macdonald recalled in a posthumous volume of Caven's addresses, "were to him not only the very essence of Christianity, but absolutely necessary alike as a ground of the Christian's hope and as a message for the evangelical preacher."[43]

The challenge to the church in the twentieth century, as Macdonald saw it, was to take these traditional themes and ideas with their focus on the Cross of Christ and present them to a new generation in terms of new movements of thought. "The changed conditions of life," he pointed out in an editorial on the eve of the twentieth century, "the widened horizons of thought, the new knowledge and the new needs have made necessary a new evangelism if the old Evangel would reach men and be again, as it was of old, a recovering and redeeming power."[44] The press, sacred and secular, was Macdonald's chosen vehicle for his enlarged vision of evangelism. He used it to exercise what he considered to be a prophetic form of social responsibility and leadership in Canadian society, crusading through his papers for the Christianization of Canadian civilization.

The role of the prophet in the minds of evangelical liberals was primarily an instructional one. For John Edgar McFadyen, the Scottish Old Testament scholar teaching at Knox who frequently contributed to Macdonald's publications, the prophets of the Old Testament had addressed a society in which religion did not have its proper place in the life of the nation. Keen and knowledgeable observers of their society, they addressed the social problems cutting away at society's religious roots. Their function was to recall a wandering people to God. The prophets, McFadyen argued, sought not to change the environment but to bring about a more basic change in the corrupt hearts of the people. They were preachers rather than politicians and social reformers, concerned primarily with the intellectual, moral, and religious well-being of their compatriots. "It was moral distinctions," McFadyen wrote, "not class distinctions, that mattered to them. They were reformers, if you like: but it was men and not the situation that they sought to reform. The reformed men could be trusted to reform the situation, and men were re-formed in God — by returning to Him."[45] The prophetic ideal was a society of brothers and sisters, living in peace and harmony while serving God through the faithful and humble discharge of their social obligations. McFadyen's ideal prophet bore a marked resemblance to Macdonald's ideal editor. Both provided the ethical leadership that made an essential contribution to the creation of a Christian collective conscience.

Macdonald's commitment to discuss the great moral questions of the age was evident throughout his term as editor of *The Westminster* and *The Presbyterian*. Editorials, articles, reviews, and news kept the readers in Presbyterian homes informed about a wide range of moral and social reforms, as well as about recent ideas and developments in the progressive Christianization of civilization. The underlying purpose was to produce an informed and stable public opinion rooted in the values of Anglo-Saxon Protestantism. Macdonald feared the stampeding of public opinion by demagogues. He hoped that "slowly but surely the people are coming into their inheritance, and when the day of their enfranchisement dawns the demagogue's sun will have set. Intelligence and conscience are the steadying forces in public opinion."[46] The social responsibility of the press was to spread the ideas that would enable the citizens of Canada to live in harmony as an organic community. Ideas were seen to be the most potent force in human history. Things happened when ideas were at work and those who dealt with ideas, especially preachers, teachers, and editors, were the most influential formulators of public opinion outside the home.[47]

Macdonald decided to accept the offer of the Jaffray family to edit the Toronto *Globe* at the beginning of 1903. In a farewell editorial in *The Presbyterian*, he admitted to moral doubts about assuming editorial control of a secular newspaper with such strong political connections. But he defended his decision by arguing that people, not services such as the press, were sacred or secular. He was confident that he would bring the right spirit to his new position. "It has been pressed upon men," he told his readers, "that in inspiring and directing a great daily newspaper like the *Globe* — admittedly the greatest and most influential in Canada — the things for which the pulpit and the journalism of the Church stand would be more effectively servedat such a time as this in the history of Canada, than by any service possible to men in any other sphere." He claimed that political corruption was the primary issue on his mind and vowed "to stand steadfastly for those things which to me seem first and best in the life of Canada." He was certain that his intentions coincided with the best traditions of the *Globe* and the outlook of its present owners. "The *Globe*," he assured his readers, "has been, not at all a mere party organ, but a great newspaper, true in motive and purpose to the ethical principles and moral truths underlying all sound politics and high service."[48]

A detailed assessment of Macdonald's success in maintaining his independence and moral standards as editor of the *Globe* remains to be done, but Malcolm McGregor, one of his successors at *The Presbyterian*, claimed that, while "remaining with his party and adhering to its fundamental principles, he has not allowed his paper to become its bondslave but has reserved for it the right of moulding the policy of his party and criticizing its failures and defections." Thus, McGregor concluded, Macdonald had contributed to "an honest, alert, and independent press and an informed public opinion."[49] Macdonald's reputation for honesty and independence in journalism achieved international stature among religious journalists. W.T. Ellis of *The Continent* (Chicago) was especially impressed with Macdonald's crusades against the corruption of politicians. As evidence of Macdonald's integrity, he cited a number of libel suits brought against the *Globe* and its editor.[50]

The suit that attracted the most attention among Canadian Presbyterians was brought against Macdonald by Dr. Beattie Nesbitt, a mayoralty candidate in Toronto in 1907. Both the *Globe* and *The Presbyterian* accused Nesbitt of personal immorality and of introducing Tammanyism into Toronto politics.[51] Political corruption was, in their eyes, a capital crime against the best traditions of democracy, the solution to which was "an educated and awakened public conscience."[52] McGregor had noted earlier in *The Presbyterian* that "the interests of Canada are higher than those of any party, and a patriotic press, a fearless and untrammeled pulpit, our schools and universities must work together for a public sentiment that shall make it impossible for any unscrupulous man to find a place among those who are called to bear rule over a Christian people."[53] When Nesbitt announced his candidature in December of 1907, *The Presbyterian* added its own condemnation of "a past master of all the silly arts of the professional ward politician" to that of the *Globe* and the *Toronto News*. "Unless prompt action is taken," the editors warned, "the citizens may wake up to the fact that by neglect the great religious, educational and commercial centre of Toronto is saddled with a chief magistrate whose advent into municipal politics would mean the introduction of Tammanyism which has made some of the great cities of the United States hot beds of corruption and graft."[54] On election eve, *The Presbyterian* urged its readers "to get to the polls early on New Year's morning, and consign this aspiring gentleman to a term of private life."[55]

For Macdonald, the issue of personal morality was added to that of political style. Drawing on a report in the *Stratford Daily Herald* published in 1905, he accused Nesbitt of being drunk in a restaurant, assaulting a young woman, and injuring those who tried to restrain him. The questions for decent citizens, Macdonald challenged, was whether they wanted such a man for their mayor.[56] Enough Torontonians shared Macdonald's negative response to consign Nesbitt to the desired term of private life. He finished a distant third in the mayoralty race with 6,500 votes. The *Globe's* candidate, Joseph Oliver, won the election with 14,000 votes.[57] Nesbitt took neither the charges nor the defeat lightly; he launched a suit of criminal libel against Macdonald and the *Globe*.[58]

Macdonald welcomed the results of the election as a vindication of popular government and a victory for integrity and morality over blind party loyalty and Tammanyism.[59] His colleagues at *The Presbyterian* defended Macdonald's actions, arguing that moulders of public opinion had a duty to inform the public of the political tactics and personal character of those seeking public office.[60] In the courts, Macdonald, represented by Newton Wesley Rowell, fought Nesbitt for a year and a half, finally winning a reserved judgement — a draw.[61] Only once in the affair, and that after the election, did Macdonald or the editors of *The Presbyterian* mention that Nesbitt was a Conservative candidate endorsed by the *Mail and Empire*.[62]

Macdonald's crusades for moral purity and social virtue were the outcome of the ethical obligations imposed by this evangelical Christianity. The cradle of such morality was the Christian home, but it stood in organic relationship with other crucial social institutions in the battle to realize Canada's destiny to become an exemplary nation for the world community. "May we not," Macdonald wrote in 1900, "cherish the hope that, in this formative period of our country's history, the teachers in our schools and colleges; the men who, in the legislative halls, are shaping our institutions; the men who, through the press, have the ear of the people every day; and the men who are called to exercise the prophetic function, shall work together as a united force to permeate our people with those great, eternal principles of righteousness which alone can make a nation strong."[63] The papers Macdonald edited, whether religious or secular, served as his pulpit from which he attempted to preserve the moral and social values of Anglo-Saxon Protestantism and shape an enlightened Christian public conscience to guide Canada's development.

The Public School and the Sunday School

To the influence of the pulpit and the press, the Presbyterian progressives added that of the school in designing their strategy for national moral uplift. In an address to the Ontario Education Association in 1898, James Gibson Hume, a student of and successor to George Paxton Young at University College in Toronto, spoke of the place of the public school in the constellation of institutions responsible for character formation in Canada. It was designed to co-operate with the home and church rather than replace them. "The Public

School teacher," he assured his listeners, "is not meant to supersede the parent, but to be his efficient and sympathetic assistant." The teacher was not simply to impart skills and information, but also to provide a mental and moral training for the pupils whereby the character of the student might be endowed with perseverance, patience, and self-denial and thus be prepared for the duties and responsibilities of home and civic life.[64]

Hume was but one of a long list of Presbyterian clergymen who exercised considerable influence and control over the educational systems in the Canadian provinces during the nineteenth century.[65] Malcolm McGregor noted in *The Presbyterian* in 1905 that the church had done well to abdicate its ancient function of direct control over non-professional education at all levels. But McGregor reminded his readers that the church had to keep a watchful eye on the educational programme of the state, especially in the light of the increasing danger that material and commercial interests would supplant the spiritual and ethical elements in education as the new Canadian nationality took shape.[66] Drawing attention to the growing consciousness of Canadians of their own nationalism, James A. Macdonald reminded the Dominion Educational Association in 1907 that teachers and educational institutions had a crucial role to play in the creation of a body of citizens who would disciplined in character, informed in mind, and trained in useful service, especially in a democracy where public opinion was so central in forming the moral standards of the nation. "It does matter," he said, "that at this time in the history of your country, with the doors all open for currents of anti-Canadian thought and ideals to enter, and with undercurrents of sectionalism and mammonism running strong in our life — it does matter that you and all others who have to do with the creating and shaping of character in the schools of the nation, should feel in every fibre of your being the thrill of opportunity and peril awakened by the present crisis in Canada's progress along the lines of nationhood."[67] When Presbyterian progressives spoke of educating the nation's citizens, they invariably emphasized moral education, and when they referred to moral education, they consistently meant religious education based on the evangelical Protestantism they associated with the best of Anglo-Saxon civilization.

T.B. Kilpatrick told the Dominion Educational Association in 1904 that Canada needed religious education in the public schools, arguing "not only that national education should be sustained by religious motives, suffused with religious influences, directed towards religious issues in life and conduct, but also that the youth of the nation ought to be educated in religion." Uppermost in Kilpatrick's mind among the problems facing Canada was the difficulty in creating a uniform Canadian nationality. Canadians were divided by differences of race, intellectual development, church, creed, and geography, with the resulting dangers of disintegration and anarchy. The true source of unity was to be found "in the truths and principles which united men in a moral order, as fellow-subjects within a realm of righteousness; and in the heightened sense of mutual obligation, and in the increase of mutual respect and mutual charity." Nationality, Kilpatrick continued, rested on the ideal and ethical sides of life. "It is rooted in truth, honesty, purity, love, self-sacrifice. It finds its function and its justification in the conservation and propagation of these, throughout the whole community."[68] Not unexpectedly, given Kilpatrick's Scottish background, he outlined a plan for the implementation of religious education in the nation's schools that was based on the Scottish Education Act.

He chose six elements from the Scottish experience that he felt would enable Canadian educationists to preserve the moral and spiritual heritage of the Anglo-Saxon race in an increasingly diverse environment. Religious education had to be encouraged, not simply permitted, by school authorities. It should be part of the curriculum and taught within school hours. School districts needed to be enlarged and the school boards needed more members, with greater press coverage and public interests in their deliberations. The preparation of the curriculum had to be entrusted to larger and more representative school boards, with the provision of a conscience clause. The curriculum in Protestant districts was to be based on the historical mediation of religion found in the Bible, which Kilpatrick claimed would prepare the students in a free and unbiased manner for true religion in the form of a personal relationship with God. Finally, teachers and students alike were to be encouraged to give religious education the primacy and honour it deserved.[69]

The stumbling block to Kilpatrick's grand design for Canadian education was the presence of Roman Catholic schools, which the government justified by arguing that religion consisted of a special creed and cultus. Kilpatrick objected to separate schools because they tended towards a deterioration of educational efficiency, proved divisive in national life, and led to "the subjection of religion and education alike to the domination of political parties, whereby they would straightway cease to be elevating influences in national life." But, in the end, Kilpatrick had to admit the current inability of Christendom to rise above its divisions, and recognize that separate schools were part of the reality of Canadian constitutional and educational life.[70] A reminder of this reality came in 1905 when the Laurier government supported separate-school clauses in the autonomy bills creating the provinces of Saskatchewan and Alberta, in spite of public and private urgings to Laurier from C.W. Gordon and James A. Macdonald to create a uniform system of public schools for the sake of Canadian unity.[71]

Similar conclusions about separate schools in Canada were reached by the Commission on Religious Education appointed in 1912 by the General Assembly "to make a scientific survey of the whole field of Religious Education in the Presbyterian Church in Canada." The Commission was chaired by W. Clark Murray, who had taught philosophy and education at Dalhousie University in Halifax before being appointed President of the University of Saskatchewan in 1908. Its secretary was W.J. Knox, a charter member of Shearer's Board and a graduate of Columbia Teachers' College in New York, which was the intellectual crossroads of the New Education in the United States at the turn of the century.[72] Part of the Commission's mandate was to survey the provisions for and practice of religious instruction in the public schools of Canada. The report reiterated that the public school was a key instrument of nation building. "In a new country like Canada, into which is being poured in hitherto unparalleled numbers people representing nearly every tongue, race, political, moral, religious and social conditions known to civilization, the national school seems to be the only effective instrument available for the welding of these diverse races into one homogeneous, self-governing people."[73] As immigrants brought different styles and ideals of family life into the country, as frontiers attracted single men and women released from the normal restraints of family life, and as urban conditions and industrial demands changed traditional Anglo-Saxon domestic patterns, the traditional role of the family seemed to disappear. Faced with this crisis, Presbyterian progressives turned increasingly to the school and its allied social agencies as surrogates for the Christian family.

The Commission on Religious Education welcomed the attempts to make national schools effective centres of moral and religious training, but had to admit that public schools in Canada were not able to offer the kind of education desired by many Presbyterians. "The public school," the Commission told the General Assembly, "is not, and cannot for this generation become an efficient instrument for religious instruction; and if it did become an active instrument in a state where creeds are diverse and antagonism strong, it would disrupt the state politically."[74] The realization that their evangelical liberal Protestantism could not provide a unifying and harmonizing force in Canadian society by designing and executing an universally acceptable place for moral instruction gained a slow and reluctant acceptance from Presbyterian progressives. But they saw this failure as a temporary setback and remained convinced that their ideals would triumph as a new generation came of age. Meanwhile, they acknowledged that the public school in Canada was not yet equipped to provide adequate religious education. Consequently, the

Commission recommended that more serious attention be given to the work of Sunday Schools and Young People's societies.

Sunday Schools had been a relatively recent innovation in the history of Christian nurture. Their origins lay in the city work of evangelicals in Great Britain in the eighteenth and nineteenth centuries as a means of providing the uplifting influences normally supplied by the home, family religion, and the church. The movement spread rapidly, especially in the United States where it became "a prep school for the whole of evangelical America" by the end of the nineteenth century.[75] Standardized and graded lesson plans, reinforced by teacher-training programmes, were developed in the 1870s and 1880s by the Chicago-based International Sunday School Association, a voluntary network closely allied with the Moody organization and serving all the evangelical churches on the continent.[76] The impact of liberalism among evangelical Protestants in the late nineteenth century led to the establishment of the Religious Education Association in 1903. Under the intellectual leadership of George A. Coe, the organization sought to integrate the insights of progressive education into Sunday School work.[77] A separate Canadian committee was not formed until 1913, but several Canadian Presbyterians, including J.E. McFadyen, Robert Falconer, and R.D. Fraser, editor and publisher of Presbyterian Sunday School material in Canada, were active in and influenced by the American organization.[78]

Commenting on the spread of Sunday School education among Canadian Presbyterians in 1903, *The Presbyterian* recognized that it was fast taking the place of the home in religious education, just as public schools had taken the place of the home in other dimensions of education. While not enthusiastic about this development, McGregor accepted it as a fact of life and encouraged his readers to make their Sunday Schools as efficient and effective as possible.[79] In 1904, J.C. Robertson was appointed full-time secretary of the Committee on Sabbath Schools. By 1914, Robertson had been joined on the national staff by C.A. Myers and had developed an extensive programme of teacher-training institutes and Sunday School resources for teachers and pupils in co-operation with R.D. Fraser.[80] These men brought to Sunday School and youth work the ideas and methods of the New Education, with its declared intention of using the best of modern insights and knowledge to make the institution a potent ally of the home and the church in shaping the character of Canada's citizens. W.J. Knox described the impact of the New Education on religious education in terms of a shift to a child-centred approach to instruction, an emphasis on nurture rather than conversion, the adoption of graded lessons plans, the provision of extensive resources for teacher training, and the encouragement of co-operative work with other social agencies.[81] The appointment of the Commission on Religious Education in 1912 was welcomed by *The Presbyterian* as a further sign that religious educators within the Presbyterian Church in Canada were making progress in modernizing their work through the principles and reforms advocated by the Religious Education Association in the United States.[82]

The Presbyterian progressives saw the expanding network of organized Sunday Schools as an important vehicle for their ideas. Several of the leading proponents of progressive religious education were members of Shearer's Board — W.J. Knox, R.A. Falconer, and W.R. McIntosh. Kilpatrick contributed a volume on Christian doctrine and Falconer one on the life of Jesus to a series of teacher-training handbooks published by Fraser which enjoyed an international circulation.[83] *The Presbyterian* ran its own series of commentaries on the International Sunday School Lessons written by such evangelical liberal apologists as Kilpatrick, McFadyen, and Pidgeon. Pidgeon, indeed, wrote a weekly commentary on the lessons in the *Globe* and frequently touched on topics of moral and social reform. The efficient organization of an active religious education system within the Presbyterian Church in Canada provided the progressives with another means of moulding the public conscience of the nation.

* * * * *

The basic strategy adopted by the leaders of the Presbyterian progressives in their defence of Christian civilization as they knew it was the creation of a Christian collective conscience embodied in the moral character of the nation's citizens. The task of forming such character was the responsibility of all Christians and best accomplished through the diligent preservation of the Christian home. But the changing social conditions led these public moralists to place more and more reliance upon agencies they saw as supplementing or replacing the home in those areas where the family was weak or parents had abdicated their responsibilities. The church, the press, and the school still had their distinct functions to perform, but they were also seen as powerful forces in the crusade for higher moral and social standards in Canadian society.

The strategy of the progressive leaders reflected the assumptions underlying their evangelical liberal apologetic: that religion was a necessary and determining component of human life and consisted, in essence, of a reconciled relationship with God made possible by the self-sacrifice of Jesus Christ; that such a religious faith was the only true and stable basis for moral character in men and women; that Christian character produced the internal motivation and discipline essential for responsible citizenship; and that the social agencies that imparted ideas and shaped character — the home, the church, the press and the schools — were the most important and influential institutions in society. Social transformations in Canada at the end of the nineteenth century and the beginning of the twentieth put these assumptions and institutions to a severe test. It was in response to this test that the Presbyterian progressives drew up their national programme.

NOTES

1. *The Westminster* (Toronto), Oct. 26, 1901.

2. A.G. Sinclair, "The Family at Home," in *Pre-Assembly Congress*, p. 162.

3. J. Thompson, "The Home: Woman's Work in the Church," *Knox College Monthly* 16, no.5 (Sept. 1892):231-232.

4. *The Westminster* (Toronto), Jan 1, 1898.

5. *The Westminster* (Toronto), Apr. 1, 1899.

6. Kilpatrick, *Christian Character*, pp. 143-144.

7. C.W. Gordon, "The W.F.M.S. as a Conserving Influence," *Knox College Monthly* 10, no.1 (May 1889):39-44.

8. Ralph Connor, *The Man From Glengarry* (Toronto: Westminster, 1901), pp. 273-287.

9. *The Westminster* (Toronto), Apr. 1, 1899.

10. *The Presbyterian* (Toronto), Apr. 1, 1909.

11. See, for example, John W. Grant's description of the Pidgeon home in *George Pidgeon* (Toronto: Ryerson, 1962), pp. 5-13.

12. *A&P*, 1909, App., p. 210.

13. *The Westminster* (Toronto), March, 1897.

14. *The Westminster* (Toronto), Nov. 6, 1897.

15. *Presbyterian Record* (Montreal), June, 1915.

16. Robert Falconer and J.G. Shearer worked closely together in the establishment of the University of Toronto's new Department of Social Work in 1914. Shearer included a complete outline of the courses offered in his report to the General Assembly that year and noted that the staff of St. Christopher House were responsible for some of the teaching. See *A&P*, 1914, App., pp. 329-330. On the emergence of social work as a profession, see R. Lubove, *The Professional Altruist: The Emergence of Social Work as a Career, 1880-1930* (Cambridge: Harvard University Press, 1965); and K. Woodroofe, *From Charity to Social Work* (Toronto: University of Toronto Press, 1968).

17. *The Presbyterian* (Toronto), May 23, 1903.

18. *The Westminster* (Toronto), Jan. 1, 1898.

19. *The Presbyterian* (Toronto), May 23, 1903.

20. Grant, *Pidgeon*, pp. ix and 5-12.

21. *Calendar of Westminster Hall, Vancouver, 1911*, p. 9. The Pidgeon Papers in the United Church Archives contain some of his lecture notes on preaching from Westminster Hall and 1,549 sermons that Pidgeon preached. Only a few of them date from prior to 1925, but there are enough to give a good indication of Pidgeon's train of thought. The earliest extant sermon was published as "God's Care For His Own," in *Presbyterian College Journal* 14, no.3 (Apr. 1913):12-13.

22. G.C. Pidgeon, "The Claims of the Christian Ministry upon the Men of the Church," *Westminster Hall and Farthest West Review* 3, no.4 (Apr. 1913):12-13.

23. G.C. Pidgeon, "Ministers' Hobbies," *Presbyterian College Journal* 13, no. 2 (Dec. 1893):108-113.

24. C.W. Gordon, "Introduction to the Art of Oratory," *Knox College Monthly* 5, no.1 (Nov. 1886):1-9. Gordon, Shearer, and Macdonald studied homiletics under J.J.A. Proudfoot, the son of William Proudfoot of the United Secession Church in London, Ont. His lectures on preaching were published in J.J.A. Proudfoot, *Systematic Homiletics* (Toronto: Westminster, 1903), following his death. For examples of the best of the preaching of the older generation of Free Church leaders, see *Canada Presbyterian Church Pulpit, First Series* (Toronto: James Campbell and Son, 1871); and *Canada Presbyterian Church Pulpit, Second Series* (Toronto: James Campbell and Son, 1873).

25. Gordon, "Art of Oratory," p. 6.

26. Kilpatrick, *New Testament Evangelism*, p. 297.

27. On Brooks, see Ahlstrom, *Religious History*, pp. 738-740. On Dale and Spurgeon, see the essays by John Kenyon and R.J. Helmstadter, respectively, in P.T. Phillips (ed.), *The View from the Pulpit: Victorian Ministers and Society* (Toronto: Macmillan, 1978), pp 161-186 and 187-210. On Bushnell, see Hutchinson, *Modernist Impulse*, pp. 43-48; and on Robertson, see S.A. Brooke, *Life, Letters, Lectures and Addresses of F.W. Robertson* (New York: Harper and Row, 1865).

28. G.C. Pidgeon, "The Teachings of Christ in their Bearing on Modern Problems," *Presbyterian College Journal* 19, no.6 (Apr. 1900):450-451.

29. G.C. Pidgeon, "The Power of the Missionary Idea," Pidgeon Papers, File 2066, United Church Archives.

30. G.C. Pidgeon, "The Church's Interest in Moral Reform, I," *Presbyterian Record* (Montreal), Feb. 1910.

31. *The Presbyterian* (Toronto), May 14, 1908; and Feb. 18 and 25, 1909.

32. Shearer and Kilpatrick, *Kootenay Campaign*, p. 4.

33. *Ibid.*, pp. 14-16.

34. *Ibid.*, p. 31.

35. Details of other campaigns can be found in the yearly reports of the Committee on Evangelism in *A&P*, 1908-1910.

36. *A&P*, 1910. App., p. 268.

37. *The Westminster* (Toronto), Sept. 29, 1900.

38. J.A. Macdonald, "The Press and the Ethical Life of the Nation," *Religious Education* 3, no.2 (June 1908):75-80. On the rise and ideal of the daily press in Canada, see P. Rutherford, *A Victorian Authority: The Daily Press in Late Nineteenth-Century Canada* (Toronto: University of Toronto Press, 1982).

39. J.M. Duncan, "The Late Managing Editor," *Knox College Monthly* 16, no.1 (May 1892):25-26.

40. On the creation and spirit of the Canada Presbyterian Church, a union of the Secessionist and Free Church branches in Canada, see Moir, *Enduring Witness*, pp. 131-150.

41. J.A. Macdonald, "Rev. Principal Caven, D.D.," *Knox College Monthly* 15, no.1 (Nov. 1891):9.

42. *The Westminster* (Toronto), Nov. 9, 1901.

43. Macdonald, "A Biographical Sketch," in Caven, *Christ's Teaching*, pp. xviii-xix.

44. *The Westminster* (Toronto), Dec. 16, 1899.

45. J.E. McFayden, "The Social Principals of the Prophets," *The Westminster* 13, no.4 (Oct. 1908):239-242.

46. *The Presbyterian* (Toronto), Oct. 11, 1902.

47. Pidgeon, in "The Power of the Missionary Idea," commented that Macdonald expressed thoughts similar to this in a speech delivered sometime in the first decade of the twentieth century. Efforts to date Pidgeon's address and find Macdonald's speech have proved fruitless.

48. *The Presbyterian* (Toronto), Jan. 10, 1903.

49. *The Presbyterian* (Toronto), Oct. 10, 1907. On Macdonald's successors at the journals published by the Westminister Company, see Pierce, *Chronicles of a Century*, pp. 183-188.

50. *The Presbyterian* (Toronto), Sept. 4, 1913.

51. *Globe* (Toronto), Dec. 7 and 28, 1907.

52. *The Presbyterian* (Toronto), Dec. 17, 1904.

53. *The Presbyterian* (Toronto), Nov. 26, 1904.

54. *The Presbyterian* (Toronto), Dec. 12, 1907.

55. *The Presbyterian* (Toronto), Dec. 26, 1907.

56. *Globe* (Toronto), Dec. 28 and 30, 1907.

57. *Globe* (Toronto), Jan. 2, 1908.

58. *Globe* (Toronto), Dec. 30, 1907; and Jan. 1, 1908.

59. *Globe* (Toronto), Jan. 2, 1908.

60. *The Presbyterian* (Toronto), Jan. 2, 1908.

61. Assize Clerks Reports, County of York, Winter 1909. Public Archives of Ontario.

62. *Globe* (Toronto), Jan. 2, 1908.

63. *The Westminster* (Toronto), June 23, 1900.

64. J.G. Hume, "Moral Training in Public Schools," *Ontario Educational Association Proceedings, 1898* (Toronto: Rowsell and Hutchinson, 1898), pp. 232-237.

65. J.D. Wilson, *et al.* (eds.), *Canadian Education: A History* (Scarborough: Prentice-Hall of Canada, 1970), pp. 24-39.

66. *The Presbyterian* (Toronto), June 17, 1905.

67. J.A. Macdonald, "The Call of the Nation," *Dominion Education Association Proceedings, 1907* (Toronto: Murray Printing, 1908), pp. 73-79.

68. T.B. Kilpatrick, "National Religious Education," *Dominion Education Association Proceedings, 1904* (Toronto: Murray Printing, 1904), pp. 106-112.

69. *Ibid.*, pp. 110-112.

70. *Ibid.*, p. 110.

71. Correspondence in the Laurier Papers, Public Archives of Canada, from Gordon and Macdonald throughout the period of debate over the autonomy bills indicates their actions in church courts and the press on the issue of education in the new provinces and their disagreements with Laurier's position.

72. *A&P*, 1913, App., p. 233. On Knox, see *The Presbyterian Witness* (Toronto), Feb. 10, 1921. On Columbia and the New Education, see L.E. Cremin, *The Transformation of the School: Progressivism in American Education, 1876-1957* (New York: Knopf, 1961), pp. 100-126 and 168-176.

73. *A&P*, 1914, App., p. 257.

74. *Ibid.*, p. 258.

75. R.W. Lynn and E. Wright, *The Big Little School: Sunday Child of American Protestantism* (New York: Harper and Row, 1971), pp. 3-16.

76. Handy, *History of the Churches.*, pp. 281-282.

77. For a survey of the background and work of the Religious Education Association, see S.A. Schmidt, *A History of the Religious Education Association* (Birmingham, Alabama: Religious Education Press, 1983).

78. *The Presbyterian* (Toronto), Nov. 17, 1913.

79. *The Presbyterian* (Toronto), Aug. 29, 1903.

80. *A&P*, 1913, App., p. 238.

81. *The Presbyterian* (Toronto), June 1, 1916.

82. *The Presbyterian* (Toronto), Sept. 12,, 1912; and Apr. 3, 1913.

83. *A&P*, 1913, App., p. 238.

CHAPTER 6

THE IMPLEMENTATION: MOBILIZING A CHRISTIAN NATION

Much of the implementation of the Presbyterian progressive programme envisaged by the leaders was indirect. Its work could perhaps be best perceived in the ways in which the moral and social obligations of citizenship were accepted by the men and women who listened to sermons in Canadian churches, read the Canadian press, studied in Canadian schools, and were raised in Canadian homes. It sought to reform the conscience of the nation by influencing the internal motivation of people as they lived in modern society. To put this programme in place, Presbyterian progressives relied primarily on the means of moral persuasion examined in the previous chapter. But they also recognized that the strength of their moral crusade would be greatly increased through associations and alliances that would enable the forces of moral and social purity to speak with a unified voice. Democratic institutions, in their minds, should be most responsive to impartial interest groups. The church, built as it was on the ideals of Jesus, best represented this disinterested stance in the face of the growing tensions among various groups within Canadian society. A unified moral sentiment, based upon what the progressives thought to be the best interests of the whole Canadian people, would then become the foundation upon which to build a legislative programme to promote and enforce the moral conscience of the community. As a result of education and organization, legislation would be passed and enforced that would remove evils from the community, encourage harmonious social relations, and improve the environment in which Christian character might be nurtured among Canada's citizens of all origins. A survey of some of the representative attempts by Presbyterian progressives to translate their views into social measures will show how they expected to harness the existing social structures and institutions to mobilize a Christian Canada.

Mobilizing the Church

The only tangible power the church had in Canada by the end of the nineteenth century was the influence of its members. It was understandable, therefore, that the leaders of the Presbyterian progressives would seek new ways to mobilize the laity in support of their moral crusade. In November of 1906, for example, J.A. Macdonald and C.W. Gordon returned from speaking engagements in the United States full of enthusiasm for the newly-formed Presbyterian Brotherhood. Macdonald saw it as an ideal means of increasing the church's "aggressive strength and practical efficiency" by tapping the expertise and influence of the church's leading laymen. "The significance of it," *The Presbyterian* noted in its editorial on the new organization, "lies in the fact that strong men in all parts of the country — men who are recognized as leaders in various walks of life — have awakened to the fact that if the church is to come to her own as a leavening and purifying force in the life of the nation, the potentialities of her manhood must be harnessed and directed into lines of practical Christian effort."[1] By February of 1907, Macdonald had established a Toronto branch in his own church, Bloor Street Presbyterian, and in June of that year the General Assembly appointed a national committee under Macdonald to promote the Brotherhood movement in congregations across the country.[2]

The national committee included prominent leaders from education, business, and law from the country's major urban centres. W.C. Murray taught philosophy at Dalhousie and S.W. Dyde the same at Queen's. G. Tower Fergusson was a prominent Toronto stockbroker and Robert Kilgour a leading Toronto manufacturer. Alexander Stuart had a thriving law practice in London, Ontario, while Judge J.S. Archibald and architect A.C. Hutchison lived in Montreal. J.R. Reid was manager for eastern Canada of Sun Life, based in Ottawa. All these laymen had been active in voluntary organizations outside the church, as well as serving as elders in their own congregations. Most had Liberal political sympathies and represented the moderate reformism of the commercial and professional classes.[3]

W.J. Knox, who succeeded Macdonald as national convener in 1909, expressed their common ideal when he wrote that the church "must infuse such a spirit of truth, justice and love into the civic body that it will be the realized Kingdom of God." Commerce, politics, social life, and education were all to be based on "the sure principles of the Kingdom."[4] The Brotherhood seemed like a natural ally for the Board of Moral and Social Reform, established by the same 1907 Assembly. "The Brotherhood idea carries with it," a report stated, "not only fellowship among the members but a helping hand to those outside. The social, benevolent and charitable work of the community too long neglected by the churches and left to other societies, should be accepted by the men of the Brotherhood as a definite part of their privilege and duty."[5] By 1909, the work of the Brotherhood had been placed under the supervision of Shearer's Board.

Little came of such high hopes for the Brotherhood. It did join with a parallel Methodist organization to sponsor social surveys of the moral and social conditions in particular cities and regions of the country, including Sydney, Montreal, Toronto, Hamilton, London, Port Arthur, Fort William, Regina, Vancouver, and Fernie. It also sponsored a report on rural conditions in Canada by John MacDougall.[6] The surveys used a broad range of methods and perspectives provided by the social sciences for an "investigation of a given area, whereby a comprehensive view is obtained of the facts and needs in their relation to human lives, and these facts and needs are then made public with corrective and constructive recommendations."[7] The London, Ontario, social survey, for example, researched and reported on juvenile court work, recreation, education, religious life and evangelism, industrial problems, social purity, charities, legislation, and civic improvement. Some civic officials, whose pride, according to survey co-ordinators W.A. Riddell and A.J.W. Myers, depended "more on whitewash than on soap," objected to the publication of the surveys, but the supporters of the surveys insisted that the purpose of the investigations was constructive.[8] The aim of the survey approach, Riddell stated, was "to set forth before the community all the facts that bear upon a problem and rely upon the common understanding, the common forethought and the common purpose of all the people as a first great source to be drawn upon in working out that problem."[9]

The fundamental problem for the Brotherhood was lack of recruits. The Board of Moral and Social Reform told the Assembly of 1910 that only 125 men's organizations of any description had been reported from across the country.[10] Several sessions in rural areas and smaller centres did not feel the need for such organizations, while sessions in larger cities found it difficult to find men with the necessary time and interest. In 1912, the Board's report on men's work was short and direct. "Your Board regrets that, largely because of the pressing claims of other work, the men of the Church do not seem disposed to organize as generally as is undoubtedly desirable for co-operative effort in the interests of the Kingdom of God and for the good of humanity."[11] The strong men in all parts of the country that *The Presbyterian* had hoped would spearhead the Brotherhood movement either were not as awake to the urgency of moral and social reform as their clerical leaders or were so involved in other activities that they had no time for the Brotherhood.[12]

The church enjoyed much greater success in mobilizing a variety of organized interest groups, notably labour organizations, in support of the Lord's Day Act in 1906. Presbyterian progressives were instrumental in attempting to keep that alliance among church, farm, labour and women's groups alive in the Moral and Social Reform Council of Canada, organized in 1907.[13] Indeed, Presbyterians accounted for ten of the twenty-four people present at the organizational meeting.[14] John G. Shearer and T.A. Moore, General Secretary for Temperance and Moral Reform for the Methodists, were joint secretaries of the new Council. In the year following the Presbyterian Pre-Assembly Congress in 1913, the Council, by then renamed the Social Service Council of Canada, sponsored its own meeting in Ottawa. C.W. Gordon, in his foreword to the printed proceedings, felt that the Congress marked the dawn of a new era in Canada. "The thoughtful men and women of the country," he wrote, "the ministers of the Gospel and Christian workers, members of parliament and civic officials, presidents of great manufacturing concerns and labour leaders, all these are focusing their eyes upon the impressive fact that in this civilized and Christian country both civilization and Christianity are challenged by the economic, industrial and social conditions upon which the fabric of our state is erected."[15] Gordon was convinced that the sense of righteousness and community was so deep-seated in Canada that reformers need only expose the evils to have effective action take place to eradicate them.

The Social Service Council believed that purity and harmony could be realized in the complex conditions of modern life only through the application of the principles of the Kingdom of God to all human affairs. Its list of goals provided a catalogue of the improvements Presbyterian progressives sought in Canadian society: the application of Christian principles to the operations of industrial associations, whether of labour or capital; a more equitable distribution of wealth; the abolition of poverty; the protection of childhood; the safeguarding of the physical and moral health of women in industrial life; the adequate protection of working people in case of industrial accidents and occupational diseases; Sunday rest for every worker; conciliation and arbitration in industrial disputes; proper housing; the adequate care of dependent and defective persons; the reclamation of criminals; wholesome recreation; the protection of society against contagious diseases; and international peace.[16] The Council failed in its attempt to hold the members of the old Lord's Day Alliance together as an effective political lobby for further moral and social reform legislation, but it did help to co-ordinate the educational efforts of its members.[17]

Another major preoccupation of the Presbyterian progressives held out the promise of greatly increasing the church's strength and efficiency as an agency of moral and social reform — the church union movement. Writing in *The Presbyterian Record* in 1906, William Patrick, chairman of the Presbyterian delegation to the joint union committee and Principal of Manitoba College since 1900, pointed out that the task of shaping Canadian society to the moral ideal evolving from Christ was a paramount reason for uniting evangelical Protestant denominations in Canada.[18] The final article of the doctrinal statement in the Basis of Union, drafted in 1906, dealt with Christian service and provided another summary of the moral and social values uppermost in the minds of its supporters. "We believe that it is our duty," the drafters wrote, "as disciples and servants of Christ, to further the extension of His kingdom, to do good unto all men, to maintain the public and private worship of God, to hallow the Lord's Day, to preserve the inviolability of marriage and the sanctity of the family, to uphold the just authority of the State, and so live in all honesty, purity, and charity that our lives shall testify to Christ."[19] T.B. Kilpatrick played an important role in drafting the doctrinal section and it faithfully reflected the evangelical liberal apologetic that underlay Presbyterian progressivism. The acknowledged mission of bringing the best in Anglo-Saxon Protestant culture and morality to perfect realization in the world demanded an aggressive assault on the moral laxity of the nation and was best achieved through a united evangelical Protestantism.[20]

The new ecclesiastical organism would create unity by synthesizing the best of the three contributing traditions — Presbyterianism, Methodism, and Congregationalism. The united church, in turn, would be a more effective agent of cultural assimilation for the heterogeneous groups that were to be found in Canada. Like a mixed race, argued Patrick, a mixed church was of higher quality and would produce a nobler form of Christianity. "There will be new knowledge," Patrick wrote, "new sympathies, new efforts. The horizons of the church's thought and aims will be widened; and the standard of spiritual attainment will rise."[21] The same law of evolutionary assimilation applied to the life of the nation. Therefore, the united church was to be the central agency in the Christianization of Canada — in practical terms, the assimilation of immigrants and the disadvantaged into the Anglo-Saxon Protestant middle classes. The Ralph Connor novels, written by C.W. Gordon, were parables of such assimilation.

For example, *The Foreigner* (1909), written with Gordon's usual blend of romance, adventure, melodrama, and moralizing, traced the Canadianization and Christianization of Kalman Kalmar, a Russian immigrant in Winnipeg who matured to Christian manhood on the Alberta frontier. Using a medical missionary named Brown as his spokesman, Gordon expressed the need for assimilation. "These people here exist as an undigested foreign mass. They must be digested and absorbed into the body politic. They must be taught our ways of thinking and living, or it will be a mighty bad thing for us."[22] Because the church was the greatest instrument in eliminating all lines of national cleavage, a new, united Protestantism received his unreserved support. It would express, according to Gordon, "those great principles and ideals for which throughout its history the Presbyterian Church has ever stood, integrity of character, lofty patriotism, spiritual independence, loyalty to scriptural truth and devotion to the onward march of the kingdom of God in the world."[23]

The campaign for a more unified, efficient, and powerful Protestantism in Canada divided Presbyterians. When the first congregational vote was taken in 1912, one-third of those voting were opposed to union and the percentage remained constant until 1925, when two-thirds of the Presbyterian Church in Canada joined with the Methodists and the Congregationalists to form the United Church of Canada. Ironically, it was the laity Presbyterian progressives had tried to mobilize in the service of moral and social reform who took the lead in resisting the movement for union with the Methodists and Congregationalists.[24] Lay resistance, and, even more, lay indifference, meant that the efforts of the Presbyterian progressives to mobilize a Christian Canada met with limited success. They revealed a naivety on the part of Presbyterian progressives about the power of public opinion, a short-sightedness concerning their own racial and cultural prejudices, and an idealism with regard to social change and stability that would be shattered following the World War I. These characteristics were most apparent in their pre-war relations with labour.

The Illusive Alliance with Labour

John G. Shearer's experience with the Lord's Day Alliance had shown Presbyterian progressives how useful an alliance with organized labour could be in gaining support for the legislative changes they wanted.[25] Yet, by the churchmen's own admission, the working classes were not attracted to the Presbyterian Church in Canada in great numbers. Although represented in ecumenical reform bodies such as the Moral and Social Reform Council of Canada by the Trades and Labour Congress of Canada, workingmen proved to be indifferent allies in the church's moral crusade. The reasons were not difficult to find. In an age when labour organizations were seeking greater control over the factors that determined wages and working conditions, the church found it impossible to identify with the cause of labour in any meaningful way.[26] It was wedded to a paternalism rooted in the assumption that its proper function was to arbitrate between conflicting groups within society to ensure the harmonious and efficient operation of the social system.

The acknowledged model for Shearer and his colleagues in their relations with labour was Charles Stelzle, head of the Department of Church and Labor in the northern American Presbyterian Church. Stelzle's department, organized in 1903, had three functions — to interpret the church to workingmen, workingmen to the church, and employer and employee to each other.[27] *The Presbyterian* described Shearer as Canada's counterpart to Stelzle in establishing ties between the church and organized labour. The Assembly of 1909 noted with pride that Shearer had been received enthusiastically by the Trades and Labour Congress "as representing a Church that by official action has shown that it cares for the struggling masses and wants to be of assistance in righting their wrongs and helping them to rise to as high a level of life as possible."[28] But the differences between Shearer and Stelzle revealed more about the attitudes of Presbyterian progressives to labour than did the similarities.

Stelzle was a son of the Bowery, born in the slums of New York's Lower East Side. He went to work in a sweatshop at the age of eight, dropped out of school at eleven, and flirted with crime throughout his early teens. He finally settled into an apprenticeship as a machinist and became a journeyman when he was twenty-one. His interest in religion grew steadily throughout his late teens and he was ordained by the Presbytery of St. Louis in 1900. His congregations were all in working-class neighbourhoods and he remained an active trade-union member throughout his life. In 1910 he opened a Labor Temple in New York, which was designed to be a church that would appeal to the average workingman. His fundamental sympathies always lay with the working classes. "I am still a workingman," he wrote, "and I care more for the welfare of the workingman than I care for the development of the church. After all, the church is simply a means to an end, and not an end in itself."[29] By 1913 Stelzle's care for his fellow workingmen led him to leave the church — where his work was under attack for not doing more to exalt the Church of Christ — to undertake independent consulting work. Shearer and his colleagues greeted this news with regret, but the *Presbyterian Record* deplored Stelzle's refusal to emphasize evangelism in his work. Citing the position of *The Presbyterian* in Philadelphia, known as a conservative journal, the *Record* claimed that evangelism and sociology could never be reconciled, because the former rightly emphasized the saved individual and the latter wrongly attempted to save society by improving the environment.[30]

In total contrast to Stelzle, Shearer was born into a prosperous Presbyterian farm family in southwestern Ontario. After teaching high school, he attended the University of Toronto and Knox College; his education was followed by pastorates in Caledonia and Hamilton. His primary loyalties lay with the church. His approach to labour was that of an evangelist, interpreting the principles of Jesus to a segment of the population alienated from the church. Moral and social reforms were a new form of evangelism, but Shearer always saw his task as first and foremost the presentation of the Gospel. Shearer's first exposure to the kind of conditions in which Stelzle grew up came as a missioner from Knox College doing door-to-door evangelism in St. John's Ward in Toronto. His interest in the labour movement was part of a larger concern with the stability and peace of the nation, a harmony he saw threatened by extremes of wealth and poverty, inadequate housing, hazardous working conditions, the exploitation of women and children, and class warfare. His own class origin understandably aligned him with the nineteenth-century liberal conviction that the lot of the poor and the oppressed could be bettered by active efforts on the part of the morally advanced elements within the socially advantaged class. It could not be forced into being by the rebellion of the lower classes against their social superiors, which would result only in godless anarchy. Organized labour could be a means to the end of a Christian nation, but only if it worked in and through those established institutions that sought a harmonious society.

Shearer felt no desire to leave the church. The split that developed between the evangelicals and the Social Gospel advocates within American Presbyterianism did not emerge in the Canadian denomination with the same intensity. By 1911, the name of the national committee was changed to the Board of Social Service and Evangelism, and *The Presbyterian* made it clear which of those two elements defined the fundamental concerns of its members. "On the one hand," the editorial read, "the institution of moral reforms removing temptation and creating a wholesome atmosphere, makes it easier for the evangelist to carry on his work. On the other hand, it is evangelism, the presentation of the Gospel of Jesus Christ, which alone is able to bring about the personal and permanent reform which is supremely worth striving for."[31] The Gospel defined the fundamental principles and offered the necessary power to make the sacrifices of self-interest needed to ensure social stability.

The welfare of the nation rather than the rights of working people were paramount in the minds of the Presbyterian reformers. Their primary thrust in interpreting the church to the working classes was to convince them of the need for self-sacrifice in the search for social harmony. Mutual understanding and mutual concessions were the solutions to disputes between employers and their employees. In an editorial entitled "The Science of Working Together," *The Presbyterian* outlined the social ideal of the progressives with reference to industrial relations. The complexity of society and the resultant variety of individual interests increased the possibility of friction. "It is the function of civilization," the editors wrote, "to oil the bearings of the intricate and complicated machine that each man shall find his true place and do his appointed work harmoniously and without friction, and that he shall help and not hinder his fellow-workers." Only as the Christian idea made its way slowly through society did people realize "that the well-being of each unit is bound up with the whole."[32]

A month later, the same paper expressed horror at the election of two socialist Members of Parliament from British Columbia. The solution such politicians favoured was revolution, *The Presbyterian* warned, "no mild remedy to be gradually applied to the bleeding sores of society."[33] The greatest threat to national unity and strength, according to *The Presbyterian* in 1905, was the kind of class hatred fed by socialism. Drawing parallels with Tsarist Russia, the paper claimed that all the conditions of bitter class struggle were present in Canada. The church's task was to appease the hatred and reconcile the opposing sides. It was not to become "the avowed champion of either side in the struggle"; rather it should "honestly and tenderly lay down the great principles which apply equally to both."[34] As both capital and labour became better organized in their own self-interest, the church's official response was to stand firm in its self-appointed role as arbitrator in the common national interest.

The priority of the common interest in the minds of the Presbyterian progressives contributed to their ambiguous attitude towards trade unions. They admitted that people had the inherent right to organize for mutual protection and social improvement. They supported the labour movement insofar as it was humanitarian, for what was humanitarian was religious. "Christian men cannot be indifferent," an editorial in *The Presbyterian* stated,

> to efforts which are directed towards improving the physical, intellectual and spiritual lot of a large portion of the community, towards the abolishing of child labor, sweating and unhealthful conditions of toil. Nor can they disregard any movement that gives hope of amending our present social conditions in such a way that the extremes of wealth and poverty shall be less glaring, that regular work and a living wage shall be more generally assured to those willing to labor, and that fewer of our fellow-men shall be crushed down below the line of comfortable and decent livelihood."[35]

Presbyterian progressives were, however, consistently opposed to the labour militancy that led to strikes. W.H. Smith focused on the cost of strikes to the community when he discussed industrial conditions in the young people's study book, *Social Service*. Industrial disputes had disrupted every branch of business in every part of Canada. Eight hundred and twenty companies had lost time equivalent to 614,000 working days through strikes in 1907. Thirty thousand employees were directly affected and 5,000 indirectly. "The loss to both capitalist and laborer," Smith pointed out, "was great, while the general public suffered perhaps more, on account of the inconvenience occasioned by these disputes and strikes."[36] Smith offered no statistics on the gains made by those unions that had been involved in such collective actions.

Smith acknowledged that the conflict between capital and labour was complex because of the many factors entering into it, but he was convinced that "the key to the situation is held by men who are in touch with Christian ideals and institutions," who would educate both parties in the principles of community love, sacrifice, and service.[37] Smith mentioned the conciliation work already done by the Laurier government, formulated in large part by William Lyon Mackenzie King, editor of *The Labour Gazette* since 1900, chief architect of the Department of Labour in 1909, and drafter of the Lemieux Act of 1907, which introduced a minor degree of compulsion into conciliation proceedings. Mackenzie King was also an active member of Shearer's Board. The orientation of the Presbyterian progressives as regards the labour movement may well be explained by Mackenzie King's involvement in the Board's work. Indeed, the Board's lack of attention to legislative recommendations in the field of industrial relations may be attributed to its substantial agreement with King's policies.[38]

Commenting on the settlement of several strikes under King's Lemieux Act, *The Presbyterian* disclosed the assumptions it shared with Canada's policy-makers. "Many of the troubles," it stated, "in public as in private life are due to misunderstanding and to looking at the question exclusively from one point of view. When men who are not utterly wrong headed are brought face to face and discuss the situation from all points of view, some working compromise is almost certain to be found." The people who served on the conciliation councils were greeted as "public benefactors" who had "saved the country from bitterness, bad blood and financial loss."[39] The Presbyterian progressives were certain that such conciliation in industrial disputes was in keeping with the reforming spirit of the age and advanced the cause of social harmony and stability. The conciliatory approach indicated, above all, that the parties involved were awakening to their common interests.

J.W. Bengough, one of Canada's leading political cartoonists and a more radical Presbyterian than the progressive leaders, suggested that his church should consider a different working basis for its relations with labour. "The great fundamental principle of rectitude," he wrote in a letter to *The Presbyterian* in response to an editorial, "which, as you believe, will in due time be recognized, must, in my opinion, be simply this — that those things which of right belong to the whole people shall not be held by individuals except upon conditions of the regular payment of a full equivalent to the rightful owners, the whole people."[40] Bengough's endorsement of the single tax reformism of Henry George did not win over the ecclesiastical leaders at the centre of the church's moral and social reform efforts. Their task, as they saw it, was the preservation of national harmony and stability, not the social transformations that would result from the introduction of the single tax or any other substantial change in the economic and social structures of Canadian society. Such priorities, in the climate of tension that existed between capital and labour at the time, provided little opportunity for a meaningful alliance between church and labour.[41]

Legislation

In spite of their optimistic talk of creating a collective Christian conscience and mobilizing a Christian nation to enforce it, the Presbyterian progressives realized that some forces of evil were beyond the reach of moral persuasion. Legislation and law enforcement were necessary to control or eliminate such groups within the community. The liquor trade was a favourite example. W. H. Smith called it "a cold-blooded, clear-headed, aggressive, money-making institution, without conscience, soul or honour, . . . dead to the moral appeal of wife, mother, child, home, decency and safety."[42] Legislation, Smith argued at the Pre-Assembly Congress, was the only way in which the power of enlightened citizenship could enforce decency and protect the moral purity of the nation. It provided both restraint and elimination of evils and had an educational function by indicating the proper standards for community life.[43]

In its first report in 1908, the Committee on Moral and Social Reform affirmed the necessity of having "public opinion crystallized in law." The constitutional and legal situation with respect to moral and social reform in Canada was complicated. The Dominion alone was able to legislate directly for the suppression of gambling or prostitution and to enact any matters directly related to criminal law. The provinces, on the other hand, had sole jurisdiction in the realm of civil rights. The Committee considered itself fortunate to have Shearer as its secretary, since his experience in legislative lobbying with the Lord's Day Alliance would help the church in promoting its reform programme. The Committee promised to seek legislative changes in the areas of temperance, gambling, workmen's compensation and child labour.[44]

By the time of the Assembly of 1913, the Board's legislative strategy in relation to the Criminal Code and the Dominion Parliament had come to focus on gambling and prostitution. It listed nine specific changes for which it was lobbying:

1) Raising the age of consent in seduction from 16 to 18, and in carnal knowledge from 14 to 16.

2) Making all employers who seduce female employees under 21 punishable — not simply those in "shops, stores, mills, factories and workshops," as now.

3) Adding the penalty of whipping for men who procure girls for immoral purposes or engage in the White Slave Traffic, and giving constables power to arrest without warrant those suspected of engaging in this traffic.

4) Making the enforcement of the law against bawdy houses and landlords who allow premises to be used as such, more effective and easy.

5) Making solicitation by males or females and living in whole or in part on the avails of prostitution punishable more easily and more severely.

6) Prohibiting the business of gambling and betting in connection with horse racing.

7) Making the use of obscene or blasphemous language in any public place an offence.

8) Making living in adultery or fornication a crime.

9) Giving constables the right of entry, search and seizure in houses of prostitution, as in the case of other disorderly houses, and power to destroy forbidden matter found therein as well as immoral literature, opium, etc. , found elsewhere in raids for illicit traffic in the same.[45]

As long as the bedrooms of the nation were in the homes of the nation, the church felt the duty to demand that the state protect the sanctity of the family. As long as the business of gambling took money out of the homes of the nation, the same applied to the financial well-being of the family. When it came to questions of sexual morality and economic exploitation in the form of gambling, the Presbyterian progressives insisted that the civil rights of individuals were secondary to the rights of the family and the nation that had to be protected against the business of vice.

The other major thrust of the Board's campaign for legislative action was in the area of temperance. Presbyterian temperance supporters had been dismayed when the Royal Commission on the Liquor Traffic in 1896 had concluded that prohibition was impractical and that the moral aspects of the problem could be ignored.[46] Presbyterian reformers had to settle for the Scott Act which attempted to regulate and restrict the distribution of liquor through provincial licencing and the local veto or option clause. This stipulated that, subject to provincial legislation, a majority or percentage vote could prohibit the issuing of licenses in a local municipality or region.[47]

By 1906, however, the Presbyterian progressives had come to rationalize the advantages of the local option in terms of being faithful to public opinion. *The Presbyterian* expressed the accepted wisdom that "a sound public opinion is the only effective means" of enforcing temperance legislation. "The true way of advance for the temperance movement," the editorial continued, "lies through action by the municipalities, and with the preponderating majority of municipalities converted into practical prohibition areas, the question of prohibition as a provincial problem will be largely solved."[48] C.W. Gordon and George Pidgeon, Shearer's two co-conveners, were both active in provincial temperance movements and local campaigns.[49]

Pidgeon took a leading role in the local option campaign in Toronto Junction. He claimed that the real enemies of reform were not those who wanted to drink for their own gratification, but those who made money out of other people's wrong-doing.[50] Pidgeon's attack on the liquor trade made a direct appeal to the financial interests of the community. The closing of the bars, he argued, would mean a distinct gain for legitimate lines of business. "The money formerly wasted over the bar," he wrote, "now goes into groceries, clothing, furniture and homes. Employers find that their men lose less time, produce more goods and of superior quality, and are in better condition for their work, than when they used to squander their earnings and their energies in drink."[51] In a pamphlet issued by Shearer's office on the effects of local prohibition on business, Pidgeon used statistics from Fargo, North Dakota, and Kansas City, Missouri, to supplement his personal experience in Montreal West and West Toronto to convince his readers that prohibition made financial sense for the municipality.[52] Pidgeon's argument was aimed at the business leadership of the community and calculated to appeal to their pocket books as well as their conscience.

Pidgeon had little patience with those who argued that such legislation was an infringement on individual liberties. Those involved in the business of vice had betrayed the community and, thereby, forfeited their rights. It was wrong for the state to cultivate vice by allowing it to continue. "It is putting a premium on the destruction of our manhood. It is building up a power that will throttle our liberties. The drink traffic is the enemy of the home and the church, of purity and truth, of individual and national righteousness, and the people that does not destroy it will be destroyed by it."[53] The logical extension of this argument was to push for total prohibition again.

The success of local option campaigns across the country encouraged the Presbyterian Board that its cumulative work in municipalities was bearing fruit. By 1913, Prince Edward Island and Nova Scotia, with the exception of Halifax, were under provincial prohibitory laws. Ten out of fourteen counties in New Brunswick, 869 out of 1168 municipalities in Quebec, 502 of 835 municipalities in Ontario, and 71 of 143 in Manitoba were without licenced liquor establishments. Saskatchewan's law was reported to be weak, and Alberta and British Columbia had no temperance legislation. Presbyterian progressives believed that campaigns for the local option and against the repeal of the option once in place had generated a considerable body of public opinion in favour of stricter legislation. "The results of scientific investigation of the last decade," the Board told the General Assembly of 1913, "have aroused nations to the fact that more than any other factor alcohol is responsible for race deterioration. Evidence regarding the relation of alcohol and poverty, idiocy, insanity, vice, inefficiency and physical degeneracy has convinced rulers, statesmen and governments that their greatest enemy is not without but within their borders, and has led them to warn people regarding the evil effects of alcohol and to take action looking to the more adequate control of its sale."[54] The Board urged the Assembly to call on the church to support federal and provincial legislation that would prohibit the manufacture, importation, and sale of intoxicating liquor. Local committees and ecumenical co-operation were called for in pursuit of this new legislative campaign, but it took the pressures of a world war to finally achieve victory in 1917 under Borden's Union government.[55]

Pidgeon and his colleagues did not expect legislation to do the whole job of reforming the nation. It did restrain, it did educate, and it did create a better environment for moral development, but the ultimate improvement of a social system depended on the quality of the people that ran it. "Imperfect systems run by angels," Pidgeon said in one of his addresses, "will produce better results than a perfect system run by the devil."[56] Improving the quality of the people in public life and engaged in enforcing the law was the key to effective reform. Pure legislation required pure legislators. At the same time, as the role of the state increased and the need for accurate legislative advice grew, a non-partisan civil service became essential. Shearer's Board advocated both.

In 1908, the Committee on Church Life and Work asked the church whether its members wanted "intelligently and honorably to discharge their duties as citizens?" The question of political purity and how to best achieve it was seen to include efforts "to secure Parliamentary candidates with ability and stainless character, purity in elections, the elimination of party politics from municipal affairs, the appointment to office of men with the highest qualifications, etc." From the replies received, the Committee concluded that Presbyterians took an active interest in public affairs, but did not exert themselves enough in defending the integrity of Canadian politics. With respect to the discussion of such questions from the pulpit, most sessions noted that they should be discussed, but as moral rather than political questions. In summary, they stated "that every moral problem is the Church's problem, and that a moral question does not cease to be a moral question when it gets into party politics. People need guidance in such matters, and rightly look to the pulpit for the teaching of God's word on the principles involved." Most sessions cautioned that "great prudence and tact" were required in discussing such questions from the pulpit, with the focus properly on the principles involved rather than on the political entanglements.[57] The distinction between principled morality and partisan politics, however, was difficult to maintain in practice. Charges of partisan interference in politics against Presbyterian progressives from Conservative governments and candidates had considerable substance to them when leaders such as James A. Macdonald and C.W. Gordon were so openly involved in the Liberal Party.[58]

Shearer's Board took up the campaign for political purity. Much of its concern was directed at the corruption that resulted from the business of vice, especially prostitution and the liquor traffic. But attention was also paid to the franchise, the degrading influence of the spoils system, and the desirability of a non-partisan political spirit.[59] In 1912, the Board issued a lengthy statement on political purity prepared by W.H. Smith and Thurlow Fraser of Portage la Prairie, Manitoba. They presented four principles intended to guide the preaching of Presbyterian ministers during the forthcoming general election. First, it was the duty of every citizen thoughtfully and seriously to discharge the full responsibility of citizenship. Secondly, the law of righteousness was an imperative in politics as in every other field of human activity. Thirdly, the interest of the nation was supreme, above any party, sectional, or selfish interests. Finally, the franchise was a solemn trust, not to be bought or sold, but to be exercised as a civic responsibility in God's sight.[60]

Smith and Fraser took special note of the need for a civil service based on ability rather than on party as a remedy for political impurity. They heartily endorsed the appointment of a Civil Service Commission "composed of men of ability and unimpeachable integrity." They were disappointed that only the inside civil service was under its control and that the government retained the right to nominate men for various positions. But they felt that the Commission had taken strong ground in refusing several of the government's appointees and held out hope for a more capable civil service.[61] The dominant figure in the Commission during this period was Adam Shortt, a teacher of Fraser's at Queen's. Shortt was president of the Ottawa branch of the Moral and Social Reform Council of Canada and, though an Anglican, worked closely with three members of the Board — Robert Magill, William Lyon Mackenzie King, and

O.D. Skelton — to produce a comprehensive social science reading course for the church in 1910.[62]

In the end, however, Smith and Fraser fell back on the power of public opinion to achieve the changes they wanted in the political system. In the last analysis, the blame for dishonesty in public life lay not with public officials but with the public opinion that allowed them to remain in office. "If public opinion," they stated, "justifies any conduct, these representatives and servants of the public will practise that conduct. If on the other hand public opinion definitely pronounces certain conduct as base and dishonorable, the representatives and servants of the public will generally avoid it."[63] They, too, recognized the limitations of legislation and administrative oversight. The source of moral power, in their view, was in the Christian character of the Canadian people, expressed as a public conscience through all the channels of influence on national life. Canada was in its youth and just beginning to establish the legal and administrative institutions that would shape its future. Presbyterian progressives zealously worked to ensure that such structures be shaped by enlightened Christian public opinion.

Law Enforcement

The question of law enforcement was a constant companion of discussions of legislative reforms. A streak of anti-Americanism that assumed that Americans were less law-abiding than Canadians often informed the writings of the Presbyterian progressives. Typical of these attitudes was that of James A. Macdonald, expressed in an editorial in *The Westminster* in 1901. American politics, as Macdonald saw them, were rife with corruption, American criminal justice was characterized by "laxity and lynching," and American statesmanship was based on demagoguery and jingoism.[64] The calls for lynch law from the American religious press that followed the assassination of President McKinley struck Macdonald as typical of American attitudes. "Lynch law," he told his readers, "is itself a phase of anarchy, and until American mobs, American divines and American journals show more respect for their own jurisprudence they may expect to find America producing an abundant crop of anarchists."[65] What distinguished Canadians from their southern neighbours was their respect for law and order, rooted in the British heritage which had shaped the country.

Similar sentiments were expressed by Shearer's Board when it raised the problem of law enforcement with the Assembly of 1908. The Board argued that respect for the law was characteristic of British citizenship, while lack of respect was one of the worst features of life in several of the American states. "There is no lack of evidence," the Board warned, "of a disposition on the part of authorities in our own country to be more ready to enact legislation than to enforce it. Especially in the present formative period of our national life it is of first consequence that we inculcate on the part of all residents within our shores uniform respect for the laws of our country."[66] The key to building such respect was seen to be a uniform and impartial enforcement of the laws of the land, especially those having a moral bearing. The experience of members of the Board from across the country led them to insist that uniform enforcement required a national, or at the very least a provincial, system of law enforcement.[67]

George Pidgeon outlined the advantages of provincial or national law enforcement agencies in an article forthe *Presbyterian Record* in 1910. Such a police force would have ample authority for enforcement wherever it might be stationed. It would not be subject to local influence or pressure through municipal politics or the financial power of the merchants of vice. The internal discipline of the force would be greater and proper training would guarantee greater efficiency. Better salaries could be foreseen, drawing a better class of officers and men to the force. Finally, the deployment of such a force at various centres through the provinces would enable local law officers to receive better training in their work. Pidgeon pointed to the success of the local option movement in Ontario as proof of the effectiveness of his scheme. He argued that it gained much of its support because of the assurance people had that their local enactment would be enforced by a well-trained and impartial provincial police force.[68]

As Pidgeon's proposal demonstrates, the same principles of independence and moral integrity applied in the moral reformers' approach to law enforcement that had guided their attitudes to the civil service. The ideal among Canadian police forces was the Royal North-West Mounted Police. "The reasons why the world-famed force, the Royal North-West Mounted Police of Western Canada," the Board of Moral and Social Reform reported to the 1908 Assembly, "and certain Provincial police forces, are so much more effective than municipal forces in securing respect for the laws of our country, are that they are not subject to the whims of local public opinion, and that they are under the authority of men who have something like an adequate sense of official responsibility."[69] C.W. Gordon's fictional tribute to the North-West Mounted Police, *Corporal Cameron*, came out in 1912. The secret of what Gordon considered to be their extraordinary hold on the population of Western Canada lay in the dispatch and fairness with which justice was administered. The "Pax Britannica" that covered 300,000 square miles in Canada stood in marked contrast, in Gordon's mind, to the law of the gun and the noose that prevailed in the American states to the south. The Mounted Police cared for, rather than suppressed, the population of the area.[70]

However, the Presbyterian progressive leaders were ready to admit that in most of Canada the enforcement of many of the laws with a moral bearing were in the hands of local enforcement agencies. Shearer's Board spent considerable time and money uncovering evidence of laxity in investigation and prosecution among Canada's police forces. The greatest indignation was directed at segregated districts in which prostitution and the liquor traffic were tolerated. In 1909, for example, the Canadian Detective Agency was hired to gather evidence on prostitution in Halifax. Operator M-8 reported on the existence of 66 houses of ill-repute inhabited by 236 women. The intention was that such information would be offered to local moral and social reform agencies who would use it in the press and the pulpit to stir up public opinion and pressure law enforcement agencies to take action.[71] By 1913, the Board was able to report to the Assembly that tolerated vice had been driven out of Halifax.[72] The most publicized venture in this field of public pressure for purity came with the Winnipeg Vice Commission in 1910.

Following a visit to Winnipeg in 1910, John G. Shearer made a public statement concerning the problem of social vice in that city. His charges were published in Macdonald's *Globe* in Toronto but were not picked up by any of the Winnipeg papers. They included charges that the authorities permitted prostitution in segregated districts, that "the colony of criminal vice" had grown from nothing to some fifty houses with two hundred and fifty women in just two years, that the police made no serious efforts to enforce the law against such activities, that self-appointed regulations of restraint were made privately between the police and the prostitutes, that every brothel was an illicit liquor dive as well, and that the one hundred dollar fines that resulted from what enforcement did take place "amounted to a price paid for permission to carry on for the year these dens and dives." Shearer concluded that the whole business was "strongly suggestive of graft."[73] The rapid growth of the segregated district in Winnipeg seemed to Shearer a perfect example of the weaknesses and disadvantages of local law enforcement.

The response of the civic authorities in Winnipeg, who were in the midst of a municipal election when Shearer's charges were published, was to ask that a provincial commission be appointed to investigate. The commission was established under Justice Hugh A. Robson, a Presbyterian and a Liberal. Shearer's Board welcomed his report which upheld the charges that the mayor, the police magistrate, the commissioners, and the police chief had violated their oaths of office and blackened the good name of Winnipeg. Robson's report, the Board told the Assembly of 1911, was "a scathing condemnation of the conditions the officials of Winnipeg had permitted to develop in that good city, and more than justifies the charges made by the Secretary of this Board."[74] The Presbyterian progressives ranked the report with those of Justice

Taschereau in Montreal, the Committee of Fifteen in New York, and the more recent Chicago Vice Commission. All were seen as important steps in mobilizing public opinion against those who tolerated or profited from the business of vice. Despite the integrity of the Robson report, it is difficult not to see this particular crusade in a somewhat doubtful light. That its impact was not substantial is understandable in view of the fact that it did not appear until three weeks after the Winnipeg election. What is less understandable is the selective reporting of the Winnipeg situation by the Presbyterian progressives. No mention was made in Presbyterian reports of the political context in which the Commission was appointed — by a Liberal provincial government with a Conservative incumbent as mayor of Winnipeg being challenged by a Liberal reform candidate. The incumbent won and the segregated districts stayed, further facts not reported to the General Assembly.[75]

A telling comment on the response of Winnipeg's laity to the clean-up effort on the part of Presbyterian progressives was made by A.G. Sinclair, minister at St. Andrew's in Winnipeg, at the Pre-Assembly Congress of 1913. "When we had a great moral campaign in Winnipeg a couple of years ago," he told his audience, "and we ministers began to take off the lid, many good men occupying church pews held up their hands in protest. 'These things may be true,' they said, 'but this publicity will do still more harm. We have a right to demand that our wives and daughters shall be kept in ignorance of such things.'"[76] The gulf between the clergy and the laity on moral and social reform, whether motivated by concern for the moral sensibilities of women or by anxiety for the good name of the city, remained a nagging problem for the Presbyterian progressives.

The Board had better news for the Assembly in 1912. A new mayor had been elected in Winnipeg on a platform that included the suppression of vice. Further, the Hon. Hugh John Macdonald, whose provincial administration had passed prohibition in 1900, had been appointed Chief Magistrate, and the Board of Police Commissioners had given express orders for the suppression of all prostitution. The following year, the Board was able to report that segregated vice had been driven out of Calgary, Lethbridge, Quebec, Halifax, and Winnipeg. Houses of shame were to be found here and there, but authorities across the country were reported to have committed themselves to a policy of suppression — except in British Columbia. Five years after the Kootenay Campaign, for example, the red women and their red patrons were still going strong. The Presbytery of Kootenay deplored the shocking conditions throughout its bounds and pledged "all moral support to every legitimate effort to remove from the fair name of Kootenay the foul blot that the shameless toleration of criminal vice puts upon it, a blot made all the more offensive because the existing shocking conditions have in some instances been openly endorsed by the majority of the electors, where suppression of vice has been made the principal issue of the municipal campaign."[77] Church reports and periodicals made it clear that the suppression of vice was sporadic at best. Law enforcement remained largely a municipal responsibility and provincial authorities proved less vigorous in their efforts than hoped. Because they relied on the public conscience and its influence on elected and appointed officials, the Presbyterian reformers were at the mercy of electors who more often than not failed to share their urgency on moral issues and were more concerned with issues of civic prosperity and material improvement.[78]

Another issue that attracted considerable attention from the leaders of Presbyterian progressivism was the distribution of immoral literature. It was an issue over which the traditional ties with the Liberal Party were strained and questions raised about the support the reformers could expect from the federal government under Laurier. Tensions developed over the case of Skill and King, owners of the Toronto Antiquarian Book Company. In 1909 they were convicted of distributing immoral literature and sentenced to one year in jail. Shearer's Board expressed gratitude for the co-operation they had received from authorities in this matter, especially for the vigilance of post office and customs officials in blocking the entry of such material from the United States. Through his contacts with the Society for the Prevention of Vice in the United States, Shearer had uncovered evidence of an extensive underground business in "antiquarian books of a demoralizing character."[79] He had been instrumental in securing a conviction in the case of Skill and King. Members of the Board of Moral and Social Reform were outraged when Laurier's Minister of Justice and Ontario lieutenant, A.B. Aylesworth, pardoned the two after they had served two months of their sentence. Aylesworth claimed the books in question were classics and of scientific interest. C.W. Gordon and J.A. Macdonald wrote several letters of protest to Laurier. The Board expressed its anger at the Assembly of 1910, quoting Toronto's chief coroner, A.J. Johnson, who called the material "utterly vile, reeking with filth from beginning to end," and "absolutely without scientific value." The *Globe* added that the books' "only value to science is as samples of the erotic factors in the making of degenerates and perverts. As literature they range all the way from the scrofulous French novel, unexpurgated, vilely illustrated, and elegantly bound, to still more lecherous exposition and advocacy of the grossest unnatural sensuality.[80] It was questionable whether the novels of Balzac had anything to do with a disease producing glandular swellings, but Macdonald no doubt felt himself entitled to some poetic licence in defending the moral character of the community. The Assembly of 1910 approved a lengthy deliverance to Laurier on the Skill and King case, appealing to him "to take such action as will avert this grave peril, imminently threatening our national life."[81] Laurier, however, remained unmoved by either the personal pleadings of Gordon and Macdonald or the deliverances of the General Assembly. He did not find the matter pressing and refused to contradict or remove his Minister of Justice.[82]

Other enforcement campaigns dealt with temperance, gambling, and Sabbath observance. As with temperance legislation, the temperance enforcement machinery varied from province to province. Shearer and his Board saw their role as one of bringing national pressure and expertise to bear on local and provincial officials. The moral and social reform forces had been unable to prevent gambling at race-tracks and simply decried, from year to year, its baneful influence on the economic and moral stability of the nation's homes. Sabbath observance was violated regularly in industrial centres, in large cities, and on the frontier. The Board attributed this to unnecessary labour or business rather than pleasure-seeking, but continued to insist that all Canadians needed "their rest-day rights, including the opportunity of worship and of hearing the Gospel."[83]

The intention in all these campaigns, whether for better legislation or stricter enforcement, according to George Pidgeon, was to stop the evil. He argued that Christ himself had not relied solely on moral persuasion, but had taken vigorous measures such as ejecting the traders from the temple. "And there are men now," he continued, "engaged in destroying souls who are as hardened in their wickedness as any in Christ's time, and when our advocacy of truth does not change their conduct, we must resort, as He did, to sterner measures. This is our great apology for using all legitimate means against the liquor traffic, against Sabbath desecration, against political corruption and other giant crimes, and nothing short of a faithful use against them of all the powers at our command will justify us in the sight of God."[84] As the first decade of the new century progressed, however, the Presbyterian reformers learned that neither legislation nor law enforcement was effective unless backed by public opinion, and they were forced back again and again to their basic strategy of moral persuasion. But the social conditions of the time made the strategy more idealistic than practical. Public indifference, public reaction against the extremism of the moral reformers on some issues, and the influence of the financial interests involved in the businesses attacked by the progressives all contributed to the weakness of the campaigns to stop evil and cleanse the nation.

* * * * *

Despite their ceaseless attempts to mobilize secular institutions, the church remained, for the Presbyterian progressives, the central dynamic in their efforts to implement their vision of a righteous Canada. Robert Haddow, a classmate of Gordon, Macdonald, and Shearer at Knox in the 1880s and one of Macdonald's successors at *The Presbyterian* and *The Westminster,* wrote that the church took its stand on divine authority and was "called to promulgate the principles that underlie every part of our complex life. It is called to be the great vitalizing and energizing force in all that makes for the uplift of humanity and for the cleansing of the sewers that poison life."[85] Within the church, these leaders endeavoured to create an efficient and effective instrument of God's will, which they understood to be the application of the evolving principles set forth by Jesus to all human affairs in the complex conditions of modern life. Attempts to mobilize the laity, form alliances with other groups, and consolidate the power and influence of the church were all part of this larger goal.

While the church provided the essential base from which the Presbyterian progressives worked, their careers and activities showed the extent to which they used every means available to them to establish and propagate the principles of national righteousness. If only people could be led to commit themselves to Christ, John G. Shearer argued, they would acquire the will and motivation to apply Christian principles to their lives. But showing people the path was only the beginning of the church's responsibility. The end was the mobilization of Christian citizens, "to lead them into the service of God, to train them for it, to keep them at it, to make them strong, vigorous Christians, and to unite them into a well-trained army to fight the King's battles and do His work of saving and serving the lost world of humanity."[86] Moral legislation and its strict enforcement would be, to the Presbyterian progressives, concrete indication of the degree to which Christian principles could shape the collective life of the country.

To translate these aims into reality was another matter. The army that the leaders of progressive Presbyterians gathered around them was less than impressive and the victories in their campaigns on the field of moral battle were scattered at best. They remained, however, defenders of the garrison of Anglo-Saxon Protestant culture. From the battlements of the suburbs of Canada's cities, they conducted their crusade for the vitality of the church, the health of the family, and the purity of personal and social life. In the perilous enterprise of preserving their moral and social values in the midst of a complex and changing Canada, they were fighters who did not question those values or the institutions through which they were expressed. Rather, they fashioned the best possible defence for those values they could and sought the perfecting of the institutions through which they were preserved and propagated.

NOTES

1. *The Presbyterian* (Toronto), Nov. 29, 1906.

2. *The Presbyterian* (Toronto), Feb. 21, 1907; and *A&P*, 1907, Minutes, p. 86.

3. For biographical information on these men, see H.J. Morgan, *The Canadian Men and Women of the Time* (Toronto: Briggs, 1912).

4. *The Presbyterian* (Toronto), Mar. 18 and 25, 1909.

5. *The Presbyterian* (Toronto), Nov. 7, 1907.

6. *A&P*, 1914, App., p. 329.

7. W.A. Riddell, "The Value of the Social Survey," *Social Service Congress*, p. 54.

8. *The Presbyterian* (Toronto), Jan 4, 1912. See also *Report on a Limited Survey of Education, Social and Industrial Life, Men's Federation, London, Ont.* (Toronto: Presbyterian Committee on Religious Education, Methodist Board of Temperance and Moral Reform, and Presbyterian Board of Social Service and Evangelism, 1913).

9. Riddell, "Social Survey," p. 56.

10. *A&P*, 1910, App., p. 284.

11. *A&P*, 1912, App., p. 322.

12. The Laymen's Missionary Movement in Canada had a similar history in its attempts to mobilize the laity in support of mission work at home and abroad. See J.S. Moir, "'On the King's Business': The Rise and Fall of the Laymen's Missionary Movement in Canada," in Andre Tihon (ed.), *Les Mouvements de Laics dans les Eglises aux XIXe et XXe Siecles* (Bruxelles: Facultes universitaires Saint-Louis, 1980).

13. By 1914, membership in the council included the Church of England in Canada, the Methodist Church in Canada, the Presbyterian Church in Canada, the Congregational Church in Canada, the Trades and Labor Congress of Canada, the Dominion Grange and Farmers' Association, the Salvation Army, the Canadian Purity Education Association, the Evangelical Association of North America, and the Dominion Women's Christian Temperance Union.

14. Minutes, Moral and Social Reform Council of Canada, Dec. 26, 1907, United Church Archives.

15. C.W. Gordon, "Foreword," *Social Service Congress*, p. vi.

16. *Social Service Congress*, p. v.

17. A focus of its educational efforts was its own magazine, *Social Welfare*, edited by Shearer.

18. W. Patrick, "Some Reasons for Church Union," *Presbyterian Record* (Montreal), Oct. 1906, quoted in N.K. Clifford, "The Origins of the Church Union Controversy," *Journal of the Canadian Church Historical Society* 18, nos. 2,3 (June-Sept. 1976):34-52. Clifford argues that Patrick, with a background remarkably similar to Kilpatrick's, was the intellectual father of the church union movement and guided Presbyterians through the initial stages of their involvement.

19. *A&P*, 1909, App., p. 273

20. *The Presbyterian* (Toronto), Feb. 10 and 17, 1910. Se also G. Pidgeon, "Foreword," in T.B. Kilpatrick's *Our Common Faith* (Toronto: United Church Publishing House, 1928), p. vi; and T.B. Kilpatrick, "A Response to Father Kelly," *The Constructive Quarterly* 5 (Dec. 1917):617-633. The latter is a detailed defense of the Basis of Union in response to a critique from Anglican Herbert Kelly of Central Theological College, Tokyo, Japan.

21. *The Presbyterian* (Toronto), May 26, 1910.

22. Ralph Connor, *The Foreigner* (Toronto: Westminster, 1909), p. 255.

23. C.W. Gordon, "The Presbyterian Church and Its Missions," in A. Shortt and A.G. Doughty (eds.), *Canada and Its Provinces, Vol. XI* (Toronto: Brook and Co., 1914). p. 300.

24. This is one of the central arguments in N.K. Clifford, *The Resistance to Church Union in Canada, 1904-1939*, (Vancouver: University of British Columbia Press, 1985).

25. Waterman, "The Lord's Day Act."

26. C. Heron and B.D. Palmer, "Through the Prism of the Strike: Industrial Conflict in Southern Ontario, 1901-1014," *Canadian Historical Review* 8, no.4 (Dec. 1977):423-458.

27. Nash, "Charles Stelzle," p. 209.

28. *The Presbyterian* (Toronto), Dec. 5, 1907; and *A&P*, 1909, App., p. 252.

29. Nash, "Charles Stelzle," p. 210.

30. *Presbyterian Record* (Montreal), Sept. 1913.

31. *The Presbyterian* (Toronto), May 18, 1911.

32. *The Presbyterian* (Toronto), Sept. 19, 1903.

33. *The Presbyterian* (Toronto), Oct. 24, 1903.

34. *The Presbyterian* (Toronto), Aug. 31, 1905.

35. *The Presbyterian* (Toronto), Sept. 17, 1908.

36. W.H. Smith, "The Church and Industrial Society,"

37. Smith, "Industrial Society," pp. 124-125. This position had deep roots in Canadian Presbyterianism. For its origins in earlier social statements, see E.A. Christie, "The Official Attitudes and Opinions of the Presbyterian Church in Canada with Respect to Public Affairs and Social Problems, 1875-1924" (unpublished M.A. thesis, University of Toronto, 1955).

38. On King's labour policies, see R.M. Dawson, *William Lyon Mackenzie King, A Political Biography, 1874-1923* (Toronto: University of Toronto Press, 1958), pp. 94-221, and P. Craven, *'An Impartial Umpire': Industrial Relations and the Canadian State, 1900-1911*(Toronto: University of Toronto Press, 1980). Neither Dawson nor Craven mentions anything about King's religious background in relation to his views on industrial relations, yet he appears to have many sources of contact with the leaders of Presbyterian progressivism. See, for example, Shearer to King, Oct. 27, 1908; King to Shearer, Nov. 3, 1908, Gordon to King, June 25, 1908; King to Gordon, July 2, 1909; King to Shearer, June 2, 1909; Gordon to King, July 7, 1911; and Gordon to King, July 18, 1911. William Lyon Mackenzie King Papers, Primary Correspondence Series, Public Archives of Canada. Much of this correspondence deals with work members of Shearer's Board did for King on conciliation boards.

39. *The Presbyterian* (Toronto), Oct. 17, 1907.

40. *The Presbyterian* (Toronto), Mar. 7, 1903.

41. On the reception of Henry George's ideas in Canada by Bengough and others, see Cook, *The Regenerators*, pp. 105-124 and 144-149.

42. *The Presbyterian* (Toronto), May 5, 1903. The passage quoted is from a book written by Smith for use by Presbyterian Brotherhoods, *The Church and Men* (Toronto: Presbyterian Publications, 1910).

43. W.H. Smith, "Legislation as a Means for the Suppression of the Liquor Traffic," *Pre-Assembly Congress*, p. 257.

44. *A&P*, 1908, App., p. 320. For a detailed report on Shearer's views on legislative and enforcement problems in Canada, see Minutes, Board of Moral and Social Reform, Presbyterian Church in Canada, Sept. 7, 1909. United Church Archives.

45. *A&P*, 1913, App., p. 284.

46. *A&P*, 1895, App. 27, p. 4.

47. See R. Allen, "The Triumph and Decline of Prohibition," in J.M. Bumstead (ed.), *Documentary Problems in Canadian History, II* (Georgetown: Dorsey, 1969), pp. 185-214.

48. *The Presbyterian* (Toronto), Apr. 19, 1906.

49. On Gordon's involvement in the Manitoba temperance movement, see J.H. Thompson, "The Prohibition Question in Manitoba, 1892-1928" (unpublished M.A. thesis, University of Manitoba, 1969); and E.H. Wood, "Ralph Connor and the Canadian West" (unpublished M.A. thesis, University of Saskatchewan, 1975). On Pidgeon's involvement, see Grant, *George Pidgeon.*

50. G. Pidgeon, "The Business of Vice," *Presbyterian Record* (Montreal), May 1910.

51. G. Pidgeon, "Problems of Moral Reform," in W.R. McIntosh (ed.), *Canadian Problems* (Toronto: Presbyterian Publications, 1910), p. 65.

52. G. Pidgeon, *Local Prohibition: Its Effect on Business* (Toronto: Board of Moral and Social Reform, Presbyterian Church in Canada, n.d.).

53. Pidgeon, "Problems," p. 66.

54. *A&P*, 1913, App., p. 279.

55. See R.C. Brown, *Robert Laird Borden, A Biography, Vol. II* (Toronto: Macmillan, 1980), pp. 50-51.

56. G. Pidgeon, "The Church and Moral Reform," Pidgeon Papers, File 2070, p. 27, United Church Archives.

57. *A&P*, 1908, App., pp. 272-273..

58. *The Presbyterian* (Toronto), Mar. 14, 1907.

59. *A&P*, 1910, App., p. 291.

60. *A&P*, 1912, App., p. 319.

61. *Ibid.*, p. 317. On the history of the Civil Service Commission, see J.E. Hodgetts *et al.*, *Biography of an Institution: The Civil Service Commission of Canada, 1908-1967* (Montreal: McGill University Press, 1972).

62. *A&P*, 1910, App., pp. 293-298.

63. *A&P*, 1912, App., p. 318.

64. *The Westminster* (Toronto), Sept. 7, 1901.

65. *The Westminster* (Toronto), Sept.21, 1901.

66. *A&P*, 1908, App., pp. 321-322.

67. Minutes, Board of Moral and Social Reform, Presbyterian Church in Canada, Sept. 7, 1909, United Church Archives.

68. G. Pidgeon, "The Church and Moral Reform, Vi, Law Enforcement," *Presbyterian Record* (Montreal), Sept. 1910.

69. *A&P*, 1908, App., p. 322.

70. Ralph Connor, *Corporal Cameron* (Toronto: Westminster, 1912), especially pp. 375-398.

71. Minutes, Board of Moral and Social Reform, Presbyterian Church in Canada, Sept. 7, 1909; and Minutes, Executive of the Board of Moral and Social Reform, Presbyterian Church in Canada, Sept. 15 and 28, 1909 and Jan. 31, 1910, United Church Archives.

72. *A&P*, 1913, App., p. 238.

73. *A&P*, 1911, App., p. 259.

74. *Ibid.*, p. 260.

75. Artibise, *Winnipeg*, pp. 258-264.

76. A.G. Sinclair, "The Family at Home," *Pre-Assembly Congress*, p. 168. Sinclair had graduated from Toronto and Knox before studying in Scotland and Europe. He earned a Ph.D. in philosophy from Heidelberg in 1906 and sat on Shearer's board.

77. *A&P*, 1913, App., p. 283.

78. For examples of the reception of moral reform campaigns by urban populations in Western Canada, see James Grey, *Red Lights on the Prairies* (Toronto: Macmillan, 1971), and *Booze* (Toronto: Macmillan, 1972).

79. For a sample list of the books seized, see M. Prang, *N.W. Rowell: Ontario Nationalist* (Toronto: University of Toronto Press, 1975), pp. 98-99.

80. Quoted in *A&P*, 1910, App., pp. 285-286.

81. *Ibid.*, Minutes, pp. 45-57.

82. On Laurier and Aylesworth, see P. Stevens, "Laurier, Aylesworth, and the Decline of the Liberal Party in Ontario," *Historical Papers, Canadian Historical Association, 1968*, pp. 94-113. The other major issue that alienated moral and social reformers in the Liberal Party from Aylesworth was race-track gambling.

83. *A&P*, 1910, App., p. 279.

84. Pidgeon, "Teachings of Christ," pp. 449-450.

85. *The Presbyterian* (Toronto), Oct. 10, 1907.

86. J.G. Shearer, "Simultaneous Evangelism," in Kilpatrick, *New Testament Evangelism*, p. 278.

CHAPTER 7

THE TESTING: THE ORDEAL OF WORLD WAR I

World War I proved to be a time of testing for the culture and the institutions in which the Presbyterian progressives had placed their hopes. Until the outbreak of the war in 1914, they had been able to point to the seldom-interrupted advance of the "Pax Britannica" around the world as proof of their belief in providential progress. The history of the nineteenth century was read as the steady and inevitable evolution of God's kingdom of peace and harmony under the pervading influence of Anglo-Saxon Protestant culture. Canada had a special place in that evolution: the exemplary nation for Europe in its declining old age, for the United States in its exuberant youth, and for other cultures in their gradual awakening to the advantages of Anglo-Saxon Protestant values. The Presbyterian progressives supposed war to be a thing of the past. It was something that the civilized nations had outgrown, just as individuals within those nations outgrew their "lower natures" as the social instruments of character formation exerted their influence.

It was not that the possibility of war had not occurred to the Presbyterian progressives. Indeed, it was very much in their minds as they considered the issues of nationalism, imperialism, and social reform in the years immediately preceding the outbreak of the war. But they maintained an unswerving belief that the Hague proposals — international arbitration, decided by an international court and enforced by international public opinion — would offer an alternative that no reasonable, moral person or nation could reject. The nightmare in Europe following August of 1914 strained that belief beyond the limit. As the rhetoric and propaganda of war intensified in Canada, moving the Presbyterian Church in Canada from reluctant support for a just war in defence of British liberties and peace to fervent backing for a holy crusade against barbarism,[1] the progressives saw their dreams of world peace and national harmony crumble.

Responses to this cataclysm varied from one to the other leaders of the Presbyterian progressives. Their individual reactions to World War I revealed differences of temperament and thought hitherto hidden. The war also brought to a head the problem of the level of support for the Presbyterian social service efforts. Financial contributions to Shearer's Board remained so inadequate and the laity displayed such indifference to its work that it had to be amalgamated with the Board of Home Missions in 1915. By the end of the fighting in 1918, the institutional framework the progressives had created to mobilize Canadian Presbyterians no longer existed. They had accomplished many of the social reform measures for which they had fought prior to the war, the most notable of which was temperance, but there were few indications that the experience of the war had wrought the conversion of conscience they deemed essential to national morality. Some of the progressives were broken by the war; some struggled to revive the pre-war vision, especially through the church union movement; some continued to work for conciliation and harmony in a divided world; and some found solace and hope in a more individualistic pietism. None of the Presbyterian progressives based in Toronto followed the more radical Western Methodists into "The New Christianity," alienated from the church, allied with farm and labour interest groups, and active in third-party politics.[2] Many of them wished to believe that Canadians had come through the test of battle with their vision of moral progress strengthened and that reconstruction after the war would usher in the commonwealth for which they had worked. But the world refused to co-operate and proved even less malleable to their ideals than prior to the war.

Progressive Peace-making

True to their ideals of achieving social goals through an enlightened conscience, the Presbyterian progressives had put their objections to war before the church. A Peace Manifesto was drafted by Principal John Mackay of Westminster Hall in Vancouver and circulated nationally by the Presbytery of Westminster in early 1913.[3] It argued that war was "a relic of barbarism," the cost of which fell largely on the producing classes, their wives and their "helpless children." The cost of producing armaments, the Manifesto continued, would be better redirected to alleviating the poverty of the civilized world. A European war would have disastrous effects in Canada and the United States "because of the complete inter-dependence of the world's financial and commercial centres." Addressing the Parliament of Canada directly, the Presbytery conceded that Canada should be ready, in the event of war in

Europe, "to stand or fall with the Empire." But this would be a necessary evil at best and every effort should be made to avoid war. Canada and the United States should take joint action in convening an international council that would "honestly and earnestly seek to find some method of adjusting international differences more in harmony with the spirit of modern civilization" and would recognize the fact "that the ties that bind all people into one world family are now so many and so intricate that no two nations can even prepare for war without seriously affecting all others." In addition, once Canada and the United States had arranged for an understanding among the European powers, a further council should be called "to establish a permanent court for the settlement of international disputes by reason and righteousness and not by blind passion and brute force."

The Manifesto drew national attention. *The Presbyterian,* for a long time the paper of Presbyterian progressivism, greeted the statement as a sign that the church was assuming its responsibility to lead the world in the enterprise of international peace.[4] Prominent British generals, the editor informed his readers, admitted that war was "murder" and "hell." "If the Church has nothing to say against murder," he continued, "if she has no fight to wage against the powers of hell, her occupation is gone and her doom is sealed." The editorial noted that the sentiments expressed agreed with those of farm and labour groups across Canada and the International Socialist Congress and created the opportunity for new alliances with these groups. James A. Macdonald, writing in the *Globe*, claimed the statement was a sign of the continuing courage of Presbyterians to take a clear stand on issues of vital importance.[5] Some might scoff at the power of the church, but Macdonald remained firm in his belief in the power of its ideas. "The Church's weapons," he wrote, "are not carnal but spiritual; not cannons and battleships, but ideas and compelling motives. But ideas are the dynamic of every great revolution and reform. Let the Church, in every pulpit and class throughout all Canada and all the United States, release and drive home the idea of war's barbarity and paganism and sin, and international war, like dueling between individuals, will collapse like a thing uncivilized and intolerable." J.F. McCurdy greeted the Manifesto as a "revival of genuine prophecy."[6] There were a few who raised their voices against the Manifesto. Lt. Col. J.B. Mitchell of Winnipeg, a member of C.W. Gordon's congregation, considered the Peace Manifesto "the most wishy-washy, meaningless conglomeration of words without practical ideas that has been drawn up for some time."[7]

The Peace Manifesto was, in fact, at once a general counsel against war and a focused argument against a particular political action. It arose in response to the debate raging across Canada over the appropriate response to Britain's request for help in countering the expansion of German naval power.

Laurier's Naval Service Bill of 1910 had provided for the creation of a small Canadian navy, to be built, manned, and maintained at Canadian expense and committed to action by decision of the Canadian Parliament. When Borden and the Conservatives came to power in 1911, in part because of opposition from a variety of quarters to Laurier's "tin pot navy," they cancelled the Liberals' naval programme. A variety of alternatives were suggested by various groups.

The Presbyterian summarized its view of the options just prior to the publication of the Peace Manifesto.[8] The Conservative government wanted to make an emergency contribution of $35,000,000 to Britain for the construction of more dreadnoughts. The Liberal opposition wanted the same amount spent on the Canadian navy, with control remaining in the hands of the Canadian Parliament. The Graingrowers' Association of Manitoba was opposed to the expenditure of any public monies on the construction of naval armaments. It called on the government to turn its energies to the promotion of international peace and disarmament by the creation of the international court of arbitration suggested by the Hague conferences. At the very least, the Graingrowers' Association argued, the question of naval spending should be put to a national referendum. *The Presbyterian* did not endorse the idea of a referendum, but it did commend the call to seek international peace and disarmament as the sanest approach.[9]

The Manifesto expressed ideas that had become commonplace among Canadian anti-militarists and anti-imperialists in the decade prior to the outbreak of war. The mid-Victorian liberalism in which most of the Presbyterian progressives were rooted has been shown to be the seedbed for the peace movement in Canada.[10] Militarism, seen as almost any kind of preparedness for war, was viewed as an old-world disease that the new-world democracies had the responsibility to eliminate. Canada and the United States, the argument went, had achieved one hundred years of peace and international neighbourliness across the world's longest undefended border and had the duty to persuade the world to adopt "the North America idea." The peace advocates argued that the root cause of war was economic. As freer trade and the resulting economic interdependence spread, the commercial competitiveness that led to war would be greatly reduced. The autocratic attitudes of the older ruling classes of Europe posed another problem. As democratic institutions evolved in civilized nations, the beneficent power of the people would replace the arrogant ambition of the aristocratic classes.

This, in brief, was the North American peace sentiment and James A. Macdonald was one of its most effective popularizers. The peace movement provided Macdonald with a means of applying the ideals of national righteousness, which grew out of his social Christianity, to the international scene. W.T. Stead, the English advocate and practitioner of a new social journalism, was a model for Macdonald.[11] In a eulogy delivered in New York following Stead's drowning on the Titanic in 1912, Macdonald paid tribute to "one of my best friends in British journalism."[12] Stead's contribution to international peace, Macdonald claimed, began with the life-long campaign he carried on against "the armour-plate press," those papers controlled by special interests, made up of the aristocracy, the military and armament manufacturers, who had great influence in Parliament and whose well-being depended on the expenditures of public money for military and naval expansion. Macdonald wished Canada and the United States had a second Stead. "When the ugly truth is out," he said, "the war scares will cease to terrify, and the full blood profits of the war syndicates will not be paid." Further, Stead's devotion to "the common people, the downtrodden and the distressed" provided the true imperialism. The disgrace of the governments of the Empire, Macdonald stated, was not to be found in the absence of military glory, "but in the existence of social evils, in the haggardness of common poverty for the old and the hopelessness of life for the young." Finally, Stead did much to promote "a world federation of free, sovereign, autonomous nations" in which disputes would be resolved by arbitration. For proof that Stead's idea was "no mere poetic fancy," Macdonald cited the evolution of the British Empire into an association of fraternal nations governed by the highest ideals of justice. Also offered as evidence by Macdonald was a treaty between Britain and the United States, then before the United States Senate, which would forge closer ties between the two nations.

Macdonald's address gained wide circulation in the pamphlet series published quarterly by the World Peace Foundation, an organization founded by American publisher Edwin Ginn. Macdonald sat on the Foundation's Board of Directors with David Starr Jordon of Stanford University and missions promoter John R. Mott among others. Edwin Mead, secretary of the Foundation, made special mention in his annual review for 1912 of Macdonald's speaking tours in Canada, the United States, and Great Britain during 1912 promoting "the reliance altogether in international practice upon the instrumentalities of justice and law."[13] Mead noted that the peace movement owed much to journalists like Macdonald and politicians like William Lyon Mackenzie King in Canada.[14]

In 1913, R.P. MacKay, Secretary of the Board of Foreign Missions, and Liberal M.P. W.A. Charlton, whose speech in opposition to Borden's Naval Bill had been hailed by *The Presbyterian* as a courageous expression of the need for peace efforts,[15] presented a resolution on peace to the General Assembly. It condemned "the increasing waste of men and money by the nations of the earth for warlike purposes," and called on the church to use every reasonable effort in its power, both as individuals and as a body, to secure the abolition of war and bring about peace on earth and good-will to men.[16] When the resolution passed, *The Presbyterian* voiced approval for the intention, but found the actual wording too vague and general.[17]

During the debate over Borden's Naval Aid Bill in 1913, aimed at providing $35,000,000 in emergency aid to the British government for dreadnought construction, Macdonald and the Presbyterian progressives kept up their demand for greater efforts to promote peace. Their pleas, however, fell on deaf ears. The government invoked closure in the Commons to pass the bill, only to have it defeated by the Liberal majority in the Senate. Borden's response was to draft legislation that would provide for an elected Senate. But before any action could be taken, war was declared in Europe.[18] The worst fears of many of the Presbyterian progressives became a reality.

Presbyterian Progressives at War

The August 6, 1914, issue of *The Presbyterian* epitomized the ambiguity with which Presbyterian progressives responded to the outbreak of war. In an editorial warning against a militarism that could turn sober patriotism into a war fever, a fever that would drain wealth from the global neighbourhood and would be quelled only by the letting of blood, the paper maintained its hope for peace. "In spite of all discouraging signs," concluded the writer, "we cannot but believe that reason and mercy will yet govern the relations of mankind." Elsewhere in the same issue, however, the news was reported that Germany's invasion of Belgium would probably draw Britain into the conflict. The editors expressed approval for the "great enthusiasm" with which offers of military support had come from all the British dominions. In their initial reactions to World War I, none of the Presbyterian progressives questioned the rightness of Canada's entry into the war at Britain's side. All agreed that the war was a test of the values at the heart of their social Christianity. But they differed in their individual understandings of what the war meant to the Christian conscience even as they urged Canadians to defend Christian civilization.

C.W. Gordon, undoubtedly the most enthusiastic of the progressives in his readiness to go to war, called it a war of principles: the will of a free people against force as the principle of imperial relations; honour against convenience as the principle of national action; and justice against might as the principle of international relations.[19] "The gage of the German Kaiser and of his Prussian Junkerdom, hurled in the teeth of Christian civilization, has been taken up, and the fight will go on until Democracy, Liberty and Law among the nations will triumph. . . . These things make peace impossible, and these things make the war worth while." Gordon went overseas with the 79th Cameron Highlanders in the spring of 1915 and within six months was senior chaplain to the

Canadian forces in England. In the first few months of war, 160 members of his Winnipeg congregation enlisted in the armed forces. By July 1915, eighty-seven had been killed in action, the largest number of casualties from any single congregation in Canada.[20] Throughout the war, Gordon offered unquestioning support to the Allied cause and greeted victory as the triumph of the spiritual values of freedom, honour, and international law.

Robert Falconer had similar ideals in mind when he addressed the students at the University of Toronto during the first few months of the war.[21] Honour, freedom, law, and agreements among nations were in danger of perishing if men were not willing to struggle to the death to maintain them. "For Britons," Falconer claimed, "the war is a sacred campaign."[22] Germany's real God had been revealed as Force, and it had shown itself to be the outlaw of civilization. The self-sacrifice Canadians were making willingly was an unprecedented moral act in support of "ordered freedom which finds its realization in law based on righteousness."[23] The real causes of the German tragedy were to be found in the character of Bismarck and his Junker bureaucracy who ruled Germany for the forty years prior to the war. "The wrong kind of people have been ruling and teaching and preaching," Falconer informed his audience. "Their ideas were not sufficiently human to train a nation to play her part in the civilized world. Wherefore we have again a justification of the view that the highest aim of education is to produce a thoroughly disciplined character directed by spiritual conceptions."[24] These spiritual conceptions inspired the kind of patriotism that sought to preserve the British heritage in the war. Canadians were fighting for

> the real spiritual Britain, a corporate life of virtue that speaks through each true citizen and perpetuates itself from generation to generation. To justify their pure heroism our soldiers must have caught a glimpse of the spiritual realm in which the virtues of our race are set like stars, and from which, as this dread night passes, there will come the dawning light of a righteousness and justice and liberty that will shine more and more into the perfect day.[25]

Falconer noted that prior to the war those connected with the universities had assumed that barbarism had been driven from the Western world. "We cannot contemplate the tragedy of this war," he said, "without being startled by the facility with which, when once moral ties are cut, civilized men can slip back into savagery."[26] Falconer went to the heart of the irony of the war for the Presbyterian progressives with this admission that a conscience enlightened by Christian morality and truth did not guarantee the Kingdom of God.

The fragility of civilization that Falconer noted lay also at the heart of T.B. Kilpatrick's initial response to the war. It was a demonstration, he felt, of the weaknesses of cultures based on human effort alone. God was using the war to call all people to religious revival, to a confession of sin and a "deep and practical repentance." To answer this call faithfully, Christians in all lands would have to seek "for deeper causes of the war than the mistakes, or even the sins, of diplomatists." They would find them in the individual and national guilt which all people shared. "A new evangelism," Kilpatrick suggested, "in which God is the preacher, reasoning 'of righteousness, and temperance, and the judgement to come,' and unfolding the greatness at once of the promises and the obligations of the Gospel, this is now being carried on amongst us, through the instrument of the war, by the power of the Divine Spirit."[27] Kilpatrick had no doubt the Britain was acting out of the highest moral motivation. He agreed with his brother, a minister in Scotland, that never had a nation or empire embarked on a life and death struggle with a clearer conscience or a loftier and more unselfish purpose.[28] The war was necessary to preserve Christian civilization.

But necessity did not absolve the participants of guilt. Indeed, Kilpatrick urged the readers of *The Presbyterian,* it was not enough to blame the Kaiser alone. The war was an universal calamity for which all humankind was accountable. The need for confession and repentance for all combatants found further expression in Kilpatrick's work with the Commission on the war appointed by the General Assembly in 1917. Among the other members of the Commission were George Pidgeon, J.G. Shearer, and John Mackay. The report, published as *The War and the Christian Church*, went well beyond endorsing the unqualified support of many Christians in Canada for the war effort and provided a penetrating analysis of the universality of sin and the judgement that the war brought on the whole of Western culture.[29]

Troubled as he was by the horrors of war, James A. Macdonald offered reluctant support to the war effort and lost few opportunities to press his peace platform in the midst of the hostilities. He wrote a series of editorials for the *Globe* on the issues raised by the war which brought a letter of appreciation from Mackenzie King, who was then in the United States working at the Rockefeller Foundation.[30] "As the inheritor and custodian in America of Britain's idea of freedom and self-government," Macdonald wrote the week after war broke out in Europe,

> Canada sends into this war against despotism and autocracy in Europe the flower of her youth backed by the strength of her resources and the solemn conviction of her united public opinion. This Canada does not for the sake of war and of war's glory, but of peace for the world. That war may be ended, its power destroyed, its sword broken, Canadians dare to fight, to sacrifice, to die.[31]

The war, Macdonald told his readers, had thrust the emerging international neighbourhood back into a jungle.[32] But Macdonald insisted that the outbreak of war had not disproved the peace policy of the church. Rather, the event had proved that the war policies of the state must be forever condemned. "Peace and neighborliness," he continued, "as a policy between nations, as in North America, have triumphed wherever they have been tried, but War and the war-policy of Armed Peace, as in Europe, have brought the civilized world face to face with collapse into barbarism." Wherever democracy, freedom, and the ideals of social brotherhood had a chance in a nation's policies, Macdonald argued, "the jungle has been pushed back and the desert has become something of a garden." British diplomacy in the years just before the war, guided by men like Asquith and Grey "in the spirit of neighborhood-service and not of jungle-deceit," provided an example of the Christian principles and purpose that should continue to guide international relations. Germany, Macdonald concluded, suffered from a rationalism that had "honeycombed the State Church and eaten away the heart and motive-power of German Christianity,"with the tragic result that "the garden of the old German evangelicalism has been overrun by the materialistic and arrogant growths of social selfishness, military autocracy, and the lust for national power." Elsewhere in the series, Macdonald quoted Tennyson to indicate the motive and purpose of British democracy for which the Allies were fighting: "Move upward, working out the beast,/And let the ape and the tiger die."[33]

Macdonald's acquiescence to the necessity of the war to defend the ideas of liberty, democracy, and internationalism did not lead to unqualified support for Britain. The rightness of the values for which Anglo-Saxon culture at its best stood did not absolve those militaristic elements in British society from their share of blame for the war. In a speech at the World Congress on Internationalism held in San Francisco in October 1915, he held out yet again the example of North American peace to a "war-stricken Europe." "Europe!"he said, with all the fervour his Celtic oratory made possible,

> bristling with guns from the Hebrides to the Dardanelles, bleeding at every boundary with death-wounds none can stanch - O Europe!how often would America have come to you with the gospel of international good-will, teaching you the secret of Anglo-American peace, proving to you the power of international disarmament, and helping to gather your shattered nationalities into a United States of Europe! How often! But ye would not. Now, no matter who among you is to blame, we, too, must suffer in your agony. The national peace of this American Republic is threatened by your madness. The best red blood of the Canadian Dominion is being soaked into your battlefields because of the blood-guiltiness of your sin.[34]

The guilt, Macdonald thought, might not be equal but it could be laid at everybody's door. This refusal to distinguish between German and British militarism, a common theme in Macdonald's speeches, was to have serious consequences for him at home.

The Toronto *News* led the attack on Macdonald's alleged pacifist position expressed on the San Francisco platform. "A British editor," the October 15 editorial read, "supposedly in a position of leadership in this country, goes to the United States and delivers a list of denunciations, not against Germany, not against Austria, but against Europe.... Dr. Macdonald's friends in the United States declare roundly that the British navy is as much a militaristic organization as the German army.... Does he agree? What is the meaning of his furious attacks on 'European' militarism?"[35] The controversy led to Macdonald's resignation as managing editor of the *Globe*, to be replaced by someone perceived to be more supportive of Canada's war effort.[36] Macdonald's attempts to distinguish the ideals for which the Allies were fighting from the practice of militaristic elements within Western nations became less and less acceptable as Canadians began to realize the probable length of the war and the degree of sacrifice that would be demanded. But the lack of public understanding could not dislodge Macdonald from his moral stand. He continued to write and lecture in the United States and Canada and write occasionally for the *Globe*, until his health gave out in 1917.[37]

Responses to the outbreak of the war varied from C.W. Gordon's manly enthusiasm to J.A. Macdonald's North American pacifism. Not only did the war bring to the surface differences in thought and temperament among the Presbyterian progressives, but it also brought changes in their relationships to each other and the social service work of the church. Falconer and Kilpatrick spent most of the war in Toronto at the University of Toronto and Knox College, respectively. Pidgeon returned to Toronto from Westminster Hall in Vancouver to assume responsibilities at Bloor Street Presbyterian Church, but spent much of 1917 with the Canadian forces in Europe under the auspices of the Y. M. C. A. Gordon added efforts to bring the United States into the war to his chaplaincy duties in Europe and did not return to Canada until September 1919. Macdonald left the *Globe* in 1915, spent much of the next two years in the United States, and left for Japan in late 1917 to restore his health. Shearer remained in Toronto, but the war coincided with significant changes in the structures he had been instrumental in creating within the Presbyterian Church to propagate moral and social reform. Events during the early course of the war also brought into sharper focus one of the central issues in the progressivist platform. An aggressive programme of rescue homes and settlement houses in Canada's major cities began in 1911 and continued through the early years of the war. The underlying strategy was enlightenment and regeneration of the poor and the immigrants through the personal influence of those formed by Christian culture. A crisis developed, however, when the financial support needed for such work did not materialize. The battle of principles in Europe was not the only ordeal John G. Shearer faced in the opening years of the war.

Progressivism in Crisis

Meeting in June 1914, the General Assembly directed the Board of Social Service and Evangelism and the Board of Home Missions to amalgamate during the upcoming year. The overlap between the Boards in certain areas of concern, given the progressives' belief that full-fledged churches were the ideal vehicles for Christianization, provided some logic to the directive. It might also have been influenced by increasing pressure from conservative factions in Canada and the United States who denied the possibility of integrating the insights of sociology with the principles of Christianity.

This pressure was so strong that Charles Stelzle, the director of the Department of Church and Labour in the Presbyterian Church (North) in the United States, to whom the Canadian progressives often turned for advice on social programmes, was forced out of his job in 1913. He became an independent consultant on Christianity and social issues and was recommended by James A. Macdonald to Mackenzie King for his staff at the Rockefeller Foundation.[38] *The Presbyterian* noted that there was a strong movement within the southern Presbyterian Church to withdraw from the Federal Council of Churches because of the Council's social programmes.[39] In an editorial on the annual report of the Council, Robert Haddow acknowledged that a more conscious effort in the realm of evangelism was necessary, but cautioned that this should not be done in isolation from the social mission of the church.[40]

The progressives invoked the authority of Christ himself to insist that social service and evangelism belonged together. Gordon and Pidgeon introduced the Social Service and Evangelism report to the Assembly in 1914 by stressing that the two were united in the ministry of the Master. "What God has joined together," they wrote, "let no man put asunder."[41] Amalgamation with home missions work stressed even further the integrated and holistic nature of the church's approach to the world. *The Presbyterian* expressed concern that the church not lose its commitment to social uplift at the very moment it was fighting for the social principles of Christianity in Europe. "The Church must continue to furnish leadership," Haddow urged,

> in the conflict with the enormous social evils of intemperance, impurity, political corruption, public gambling, and the like. The attempt to sweeten and elevate the life of those who are crowded down in the crush of the great cities must be pursued. The door of hope must be held open to the outcasts of society. The spirit of Jesus must be invoked to quell the fierceness of industrial strife, and to usher in a new era of brotherhood, both among the classes of society and the nations of the world. All this is social service. It is Christianity in action. It is an essential part of the Church's task.[42]

In the midst of a real war, the progressives continued to press the church to take seriously "the moral equivalent of war" within Canadian society. In spite of their best efforts, however, work among the urban poor did not find adequate financial support.

The largest single reason for the amalgamation, in the final analysis, was the financial crisis Shearer and his Board created with the rapid expansion of their work.[43] In 1913, the Board wanted to spend $80,000, actually spent $65,000, and raised only $50,000. In 1914, the General Assembly gave the Board a budget of $100,000. The Board spent $89,000, but raised only $49,000. The balance sheet indicates that the idealism and enthusiasm for the work of Shearer's Board, so apparent in the writing and speaking of the Presbyterian progressives, had not been fully accepted by the laity of the church upon whom they depended for financial support.

Initially, the growth of support for the Board of Social Service and Evangelism was impressive. Contributions tripled between 1907 and 1909, growing from $2,366 to $7,877. The amalgamation of evangelistic work with the moral and social reform programmes brought another significant increase in support, from $7,877 in 1909 to $21,288 in 1910. Buoyed by the rapid increase in support, the Board took some bold and costly initiatives. F.A. Robinson was added to the staff as Associate Secretary for Evangelism in 1910, with the promise of an annual contribution of $1,000 towards his salary from the American Presbyterian Church in Montreal. In 1911, D.C. MacGregor came from Knox Church in Orillia to assume responsibilities as Associate Secretary for Social Service, with the commitment from his old congregation to pay half of his salary($1,200) each year. In 1911, the Board also opened a number of rescue homes for girls who became victims of the evil environment in Canada's cities. By 1913, the Board had seventeen workers in five homes located in Sydney, Montreal, Toronto, Winnipeg, and Calgary. In 1912, it established the national chain of settlement houses, and by 1913 there were four institutions with a combined staff of nineteen. In six short years, Shearer and the Board had built the largest bureaucracy in the national offices of the Presbyterian Church in Canada. They had a large field staff in a variety of urban mission work and conducted evangelistic campaigns across Canada. Contributions to the work of the Board in 1913 did increase by $18,000, from $32,000 in 1912 to $50,000, but the cost of running the homes and the settlements alone in 1913 totalled $28,000. The administrative costs were almost $10,000. Robinson's evangelism department cost over $9,000 and MacGregor's co-ordination of social service work, over $7,000. The Board continued to expand its work, however, hoping that support was forthcoming from congregations across the country. Rescue home and settlement work cost over $44,000 in 1914, an increase of $16,000 over the previous year and fully one half of the $88,000 spent by the Board. But the level of financial support from the congregations in 1914 not only did not rise but actually declined to $49,000.

An analysis of the sources of support from congregations across the country shows that the Presbyterian progressives had not done an effective job of selling their work to the whole church. The bulk of support for social service and evangelism between 1910 and 1915 came from nine congregations in the three urban presbyteries of Montreal, Toronto, and Winnipeg (see Table 6). The most generous congregations were either those, such as St. Stephen's in Winnipeg, and St. James Square and Bloor Street in Toronto, where prominent progressives were ministers or members of the congregation, or those, such as American in Montreal and Knox in Orillia, where specific commitments had been made for support of a person's salary. In 1913, for example, the five congregations named above contributed $6,951, or 14 per cent of the total money raised across the country. The vast majority of congregations outside the urban centres of Canada gave nothing to the work of Shearer's Board and most of the congregations that did contribute gave less than $25 a year.

TABLE 6
Financial Support for Social Service and Evangelism

	1910	1911	1912	1913	1914	1915
Total $	21,805	24,488	31,859	50,425	49,416	50,456
$ from Urban Presbyteries	6,178	8,486	9,783	14,801	10,768	12,149
$ from 9 Urban Congregations	4,034	4,847	5,054	7,998	4,239	4,713

The report of the Board of Social Service and Evangelism to the General Assembly in 1915 informed the church that the growth of the various forms of ministry was "sufficient evidence of God's guidance and favour and blessing."[44] There was, however, one cause for "anxiety, not to say discouragement," and that was the lack of financial support. Examination of these statistics, gleaned from congregational reports to the General Assembly, reveals that wide spread support for the work of Shearer's Board never appeared on the collection plates of local congregations across the country. Early in 1915, the Board of Finance, under A.S. Grant, had directed them to keep their expenditures within $50,000 until their revenues exceeded that sum and they had repaid the accumulated deficit of $36,000.[45] The Board appealed to the Assembly to relieve it from giving effect to that order and help raise the money to continue its work. Rather than reply directly to the request from Shearer's Board, the Assembly, through a special committee, told the Board to effect the amalgamation with the Board of Home Missions ordered by the previous Assembly.[46] The difficulties experienced during 1914 and 1915 in amalgamating the Board of Social Service and Evangelism with the Board of Home Missions, headed by the same A.S. Grant responsible for the Board of Finance, stemmed from tensions created by the large deficits built up by Shearer's Board.

The financial crisis brought on by the rapid expansion of the work and the slow response of the congregations was apparent prior to the war. The recession that hit Canada in 1912 might explain some of tardiness in growth of support, and there can be no doubt that the war effort soon began to drain support from many areas of the church's work. But even when allowance is made for circumstances beyond its control, the Board was simply irresponsible in persisting with its ambitious schemes when it was incapable of keeping the work on a sound financial footing. Idealism seemed to blind its members to the financial realities which the whole church, not just the Board, was being forced to face. It was inevitable that the church should curb the Board's rash meliorism by merging its work into the responsible pattern of a better regulated body. The need was pressing, for the times were grim. The devastation of war was upon the world, and the church needed to husband its resources while it pondered the significance of the war.

What the war signified for the church was a crisis of the Christian conscience. It was to define its response to that crisis that the Presbyterian Church set up a commission on the war in 1917, a commission that would at the same time discover the war's social implications from a Christian point of view. Shearer sat with George Pidgeon and T.B. Kilpatrick on the commission, the report of which followed a moderate path between Gordon's enthusiasm and Macdonald's caution. Following the amalgamation and retrenchment of social work that financial stringency imposed, Shearer turned more and more to the Social Service Council of Canada as the best vehicle for continuing his efforts at social uplift. In June 1918, just before the war ended, Shearer left the national office of the Presbyterian Church in Canada and became General Secretary of the Council. The official voices of Presbyterian progressivism mourned his parting and gave assurances that the work for the elevation of Canadian society would continue unabated. But the denomination in whose service Shearer had spent the previous eleven years proved unwilling to pay the cost of the particular programmes the progressives inaugurated and was itself becoming more and more divided by the debate over union with the Methodists and Congregationalists.

* * * * *

The programmes instituted or proposed by the Presbyterian progressives fell before the contingencies of the war but the ideals espoused by the progressives survived the test of the war, at least in the minds of most of them. J. A. Macdonald was the only one whose career was ended by the war. After five years of frail health, he died in 1923. C.W. Gordon returned as Senior Minister of St. Stephen's in 1919 and continued to write popular novels as Ralph Connor until his death in 1937. He found several opportunities — in labour relations in Manitoba, through support for the League of Nations, and by promoting church union — to continue to seek the conciliation and harmony inspired by the liberal principles developed by the progressives prior to the war. George Pidgeon, Robert Falconer, and T.B. Kilpatrick directed much of their energy to the consummation of organic union with the Methodists and the Congregationalists. Falconer and Kilpatrick died before the outbreak of World War II, but Pidgeon lived until the 1960s. Shearer's work with the Social Service Council of Canada was cut short by his death in 1925. These Presbyterian progressives had maintained their moral and social vision through World War I, but those ideals had to prove themselves in a world very different from the one that had given them birth and that had nurtured them.

NOTES

1. S. Macdonald, "The War-Time Sermons of the Rev. Thomas Eakin," *Canadian Society of Church History 1985 Papers*, pp. 58-78.

2 .R. Allen, *The Social Passion*, picks up the story of both the progressive and the radical wings of the Social Gospel in Canada following the outbreak of World War I.

3. The text of the Manifesto was first published in *The Westminster Hall Magazine and Farthest West Review* 3, no.1 (Jan. 1913):31-32.

4. *The Presbyterian* (Toronto), Jan. 30, 1913.

5. *Globe* (Toronto), Jan. 24, 1913.

6. *The Presbyterian* (Toronto), Feb. 6, 1913.

7. *The Presbyterian* (Toronto), Feb. 27, 1913. Letters debating the issues of peace and preparedness in Canada appeared in *The Presbyterian* until the end of May 1913.

8. *The Presbyterian* (Toronto), Jan. 16, 1913.

9. *The Presbyterian* (Toronto), Jan. 30, 1913. Similar stands, it was noted, had been taken by the Dominion Grange, the United Farmers of Alberta, and various labour groups.

10. C. Berger, *The Sense of Power: Studies in the Ideas of Canadian Imperialism, 1867-1914* (Toronto: University of Toronto Press, 1970), pp. 239-242.

11. On Stead, see J.O. Baylen, "W.T. Stead and the Boer War: The Irony of Idealism," *Canadian Historical Review* 40, no.3 (Oct. 1959):304-314; and W.T. Stead and the New Journalism," *Emory University Quarterly* 21, no.3 (1965):196-197.

12. J.A. Macdonald, "The Peace Message of W.T. Stead," in *Messages of the Men and Religion Movement, Vol. 1, Congress Addresses*(New York: Funk and Wagnalls, 1912), pp. 104-124.

13. Edwin D. Mead, "The World Peace Foundation: Its Present Activities," in *World Peace Federation: Pamphlet Series, Vol. 2, 1912* (Boston: World Peace Foundation, 1912).

14. On King and the peace movement, see J.E. Esberey, *Knight of the Holy Spirit* (Toronto: University of Toronto Press, 1980), pp. 196-206. See also D.M. Page, "Canada as the exponent of North American Idealism," *The American Review of Canadian Studies* 3, no.2 (Autumn 1973):30-46.

15. *The Presbyterian* (Toronto), May 22, 1913.

16. *A&P*, 1913, p. 73.

17. *The Presbyterian* (Toronto), June 19, 1913.

18. R.C. Brown and R. Cook, *Canada, 1896-1921: A Nation Transformed* (Toronto:McClelland and Stewart, 1974), pp. 205-211.

19. *The Presbyterian* (Toronto), Nov. 12, 1914.

20. *The Presbyterian* (Toronto), May 27, 1915; July 1, 1915; and Dec. 2, 1915. A considerable portion of Gordon's autobiography, *Postscript to Adventure*, is devoted to his promotion of the British cause during World War I.

21. R.A. Falconer, *The German Tragedy and its Meaning for Canada* (Toronto: University of Toronto Press, 1915).

22. *Ibid.*, p. 3.

23. *Ibid.*, p. 68.

24. *Ibid.*, p. 89.

25. *Ibid.*, p. 8.

26. *Ibid.*, p. 17.

27. *The Presbyterian* (Toronto), Oct. 8, 1914.

28. *The Presbyterian* (Toronto), July 22, 1915.

29. Allen, *The Social Passion*, pp. 43-45.

30. Mackenzie King Papers, King to Macdonald, Nov. 20, 1914, Public Archives of Canada.

31. *Globe* (Toronto), Aug. 17, 1914.

32. *Globe* (Toronto), Sept. 7, 1914.

33. *Globe* (Toronto), Sept. 2, 1914.

34. J.A. Macdonald, *Democracy and the Nations: A Canadian View* (Toronto: S.B. Gundy, 1915), pp. 241-242.

35. Quoted in A. Bridle, *Sons of Canada: Short Studies of Characteristic Canadians* (Toronto: J.M. Dent and Sons, 1916), pp. 279-280.

36. *Ibid.*, p. 280. See also *The Presbyterian* (Toronto), Dec. 2, 1915; and C. Hopkins, *The Canadian Annual Review, 1915* (Toronto: Annual Review Publishing, 1916), pp. 338-353.

37. *Globe* (Toronto), May 15, 1923.

38. King Papers, Macdonald to King, Oct. 5, 1914, and King to Macdonald, Oct. 9, 1914, Public Archives of Canada.

39. *The Presbyterian* (Toronto), Oct. 30, 1913.

40. *The Presbyterian* (Toronto), Dec. 26, 1912.

41. *A&P*, 1914, App., p. 296.

42. *The Presbyterian* (Toronto), Mar. 15, 1915.

43. Information on the decisions to expand the work and the financial figures analysed in this chapter are gleaned from *A&P*, 1907-1916.

44. *A&P*, 1915, App., p. 327.

45. *Ibid.*, p. 362.

46. *A&P*, 1915, Minutes, pp. 60-61 and 91-92.

CHAPTER 8

THE SOCIAL UPLIFTERS IN PERSPECTIVE

The Presbyterian progressives examined in this work can best be understood against the background of the religious traditions in which they were raised and to which they remained loyal throughout their careers. They were heirs and successors to a generation of evangelical Presbyterians who, like William Caven and Donald MacVicar, fought to preserve the purity and righteousness of a Protestant Canada by means of an aggressive assault on what they considered to be the un-Christian elements of Canadian society. Following in the steps of the "Protestant Saints" who battled to keep Sunday streetcars off the tracks in Toronto in the 1880s and the 1890s, "they were concerned social critics who discerned (quite correctly) that industrialization and urbanization had unleashed powerful secular forces in the community. Against these influences, they struggled to anchor society to its Christian foundations, thrusting the churches more prominently into public life in an effort to stem the tide."[1] By the first decade of the twentieth century, when Caven's place in the Protestant crusade had been taken by his students, the tide of materialism was in flood and the sandbags of a former generation had to be replaced by the dikes of a new one.

The new defence was found in the new Christian apologetic imported from Scotland, best articulated by T.B. Kilpatrick. It took with the utmost seriousness the collectivization of society that came in the wake of industrialization and urbanization. The moral defence against these forces was provided by the social philosophy of British Idealism, "Evangelicalism modernized" as one historian has described it.[2] This philosophy offered Kilpatrick and his colleagues a collective liberal morality that continued to stress individual self-realization as the avowed goal of civilized society. But this goal was placed in a broader perspective showing society itself as a collective organism that often required the sacrifice of self-interest for the advancement of the common good and the stability of the community. Only on the basis of such a collectivist liberalism, argued the Presbyterian progressives, could the social order remain harmonious and secure. The moral and social values endorsed by Idealist moral philosophy were those embodied in the prosperous and educated Protestant middle classes of the Anglo-Saxon world and were articulated to meet the crisis of identity produced by new social conditions.

The Scottish liberal evangelical apologists were unwilling, however, to follow their Idealist mentors in their indifference to or rejection of many of the traditional doctrines of the Christian faith, or in their abandonment of the church as the primary means of moral improvement and social stability. They used new historical insights and methods of study to trace the evolution of doctrines within the biblical literature and through the history of the Christian Church. Highlighting the periods and writings in which they felt the faith reached its highest expression, they claimed to have found the essential meanings of the traditional doctrines. These, in turn, were expressed in modern categories of thought and applied to the problems of modern life, analysed within the framework of Idealist social philosophy. Nor were the Scottish apologists willing to turn their backs on the church as the central dynamic in their crusade to anchor national development to Christian moral and social foundations. The evangelical mission was one of winning the souls of the country's citizens, as well as the collective conscience of the nation, for Christ remained at the heart of their efforts. The church was not to be replaced by other social, educational, and political associations and institutions, but rather was to be the senior and determining partner in a collective assault on indifference, immorality, and instability in personal and community life.

At the end of the Victorian era in Canada, the task of forging the ethics of the nation was thought to rest upon the professors of mental and moral philosophy at Canadian universities, who saw themselves as a group of public moralists.[3] From their classrooms came another group of public moralists who had the same goal but a different base of operation. These were the Presbyterian progressives discussed in this study. They worked primarily in and through the church and sought to unify spiritual and social progress within the programme of their church. They consciously sought to use a variety of means to conserve and propagate the influence of Christianity — the public school, the secular university, the popular novel, and the secular press, as well as the pulpit, the theological college, and the religious press. Because of such wide access to the Canadian public, they exercised greater influence on the popular loyalties and morality of the English-speaking Protestant middle classes than did the professorial moralists.

The public writings and addresses of the Presbyterian progressives, all derivative in nature and popular in appeal, revealed little of the ambiguity and tension between critical inquiry and faith evident in other social critics of the age.[4] Idealism did not pose questions for them, but rather provided answers to the dilemmas of their age. They all echoed the sentiments of Alfred Gandier — a gold medallist under John Watson, Robert Falconer's brother-in-law, and Principal of Knox College from 1908 until 1925 — who found in Idealism a spiritual conception of the universe and an intellectual basis for religious faith.[5] It provided the solution to the conflicts and tensions they experienced in thought and social conditions. Since all reality originated in the Divine Mind, all intellectual quandaries and social divisions were ultimately to be resolved as people became reconciled with God and as the Kingdom of Heaven advanced on earth. Idealism acted as a sponge, absorbing all the complexities and contradictions of modern life and holding them together in a moral and religious whole. In the final analysis, Idealism was a supportive rather than a determining factor in their thought. A new source of moral nourishment, it was integrated into a more fundamental faith in Christianity and loyalty to the church that was rooted in their early evangelical experience and nurture.

The new forms in which they cast the traditional doctrines of their Christian faith were paralleled by the new organizational structures through which they continued the traditional work of the church. National consolidation in 1875 triggered a new spirit in Canadian Presbyterianism. With membership concentrated in the expansionist districts of Ontario, and control of the new denomination shifting from Montreal to the centre of Ontario nationalism in Toronto, the Presbyterian progressives who gained the respect and trust of the church in the early twentieth century assumed more initiative and authority in directing the affairs of the church than had their predecessors. These structural changes were forced upon them, in part, by the increasing amount of work required to co-ordinate a rapidly growing enterprise and by the need to respond to the new challenges posed by radical changes in the composition and structure of Canadian society. But the ecclesiastical reforms they initiated or supported also reflected their determination to thrust the church more prominently into public life. The generation of Presbyterian leaders that succeeded Caven gave evidence of this not only in the new committees they established and the new bureaucracy they appointed, but also in their use of voluntary associations, secular education, the secular press, and popular fiction to defend and propagate the moral and social values upon which they felt civilization rested.

The Presbyterian progressives sought to bring to the task of Christianizing Canada the same spirit of efficiency and expertise that a new generation of progressive businessmen were introducing to Canadian economic life. Indeed, they lived in the same neighbourhoods, belonged to the same voluntary associations and benevolent societies, and served on the same civic boards and government commissions as Canada's business and professional leaders. There was nothing in Presbyterian progressivism prior to World War I that demanded from the church's laity a substantial change in the values they held or the institutions through which they worked. Although the religious progressives were more adamant, at times, in pressing for moral purity among Canadians than many of their neighbours, the men examined in this study shared the same goals of national prosperity, efficiency, and stability that guided Canada's progressive businessmen and professionals. The best interests of everyone in the country, they believed, were served by a stable economic climate, a legal and political system devoid of graft and corruption, a safe and healthy industrial system, a planned urban environment and a harmonious social order built on co-operation, compromise and self-sacrifice.[6] However, with all the sincerity of their moral reformism and social criticism, this group of Anglo-Saxon Protestant ecclesiastical professionals, based as they were in the prosperous middle-class suburbs of central Canada's leading city, exhibited a notable blindness to the religious, cultural, and economic narrowness of their vision. The Kingdom of God would be realized, they firmly believed, when everyone was assimilated into their Anglo-Saxon Protestantism.

There was remarkably little controversy over the moral and social views of the Presbyterian progressives within the church. This was due, in large part, to the conscious effort on their part to preserve and defend the essence of traditional Christianity through their new apologetic. Their careful balance between the traditional and the innovative, between evangelism and social reform, and between personal and social Christianity did much to prevent the polarization of parties that characterized the rise of the American Social Gospel.[7]

Another important factor in the unified moral outlook characterizing Presbyterians in Canada was the close relationship between all Presbyterian colleges and the universities.[8] By the 1880s, all Presbyterian theological students had been through the classrooms of professors of mental and moral philosophy, all of whom developed their teaching within the same metaphysical and ethical framework — British Idealism. The Presbyterian Church in Canada was not without its controversies, but they had little to do with the moral ideals and social philosophy of Presbyterian progressivism. It might be argued that an important exception to this claim was the church union debate, but ardent opponents of union, such as R.G. MacBeth, found themselves in substantial agreement with the progressives on the substance of questions of moral and social reform, if not on the strategy of an organic union among Protestant denominations in Canada as a means to accomplish these goals.[9]

In the final analysis, the leaders of Presbyterian progressivism owed more to their social and intellectual roots than they did to social conditions at the turn of the century in Canada in formulating their thoughts and strategies. They were knowledgeable about and sensitive to the social transformations going on about them, but they relied primarily on the moral, social, and intellectual resources of the Free Church Presbyterianism in which they were raised. Industrialization, immigration, and new currents of thought contributed to significant changes in the way these men articulated their Christianity, but these changes were viewed as a means of adapting the essentials of the Christian message to a new environment. They saw themselves as agents of the progressive perfection of Christianity rather than as discoverers of a new Christianity. Continuity rather than change characterized their approach to the basics of their faith and morality.

The portrait painted here is of a group of prominent Presbyterians who made a sincere but naive attempt to Christianize Canadian civilization in the early years of the twentieth century. James A. Macdonald captured both the depth of their sincerity and the breadth of their innocence in a speech to Canada's Missionary Congress in 1909. "Men who themselves are thrilled by the Christ-life and inspired by the Christ-spirit and constrained by the Christ-motive," he urged his audience, "must go into the social life and into the business life and into the political life, and into all other avenues of thought and life, and there live out the Christ-idea. . . . Four thousand Christ-men could redeem Canadian civilization in this generation."[10] Raised in the confident and aggressive culture of nineteenth-century Protestantism, the Presbyterian progressives encountered nothing in their upbringing or careers prior to World War I that caused them to question the rectitude or universality of their moral and social ideals. While aware of growing divisions and tensions within Canadian society and conscious of the waning power and prestige of Protestantism, they nevertheless rationalized or ignored their weaknesses in the light of their strengths — real or imagined, achieved or hoped for. World War I created the first crisis that produced acknowledged nightmares amid their national dreams.

The Presbyterian progressives dreamed of a permanence for their vision of Canada, which the historical circumstances did not warrant. Wilfrid Laurier's years as Prime Minister gave him a much more realistic understanding of the character and destiny of Canada. Writing to C.W. Gordon to acknowledge the receipt of a Christmas copy of *Corporal Cameron*, Laurier pronounced a fitting epigram for Presbyterian progressivism. "Your books," he wrote, "are particularly attractive to me because they will preserve a special phase of our national history, and customs which are rapidly passing away."[11]

NOTES

1. C. Armstrong and H.V. Nelles, *The Revenge of the Methodist Bicycle Company* (Toronto: Peter Martin Associates, 1977), p. 180.

2. M. Richter, *The Politics of Conscience: T.H. Green and his Age* (London: Weidenfeld and Nicolson, 1964), p. 15.

3. McKillop, *Disciplined Intelligence*, p. x.

4. *Ibid.*, pp. x-xi; and Cook, *The Regenerators*, pp. 7-40.

5. J. Dow, *Alfred Gandier: Man of Vision and Achievement* (Toronto: Ryerson Press, 1951), p. 9.

6. See J.C. Weaver, "Tomorrow's Metropolis Revisited: A Critical Assessment of Urban Reform in Canada, 1890-1920," in Stelter and Artibise, *Canadian City*, pp. 393-418. A more conclusive appraisal of the involvement of ecclesiastical figures in urban reform movements awaits a more detailed study of their role in the campaigns for civic improvement in their respective cities.

7. M.E. Marty, *Righteous Empire: The Protestant Experience in America* (New York: Dial, 1970), pp. 177-187.

8. See R.T. Handy, "Trends in Canadian and American Theological Education, 1880-1980," *Theological Education* 18, no.2 (Spring 1982):190-196.

9. See, for example, R.G. MacBeth, *Our Task in Canada* (Toronto: Westminster, 1912).

10. J.A. Macdonald, "The Christianization of our Civilization," *Canada's Missionary Congress* (Toronto: Canadian Council, Laymen's Missionary Movement, 1909), p. 119.

11. Laurier to Gordon, December 19, 1912, Laurier Papers, Public Archives of Canada.

SELECTED BIBLIOGRAPHY

PRIMARY SOURCES

1. Church Records

Acts and Proceeedings of the General Assembly, Presbyterian Church in Canada.

2. Periodicals and Magazines

The Christian Guardian (Toronto)

The Dominion Presbyterian (Toronto)

The Globe (Toronto)

The Home and Foreign Record of the Canada Presbyterian Church (Toronto)

The Knox College Monthly (Toronto)

The Presbyterian (Montreal)

The Presbyterian (Toronto)

The Presbyterian and Westminster (Toronto)

The Presbyterian College Journal (Montreal)

The Presbyterian Record (Montreal)

The Presbyterian Witness (Halifax)

The Queen's University Journal (Kingston)

The Queen's Quarterly (Kingston)

The Westminster (Toronto)

The Westminster Hall and Farthest West Review (Vancouver)

3. Manuscript Collections

British Columbia Conference Archives,
United Church of Canada:

Westminster Hall Collection

Knox College Archives:

Minutes, Senate of Knox College, Toronto

Public Archives of Canada:

Wilfrid Laurier Papers
William Lyon Mackenzie King Papers

Queen's University Archives:

John Watson Papers
George M. Grant Papers

United Church of Canada Archives:

Biographies Collection
Church Union Collection
G.G.D. Kilpatrick Papers
George Pidgeon Papers
Minutes, Board of Evangelism and Social Service, Presbyterian Church in Canada
Minutes, Social Service Council of Canada

University of Toronto Archives:

Robert A. Falconer Papers

4. Books and Pamphlets

Aberdeen, Lord and Lady. *We Twa, Reminiscences of Lord and Lady Aberdeen*. London: W. Collins Sons, 1925.

Blewett, G.J. *The Study of Nature and the Vision of God: with other essays in philosophy*. Toronto: William Briggs, 1907.

Brown, W.A. *Christian Theology in Outline*. Edinburgh: T.& T. Clark, 1908.

--- . *Modern Theology and the Preaching of the Gospel*. New York: Charles Scribner's Sons, 1914.

Bruce, A.B. *Apologetics, or Christianity Defensively Stated*. Edinburgh: T.& T. Clark, 1892.

Caird, E. *Essays on Literature*. Glasgow: James Maclehose and Sons, 1909.

--- . *Hegel*. Edinburgh: William Blackwood and Sons, 1892.

--- . *The Social Philosophy and Religion of Comte*. Glasgow: James Maclehose and Sons, 1893.

Caird, J. *An Introduction to the Philosophy of Religion*. Glasgow: James Maclehose and Sons, 1910.

--- . *The Fundamental Ideas of Christianity* (2 vols., with a Memoir by Edward Caird). Glasgow: James Maclehose and Sons, 1899.

--- . *University Sermons*. Glasgow: James Maclehose and Sons, 1899.

Canada Presbyterian Church Pulpit, First Series. Toronto: James Campbell and Sons, 1871.

Canada Presbyterian Church Pulpit, Second Series. Toronto: James Campbell and Sons, 1873.

Canada's Missionary Congress. Toronto: Canadian Council, Laymen's Missionary Movement, 1909.

Caven, W. *Christ's Teaching Concerning the Last Things and other Papers*. Toronto: Westminster, 1908.

Chapman, J.W. *The Life and Work of Dwight L. Moody*. Toronto: Bradley-Garretson, 1900.

Christianity Practically Applied (2 vols.). New York: Baker and Taylor, 1893.

Connor, R. *Black Rock: A Tale of the Selkirks*. Toronto: Westminster, 1898.

--- . *Corporal Cameron*. Toronto: Westminster, 1912.

--- . *The Doctor: A Tale of the Rockies*. Toronto: Westminster, 1906.

--- . *The Foreigner*. Toronto: Westminster, 1909.

--- . *The Man From Glengarry*. Toronto: Westminster, 1901.

--- . *The Sky Pilot: A Tale of the Foothills*. Toronto: Westminster, 1899.

Cunningham, W. *Christianity and Economic Science*. London: John Murray, 1914.

--- . *Christianity and Social Questions*. London: Duckworth, 1910.

--- . *The Gospel of Work, being four lectures on Christian Ethics*. Cambridge: Cambridge University Press, 1902.

Drummond, H. *Addresses* (with a biographical sketch by W.J. Dawson). New York: Fleming H.Revell, 1891.

--- . *Natural Law in the Spiritual World.* London: Hodder and Stoughton, 1887.

--- . *The Ascent of Man.* London: Hodder and Stoughton, 1894.

--- . *The Ideal Life and other unpublished addresses.* London: Hodder and Stoughton, 1897.

--- . *The New Evangelism and other papers.* London: Hodder and Stoughton, 1899.

Falconer, R.A. *Idealism in National Character.* London: Hodder and Stoughton, 1920.

--- . *The Truth of the Apostolic Gospel.* New York: YMCA, 1904.

Gordon, C.W. *Postscript to Adventure: The Autobiography of Ralph Connor.* Toronto: McClelland and Stewart, 1975.

--- . *The Life of James Robertson.* Toronto: Westminster, 1908.

Green, T.H. *Prolegomena to Ethics.* London: Oxford University Press, 1883.

Herridge, W.T. *The Orbit of Life.* Toronto: Fleming H. Revell, 1906.

Hughes, H.T. *Social Christianity.* London: Hodder and Stoughton, 1890.

Jones, H. *Browning as a Philosophical and Religious Teacher.* London: Thomas Nelson and Sons, 1891.

--- . *Idealism as a Practical Creed.* Glasgow: James Maclehose and Sons, 1909.

Jones H., and Muirhead, J.H. *The Life and Philosophy of Edward Caird.* Glasgow: Maclehose, Jackson, 1912.

Jordon, W.G. *Biblical Criticism and Modern Thought.* Edinburgh: T.& T. Clark, 1909.

--- . *Prophetic Ideas and Ideals.* Toronto: Westminster, 1902.

Kilpatrick, T.B. *Christian Character: A Study in New Testament Morality.* Edinburgh: T.& T.Clark, 1904.

--- . *New Testament Evangelism.* Toronto: Westminster, 1911.

King, W.L.M. *Industry and Humanity.* Toronto: University of Toronto Press, 1973.

--- . *The Secret of Heroism.* New York: Fleming H. Revell, 1906.

MacBeth, R.G. *Our Task in Canada.* Toronto: Westminster, 1912.

Macdonald, J.A. *Democracy and the Nations, a Canadian View.* Toronto: S.B.Gundy, 1915.

--- . *The Interests of the Nation in the Missions of the Church.* Toronto: Canadian Council, Laymen's Missionary Movement, n.d.

--- . *The Message of the Strenuous Life: in memoriam of the Rev. George Munro Grant.* Toronto: Friends of St. Andrew's, 1902.

--- . *The North American Idea.* Toronto: McClelland, Goodchild and Stewart, 1917.

--- . *What A Newspaper Man Saw in Britain.* Toronto: The Globe, 1909.

MacDougall, J. *Rural Life in Canada.* Toronto: University of Toronto Press, 1973.

MacFarland, C.S. *Spiritual Culture and Social Service.* New York: Fleming H. Revell, n.d.

Mackay, J. *Religion as Friendship with God: A New Statement of Old Doctrines.* Toronto: Westminster, 1906.

MacLaren, W. *Sixty Years' Retrospect.* Toronto: Armac Press, 1907.

McCurdy, J.F. (ed.). *Life and Work of D.J. Macdonnell.* Toronto: William Briggs, 1897.

McFadyen, J.E. *A Cry For Justice: A Study in Amos.* New York: Charles Scribner's Sons, 1912.

--- . *An Introduction to the Old Testament.* London: Hodder and Stoughton, 1905.

--- . *Old Testament Criticism and the Christian Church.* London: Hodder and Stoughton, 1903.

McIntosh, W.R. (ed.). *Canadian Problems.* Toronto: Presbyterian Publications, 1910.

--- . *Social Service: a book for young Canadians.* Toronto: Presbyterian Publications, 1911.

Muirhead, J.H. *The Platonic Tradition in Anglo-Saxon Philosophy.* London: George Allen and Unwin, 1931.

Murray, J.C. *A Handbook of Christian Ethics.* Edinburgh: T. & T. Clark, 1908.

Nichol, J. *Thomas Carlyle.* London: Macmillan, 1892.

Peabody, F.G. *Jesus Christ and Christian Character.* London: Hodder and Stoughton, 1905.

--- . *Jesus Christ and the Social Question.* New York: Macmillan, 1903.

Pre-Assembly Congress. Toronto: Board of Foreign Missions, Presbyterian Church in Canada, 1913.

Proudfoot, J.J.A. *Systematic Homiletics.* Toronto: Westminster, 1903.

Rauschenbush, W. *Christianity and the Social Crisis.* New York: Macmillan, 1907.

--- . *Christianizing the Social Order.* New York: Macmillan, 1912.

Robinson, F.A. *Religious Revival and Social Betterment.* Boston: Gorham, 1918.

Simpson, P.C. *The Life of Principal Rainy* (2 vols.). London: Hodder and Stoughton, 1909.

Skelton, O.D. *Socialism: A Critical Analysis.* New York: Houghton Mifflin, 1911.

Smith, G.A. *Modern Criticism and the Preaching of the Old Testament.* London: Hodder and Stoughton, 1901.

--- . *The Life of Henry Drummond.* London: Hodder and Stoughton, 1898.

Smith, W.H. *The Church and Men.* Toronto: Presbyterian Publications, 1910.

Social Service Congress, Ottawa, 1914. Toronto: Social Service Council of Canada, 1914.

Strong, J. *Our Country: Its Possible Future and Its Present Crisis.* New York: American Home Missionary Society, 1885.

--- . *Religious Movements for Social Betterment.* New York: Baker and Taylor, n.d.

--- . *The Challenge of the City.* New York: Young People's Missionary Movement, 1907.

--- . *The Twentieth Century City.* New York: Baker and Taylor, 1898.

Taylor, Sir W.T. *Historical Sketch of St. James Square Presbyterian Congregation, Toronto: 1853-1903.* Toronto: Brown-Searle Printing, 1903.

Toynbee, A. *Lectures on the Industrial Revolution of the Eighteenth Century in England.* London: Longmans, Green and Co., 1894.

Tulloch, J. *Movements of Religious Thought in Britain During the Nineteenth Century.* New York: Charles Scribner's Sons, 1886.

Vital Questions: The Discussions of the General Christian Conference, 1888. Montreal: William Drysdale, 1889.

Ward, W. *The Brotherhood in Canada.* London: Brotherhood Publishing House, 1912.

Watson, J. *Christianity and Idealism: the Christian ideal of life in its relations to the Greek and Jewish ideals and to modern philosophy.* New York: Macmillan, 1897.

--- . *Comte, Mill and Spencer: An Outline of Philosophy.* New York: Macmillan, 1895.

--- . *The Interpretation of Religious Experience* (2 vols.). Glasgow: Maclehose, 1912.

--- . *The Philosophical Basis of Religion.* Glasgow: James Maclehose and Sons, 1907.

Woodsworth, J.S. *My Neighbour.* Toronto: University of Toronto Press, 1972.

--- . *Strangers within our gates.* Toronto: University of Toronto Press, 1972.

Young, G.P. *Miscellaneous Discourses and Expositions of Scripture.* Edinburgh: Johnstone and Hunter, 1854.

--- . *The Ethics of Freedom* (with a biographical sketch by J.G.Hume). Toronto: University of Toronto Press, 1911.

5. Articles

Beattie, F.R. "The Materials of Apologetics," *Knox College Monthly* 12, no.5 (Sept.1890).

Campbell, J. "Scholasticism in Modern Theology," *Knox College Monthly* 11, no.2 (Dec.1889).

Cappon, J. "Edward Caird: A Reminiscence," *Queen's Quarterly* 5, no.3 (1909).

Caven, W. "Clerical Conservatism and Scientific Radicalism," *Knox College Monthly* 14, no.6 (Oct.1891).

Dods, M. "Recent Progress in Theology," *Knox College Monthly* 11, no.2 (Dec.1889).

Dyde, S.W. "A Basis for Ethics," *Mind* 13, no.52 (Oct.1888).

Falconer, J.W. "Religious Factors in Ritschl's Theology," *Presbyterian College Journal* (Montreal) 16, no.3 (Feb. 1897).

Falconer, R.A. "Christian Theology Spiritually Discerned," *Presbyterian College Journal* (Halifax) 16, no.3 (Jan.1896).

--- . "Science and Religion as Factors in Progress," *Religious Education* 8, no.4 (Oct.1915).

--- . "The Present Position of the Churches in Canada," *Constructive Quarterly* 1 (June 1913).

Frizzell, W. "Practical Aspects of Present Day Socialism," *Knox College Monthly* 16, no.1 (May 1892).

Gordon, C.W. "Introduction to the Art of Oratory," *Knox College Monthly* 5, no.1 (Nov.1886).

--- . "The New West and the New East," *Knox College Monthly* 18, no.7 (Nov.1894).

--- . "The Woman's Foreign Missionary Society as a Conserving Influence," *Knox College Monthly* 10, no.1 (May 1889).

Gregg, W. "Thomas Chalmers," *Knox College Monthly* 16, no.7 (Nov.1892).

Hume, J.G. "Socialism," *Knox College Monthly* 17, nos.11,12 (March and April 1894).

Inglis, G. "Christian Socialism," *Knox College Monthly* 7, no.4 (Feb.1888).

Jordon, W.G. "The Social Principles of Hebrew Legislation," *The Westminster* 13, no.2 (Aug.1908).

Kennedy, H.A.A. "The Social Principles of Jesus," *The Westminster* 13, no.5 (Nov.1908).

Macdonald, J.A. "Christianity and Governments." In *Messages of the Men and Religion Movement* (vol.1). New York: Funk and Wagnalls, 1912

--- . "Pietism in Germany and Evangelism in Canada," *Knox College Monthly* 8, no.2 (June 1888).

--- . "Rev.Principal Caven, D.D.," *Knox College Monthly* 15, no.1 (Nov.1891).

--- . "The Peace Message of W.T.Stead." In *Messages of the Men and Religion Movement* (vol.1). New York: Funk and Wagnalls, 1912.

--- . "The Press and the Ethical Life of the Nation," *Religious Education* 3, no.2 (June 1908).

--- . "The Vocation of North America." In F.P.Turner (ed.), *Students and the World-Wide Expansion of Christianity*. New York: Student Volunteer Movement for Foreign Missions, 1914.

MacDougall, J. "The Ritschlian Theology," *Presbyterian College Journal* (Montreal) 18, no.6 (Apr.1899).

MacVicar, D.H. "The Study of Sociology," *Presbyterian College Journal* (Montreal) 18, no.3 (Jan.1898).

McCurdy, J.F. "Modern Old Testament Criticism: A Study for Preachers and Teachers," *The Westminster*, July 6, 1901.

McFadyen, J.F. "The Social Principles of the Prophets," *The Westminster* 13, no.4 (Oct.1908).

McGill, R. "The Social Principles of the Early Church," *The Westminster* 13, no.6 (Dec.1908).

Pidgeon, G.C. "The Teachings of Christ in their Bearing on Modern Problems," *Presbyterian College Journal* (Montreal) 19, no.6 (Apr.1900).

Sinclair, A.G. "The Chapman Campaign in Winnipeg," *The Westminster* 12, no.1 (Jan.1908).

Watson, J. "Christianity and Modern Life," *Knox College Monthly* 14, no.3 (July 1891).

--- . "The Higher Life of the Scholar," *Queen's University Journal*, Dec.21, 1899.

--- . "The Ideal Life," *Presbyterian College Journal* (Montreal) 26, no.4 (Mar.1907).

--- . "The Idealism of Edward Caird," *The Philosophical Review* 18, nos.2,3 (1909).

SECONDARY SOURCES

1. Books and Pamphlets

Aaron, D. *Men of Good Hope: A Story of American Progressives.* London: Oxford University Press, 1951.

Abell, A.I. *The Urban Impact on American Protestantism, 1865-1900.* Cambridge: Harvard University Press, 1943.

Ahlstrom, S.E. *A Religious History of the American People.* New Haven: Yale University Press, 1972.

Allen, R. (ed.). *The Social Gospel in Canada.* Ottawa: National Museums of Canada, 1975.

Allen, R. *The Social Passion: Religion and Social Reform in Canada, 1914-1928*. Toronto: University of Toronto Press, 1971.

Altick, R. *Victorian People and Ideas*. New York: W.W. Norton, 1973.

Armour, L., and Trott, E., *The Faces of Reason: An Essay on Philosophy and Culture in English Canada, 1850-1950*. Waterloo: Wilfrid Laurier University Press, 1981.

Armstrong, C., and Nelles, H.V. *The Revenge of the Methodist Bicycle Company*. Toronto: Peter Martin Associates, 1977.

Artibise, A.F.J. *Winnipeg: A Social History of Urban Growth, 1874-1914*. Montreal: McGill-Queen's University Press, 1975.

---, and Stelter, G.A. (eds.). *The Usable Urban East: Planning and Politics in the Modern Canadian City*. Toronto: Macmillan, 1979.

Berger, C. *The Sense of Power*. Toronto: University of Toronto Press, 1970.

---, and Cook, R. (eds.). *The West and the Nation: Essays in Honour of W.L. Morton*. Toronto: McClelland and Stewart, 1976.

Bliss, M. *A Living Profit: Studies in the Social History of Canadian Business, 1883-1911*. Toronto: McClelland and Stewart, 1974.

Boyer, P.S. *Urban Masses and Moral Order in America, 1820-1920*. Cambridge: Harvard University Press, 1978.

Brown, R.C., and Cook, R. *Canada: 1896-1921: A Nation Transformed*. Toronto: McClelland and Stewart, 1974.

Carter, P.A.*T he Spiritual Crisis of the Gilded Age*. DeKalb: Northern Illinois University Press, 1971.

Clark, S.D. *Church and Sect in Canada*. Toronto: University of Toronto Press, 1948.

Cook, R. *The Regenerators: Social Criticism in Late Victorian English Canada.* Toronto: University of Toronto Press, 1985.

Craven, P. *'An Impartial Umpire': Industrial Relations and the Canadian State, 1900-1911.* Toronto: University of Toronto Press, 1980.

Cremin, L. *The Transformation of the School: Progressivism in American Education: 1876-1957.* New York: Vintage Books, 1961.

Crunican, P. *Priests and Politicians: Manitoba schools and the election of 1896.* Toronto: University of Toronto Press, 1974.

Crysdale, S. *The Industrial Struggle and Protestant Ethics in Canada.* Toronto: Ryerson Press, 1961.

Davie, G.E. *The Democratic Intellect.* Edinburgh: Edinburgh University Press, 1961.

Davis, A.F. *Spearheads for Reform.* Toronto: Oxford University Press, 1967.

Drummond, A.L., and Bulloch, J. *The Scottish Church, 1688-1843: The Age of the Moderates.* Edinburgh: St. Andrew Press, 1973.

--- . *The Church in Victorian Scotland, 1843-1874.* Edinburgh: St. Andrew Press, 1974.

--- . *The Church in late Victorian Scotland, 1874-1900.* Edinburgh: St. Andrew Press, 1978.

Elgee, W.H. *The Social Teachings of the Canadian Churches, Protestant, The Early Period, Before 1850.* Toronto: Ryerson Press, 1964.

Esberey, J.E. *Knight of the Holy Spirit: A Study of William Lyon Mackenzie King.* Toronto: University of Toronto Press, 1980.

Findlay, J.F., Jr. *Dwight L.Moody: American Evangelist, 1837-1899.* Chicago: University of Chicago Press, 1969.

Gerrish, B.A. *Tradition and the Modern World: Reformed Theology in the Nineteenth Century.* Chicago: University of Chicago Press, 1978.

Gilbert, A.D. *Religion and Society in Industrial England: Church, Chapel and Social Change, 1740-1914.* London: Longman, 1976.

Goheen, P.G. *Victorian Toronto: 1850-1900: Pattern and Process of Growth.* Chicago: University of Chicago Press, 1970.

Grant, J.W. *George Pidgeon.* Toronto: Ryerson Press, 1962.

--- . *The Canadian Experience of Church Union.* London: Lutterworth Press, 1967.

--- . *The Church in the Canadian Era.* Toronto: McGraw-Hill Ryerson, 1972.

Grant, W.S., and Hamilton, F. *George Munro Grant.* Toronto: Morang, 1905.

Gray, J. *Booze.* Toronto: Macmillan, 1972.

--- . *Red Lights on the Prairies.* Toronto: Macmillan, 1971.

Greengarten, I.M. *Thomas Hill Green and the Development of Liberal-Democratic Thought.* Toronto: University of Toronto Press, 1981.

Handy, R. *A Christian America: Protestant Hopes and Historical Realities.* New York: Oxford University Press, 1971.

--- . *A History of the Churches in Canada and the United States.* New York: Oxford University Press, 1982.

Harris, R.S. *A History of Higher Education in Canada, 1663-1960.* Toronto: University of Toronto Press, 1976.

Harrison, J.F.C. *Living and Learning: 1790-1960.* Toronto: University of Toronto Press, 1961.

Harvie, C. *The Lights of Liberalism: University Liberals and the Challenge of Democracy, 1860-86*. London: Allen Lane, 1976.

Hays, S. *The Response to Industrialism, 1885-1914*. Chicago: University of Chicago Press, 1957.

Himmelfarb, G. *Darwin and the Darwinian Revolution*. New York: W.W.Norton, 1962.

Hofstadter, R. *The Age of Reform*. New York: Vintage Books, 1955.

Holloway, J. *The Victorian Sage*. London: Archon, 1962.

Hopkins, C.H. *The Rise of the Social Gospel in American Protestantism: 1865-1915*. New Haven: Yale University Press, 1940.

Houghton, W.E. *The Victorian Frame of Mind*. New Haven: Yale University Press, 1957.

Hutchison, W.R. *The Modernist Impulse in American Protestantism*. Cambridge: Harvard University Press, 1976.

Inglis, K.S. *Church and the Working Classes in Victorian Protestantism*. Toronto: University of Toronto Press, 1963.

Irvine, W. *Apes, Angels and Victorians: Darwin, Huxley and Evolution*. New York: McGraw-Hill, 1955.

Jones, A., and Rutman, L. *In the Children's Aid: J.J.Kelso and Child Welfare in Ontario*. Toronto: University of Toronto Press, 1981.

Jones, P.d'A. *The Christian Socialist Revival, 1877-1914: religion, class, and social conscience in late-Victorian England*. Princeton: Princeton University Press, 1968.

Kelley, R. *The Trans-Atlantic Persuasion: The Liberal-Democratic Mind in the Age of Gladstone*. New York: Knopf, 1969.

Kesterton, W.H. *A History of Journalism in Canada.* Toronto: McClelland and Stewart, 1967.

Landon, F. *Western Ontario and the American Frontier.* Toronto: McClelland and Stewart, 1967.

Loetscher, L.A. *The Broadening Church: A Study of Theological Issues in the Presbyterian Church Since 1869.* Philadelphia: University of Pennsylvania Press, 1957.

Lubove, R. *The Professional Altruist: The Emergence of Social Work as a Career, 1880-1930.* Cambridge: Harvard University Press, 1965.

Lynn, R., and Wright, E. *The Big Little School: Sunday Child of American Protestantism.* New York: Harper and Row, 1971.

McKillop, A.B. *A Disciplined Intelligence: Critical Inquiry and Canadian Thought in the Victorian Era.* Montreal: McGill-Queen's University Press, 1979.

McLoughlin, W.G. *Awakenings, Revivals and Reform.* Chicago: University of Chicago Press, 1978.

McNaught, K. *A Prophet in Politics: A Biography of J.S.Woodsworth.* Toronto: University of Toronto Press, 1959.

Marsden, G. *The Evangelical Mind and the New School Presbyterian Experience: A Case Study of Thought and Theology in Nineteenth Century America.* New Haven: Yale University Press, 1970.

--- . *Fundamentalism and America Culture: The Shaping of Twentieth Century Evangelicalism, 1870-1925.* New York: Oxford University Press, 1980.

Marty, M.E. *Righteous Empire: The Protestant Experience in America.* New York: Dial Press, 1970.

Masters, D.C. *The Rise of Toronto, 1850-1890.* Toronto: University of Toronto Press, 1947.

May, H.F. *Protestant Churches and Industrial America.* New York: Harper Torchbooks, 1967.

Mechie, S. *The Church and Scottish Social Development, 1780-1870.* London: Oxford University Press, 1960.

Meyer, D.H. *The Instructed Conscience: The Shaping of the American National Ethic.* Philadelphia: University of Pennsylvania Press, 1972.

Milne, A.J.M. *The Social Philosophy of English Idealism.* London: George Allen and Unwin, 1962.

Moir, J.S. *Enduring Witness: A History of the Presbyterian Church in Canada.* Toronto: Presbyterian Publications, 1975.

--- . *A Sense of Proportion: A History of Biblical Studies in Canada.* Chico, California: Scholar's Press, 1984.

Noble, D.W. *The Progressive Mind, 1870-1917.* Chicago: Rand McNally, 1970.

Orr, J.E. *The Second Evangelical Awakening in Britain.* London: Marshall, Morgan and Scott, 1959.

Owram, D. *Promise of Eden: The Canadian Expansionist Movement and the Idea of the West, 1865-1900.* Toronto: University of Toronto Press, 1980.

Phillips, P.T. (ed.). *The View from the Pulpit: Victorian Ministers and Society.* Toronto: Macmillan, 1978.

Prang, M. *N.W. Rowell: Ontario Nationalist.* Toronto: University of Toronto Press, 1975.

Reardon, B.M.G. *From Coleridge to Gore: A Century of Religious Thought in Britain.* London: Longmans, 1971.

Reid, W.S. (ed.). *The Scottish Tradition in Canada.* Toronto: McClelland and Stewart, 1976.

Richter, M. *The Politics of Conscience: T.H.Green and His Age.* Cambridge: Harvard University Press, 1964.

Selleck, R.J.W. *The New Education: English Background, 1870-1914.* Melbourne: Pitman and Sons, 1968.

Semmel, B. *Imperialism and Social Reform.* New York: Anchor Books, 1960.

Sharpe, D.R. *Walter Rauschenbusch.* New York: Macmillan, 1942.

Shortt, S.E.D. *Six Canadian Intellectuals and their Convictions in an Age of Transition, 1890-1930.* Toronto: University of Toronto Press, 1976.

Smith, D.C. *Passive Obedience and Prophetic Protest: Social Criticism in the Scottish Church, 1830-1945.* New York: Peter Lang, 1987.

Smith, T.L. *Revivalism and Social Reform in mid-nineteenth century America.* New York: Abingdon Press, 1957.

Splane, R.B. *Social Welfare in Ontario, 1791-1893.* Toronto: University of Toronto Press, 1965.

Sutherland, N. *Children in English-Canadian Society: Framing the Twentieth-Century Consensus.* Toronto: University of Toronto Press, 1976.

Swainson, D. (ed.). *Oliver Mowat's Ontario.* Toronto: Macmillan, 1972.

Turner, F.M. *Between Science and Religion: the reaction to scientific naturalism in late Victorian England.* New Haven: Yale University Press, 1974.

Tuveson, E.L. *Redeemer Nation: The Idea of America's Millenial Role.* Chicago: University of Chicago Press, 1968.

Wade, L.C. *Graham Taylor: Pioneer for Social Justice, 1851-1938.* Chicago: University of Chicago Press, 1964.

Welch, C. *Protestant Thought in the Nineteenth Century, Vol.1, 1799-1870*. New Haven: Yale University Press, 1972.

--- . *Protestant Thought in the Nineteenth Century.Vol.2, 1870-1914*. New Haven: Yale University Press, 1985.

White, R.C., and Hopkins, C.H. *The Social Gospel: Religion and Reform in Changing America*. Philadelphia: Temple University Press, 1976.

Wiebe, R. *Businessmen and Reform: A Study of the Progressive Movement*. Cambridge: Harvard University Press, 1962.

--- . *The Search for Order, 1877-1920*. New York: Hill and Wang, 1967.

Wilson, R.J. *In Quest of Community: Social Philosophy in the United States, 1860-1920*. New York: Oxford University Press, 1968.

Woodroofe, K., *From Charity to Social Work: in England and the United States*. Toronto: University of Toronto Press, 1968.

2. Articles

Ahlstrom, S. "The Scottish Philosophy and American Theology," *Church History* 24, no.3 (Sept.1955).

Aiken, J.R. "Walter Rauschenbusch and Education for Reform," *Church History* 36, no.4 (Dec.1967).

Allen, R. "Providence to Progress: The Migration of an Idea in English Canadian Thought," *Canadian Issues/Themes Canadiens* 7 (1985).

--- . "Salem Bland: The Young Preacher," *The Bulletin* 26 (1977).

--- . "The Social Gospel and the Reform Tradition in Canada, 1890-1928," *Canadian Historical Review* 49, no. 4 (Dec.1968).

Angrave, J. "William Dawson, George Grant and the Legacy of Scottish Higher Education," *Queen's Quarterly* 82, no.1 (Spring 1975).

Aspinwall, B. "The Scottish Religious Identity in the Atlantic World, 1880-1914." In D. Baker (ed.), *Religion and National Identity.* Oxford: Basil Blackwell, 1982.

Bailey, W.M. "William Robertson Smith and American Biblical Studies," *Journal of Presbyterian History* 51, no.3 (Fall 1973).

Berger, C. "The Other Mr.Leacock," *Canadian Literature* 55 (Winter 1973).

Best, G. "The Scottish Victorian City," *Victorian Studies* 11, no.3 (Mar.1968).

Bliss, M. "The Methodist Church and World War I," *Canadian Historical Review* 49, no.3 (Sept.1968).

Clifford, N.K. "His Dominion: a vision in crisis," *Studies in Religion/Sciences Religieuses* 2, no.4 (1974).

Conway, J. "Woman Reformers and American Culture, 1870-1930," *Journal of Social History* 5, no.2 (Winter 1971-72).

Cook, R. "Stephen Leacock and the Age of Plutocracy." In J.S. Moir (ed.), *Character and Circumstance.* Toronto: Macmillan, 1970.

Emery, G.N. "The Origins of the Canadian Methodist Involvement in the Social Gospel Movement, 1890-1914," *The Bulletin* 26 (1977).

Forbes, E.R. "Prohibition and the Social Gospel in Nova Scotia," *Acadiensis* 1, no.1 (Autumn 1971).

Grant, J.W. "The Impact of Christianity on Canadian Culture and Society, 1867 to the Present," *Theological Bulletin* 3 (1968).

Gutman, H.G. "Protestantism and the American Labor Movement: The Christian Spirit in the Gilded Age," *American Historical Review* 72, no.1 (1967).

Handy, R.T. "Trends in Canadian and American Theological Education, 1880-1980, Some Comparisons," *Theological Education* 18, no.2 (Spring 1982).

Harevan, T.K. "An Ambiguous Alliance: Some Aspects of American Influence on Canadian Social Welfare," *Histoire Sociale/Social History* 3 (June 1969).

Hefner, P. "The Real Challenge of the Nineteenth Century," *Dialog* 22, no.1 (Winter 1983).

Heron, C. and Palmer, B.D., "Through the Prism of the Strike: Industrial Conflict in Southern Ontario, 1901-1914," *Canadian Historical Review* 8, no.4 (Dec.1977).

Hudson, W.S. "How American is Religion in America?" In J.C. Brauer, *Reinterpretation in American Church History.* Chicago: University of Chicago Press, 1968.

--- . "Protestant Clergy Debate the Nation's Vocation, 1898-1899," *Church History* 42, no.1 (Mar.1973).

Hutchison, W.R. "The Americanness of the Social Gospel: An Inquiry in Comparative History," *Church History* 44, no. 3 (Sept.1975).

--- . "Liberal Protestantism and the 'End of Innocence'," *American Quarterly* 15 (Summer 1963).

Irving, J. "The Development of Philosophy in Central Canada from 1850 to 1900," *Canadian Historical Review* 31, no.3 (1950).

Judd, W.W. "The Vision and the Dream: The Council of Social Service — Fifty Years," *Journal of the Canadian Church History Society* 8, no.4 (Dec.1965).

Kiesekamp, B. "Presbyterian and Methodist divines: their case for a national church in Canada, 1875-1900," *Studies in Religion/Sciences Religieuses* 2, no.4 (1974).

McKillop, A.B. "Nationalism, Identity and Canadian Intellectual History," *Queen's Quarterly* 8, no.4 (Winter 1974).

McLoughlin, W.G. "Pietism and the American Character," *American Quarterly* 17, no.2 (Summer 1965).

Masters, D.C. "The Rise of Liberalism in Canadian Protestant Churches," *Canadian Catholic Historical Association, Study Sessions, 1969.*

Magney, W.H. "The Methodist Church and the National Gospel," *The Bulletin* 20 (1968).

Meacham, S. "The Church in the Victorian City," *Victorian Studies* 11, no.3 (Mar.1968).

Mealing, S.R. "The Concept of Social Class and the Interpretation of Canadian History," *Canadian Historical Review* 46, no.3 (Sept.1965).

Meyer, P.R. "The Fear of Cultural Decline: Josiah Strong's Thought about Reform," *Church History* 42, no.3 (Sept.1973).

Moir, J.S. "James Frederick McCurdy: Christian Humanist," *The Canadian Society of Presbyterian History, Papers, 1981.*

--- . "'On the King's Business': the Rise and Fall of the Laymen's Missionary Movement in Canada." In A. Tihon (ed.),*Les Mouvements de Laics dans les Eglises aux XIXe et XXe Siecles.* Bruxelles: Facultes universitaires Saint-Louis, 1980.

Moore, J.R. "Walter Rauschenbusch and the Religious Education of Youth," *Religious Education* 68, no.4 (July-Aug.1973).

Muller, D.R. "The Social Philosophy of Josiah Strong: Social Christianity and American Progressivism," *Church History* 28, no.2 (1959).

Nash, G.H., III. "Charles Stelzle: Social Gospel Pioneer," *Journal of Presbyterian History* 50, no.3 (Fall 1972).

Nicholl, G. "The Image of the Protestant Minister in the Christian Social Novel," *Church History* 37, no.3 (Sept. 1968).

Rousmaniere, J.P. "Cultural Hybrid in the Slums: The College Woman and the Settlement House, 1889-1894," *American Quarterly* 22, no.1 (Spring 1970).

Rutherford, P. "Tomorrow's Metropolis: The Urban Reform Movement in Canada," *Historical Papers, 1971*, Canadian Historical Association.

Sandeen, E.R. "The Princeton Theology: One Source of Biblical Literalism in American Protestantism," *Church History* 31 (1962).

Singleton, G.H. "'Mere Middle-Class Institutions': Urban Protestantism in Nineteenth-Century America," *Journal of Social History* 6 (Summer 1973).

Soffer, R.N. "The Revolution in English Social Thought, 1880-1914," *American Historical Review* 75, no.7 (Dec.1970).

Smith, A. "American Culture and the Concept of Mission in Nineteenth-Century English Canada," *Historical Papers, 1971*, Canadian Historical Assocation.

Speisman, S.A. "Munificent Parsons and Municipal Parsimony," *Ontario History* 65, no.1 (Mar.1973).

Thompson, J.L. and J.H., "Ralph Connor and the Canadian Identity," *Queen's Quarterly* 79, no.2 (Summer 1972).

Vipond, M. "Blessed are the peacemakers: The Labour question in Canadian social gospel fiction," *Journal of Canadian Studies/Revue d'etudes canadiennes* 10, no.3 (1975).

Wallace, E. "The Origin of the Social Welfare State in Canada, 1867-1900," *Canadian Journal of Economics and Political Science* 16 (1950).

Waterman, A.M.C. "The Lord's Day Act in a Secular Society: A Historical Comment on the Canadian Lord's Day Act of 1906," *Canadian Journal of Theology* 11, no.2 (1965).

Watt, F.W. "Western Myth--The World of Ralph Connor," *Canadian Literature* 1 (Summer 1959).

Weaver, J.C. "The Meaning of Municipal Reform: Toronto, 1895," *Ontario History* 66, no.2 (June 1974).

Wigney, T. "Manifest Righteousness: The Presbyterian Church, Education and Nation Building in Canada, 1875-1914." In A. Chaiton and N. McDonald (eds.), *Canadian Schools and Canadian Identity*. Toronto: Gage, 1977.

Theses

Carter, B.N. "James L.Hughes and the Gospel of Education." Ed.D. thesis, University of Toronto, 1966.

Christie, E.A. "The Presbyterian Church in Canada and its Official Attitudes to Public Affairs and Social Problems, 1875-1925." M.A. thesis, University of Toronto, 1955.

Kiesekamp, B. "Community and Faith: The Intellectual and Ideological Bases of the Church Union Movement in Victorian Canada." Ph.D. thesis, University of Toronto, 1974.

McKillop, A.B. "English Canadian Idealism in Transition, 1872-1920." Ph.D. thesis, Queen's University, 1971.

Manson, I.M. "Serving God and Country: Evangelical Piety and the Presbyterian Church in Manitoba, 1880-1900." M.A. thesis, University of Manitoba, 1986.

Markell, K. "Canadian Protestantism against the background of urbanization and industrialization in the period from 1885 to 1914." Ph.D. thesis, University of Chicago, 1971.

Morrison, T. "The Child and Urban Social Reform in Late Nineteenth-Century Ontario." Ph.D. thesis, University of Toronto, 1971.

Williams, C.J. "The Political Philosophy of Two Canadians, John Watson and W.C.Kierstead." M.A. thesis, University of Western Ontario, 1952.

Wood, E.H. "Ralph Connor and the Canadian West." M.A. thesis, University of Saskatchewan, 1975.

INDEX

Addams, Jane, 82
Ahlstrom, Sydney, xi
Allen, Richard, x, xi, xiii
Anglicans, 55
Archibald, J.S., 128
Armstrong, A.E., 65
Aylesworth, A.B., 146-147

Baptists, 24, 53
Bengough, J.W., 136-137
Black, John, 65
Bloor Street Presbyterian Church, Toronto, 94, 128, 164
Bonsanquet, B., 4
Borden, Robert, 159-160
Briggs, Charles, 8
Bright, John, 107
British Idealism, 3-8, 25, 27-32, 173-175
Brookes, Phillips, 107
Brown, George, 23, 51, 54, 56
Bruce, A.B., xi, 2-3, 7-10, 27
Bryce, G., 65
Burton, P.H., 92
Bushnell, Horace, 107
Butler, Bishop, 31

Caird, Edward, 1-2, 3-8, 27, 37
Caird, John, 1, 27. 56
Campbell, John, 26-27
Campbell, J. McLeod, 14
Canada's Missionary Congress (1909), 177
Canada Presbyterian Church, 122n.
Careless, J.M.S., 57
Carlaw, J.A., 92
Carlyle, Thomas, 3-4
Carmichael, J.A., 65
Caven, William, 25, 110-111, 173
Chalmers, Thomas, 68, 75n.
Chapman, Wilbur, 34, 108
Christian Character, 31-32, 35-36, 38-43, 99-120
Christian Family, 35-26, 69, 88, 100-105, 117, 127

Charlton, W.A., 159
Church of Scotland, 1, 51-56
Church Union, 89-90, 131, 169
Civil Service Commission, 141
Clark, S.D., 61
Clark, W. Mortimer, 92
Clifford, N.K., 60
Coe, G., 118
Columbia Teachers' College, 118
Common Sense, Scottish, 3, 18n., 30
Congregationalists, 89
Connor, Ralph. *See* Gordon, C.W.
Conservative Party, 145, 158
Cook, R., xi
Coussirat, Daniel, 64

Dale, R.W., 107
Darwin, Charles, 13, 16
Davidson, A.B., 9, 11, 26
Delitzch, F., 26
Dods, Marcus, 8, 26
Dominion Educational Association, 115-116
Drummond, Henry, xi, 13-17, 26, 33
Duncan, J.M., 65
Dyde, S.W., 128

Edmison, J.H., 65
Ellis, W.T., 113
Erskine, Thomas, 14
Evangelical Liberalism, xi, 23-43, 174
Evangelism, 33-38, 85-86, 106-109

Falconer, R.A.:
  biographical, x, 23, 26, 49, 71, 77, 119, 164, 169
  on church union, 89
  on education, 87
  and social work, 121n.
  on war, 161
Fergusson, G.T., 92, 128
Fraser, R.D., 65, 87-88, 118
Fraser, Thurlow, 141-142
Free Church College, Glasgow, 9, 27
Free Church in Canada, xi, 1, 23-24, 51, 54-56, 69
Free Church in Scotland, 2-3, 9
French Evangelization, 64

Gandier, Alfred, 33, 175
Germany, 26, 160-165
George, Lloyd, 107
Gilbert, A.D., 55, 74n.
Glasgow, 33
Glasgow Colonial Society, 53-54
Globe:
  under G. Brown, 23, 56
  and Christian education, 119
  under J.A. Macdonald, 66, 110, 112-114, 162-164
  and peace, 157
Gordon, C.W.:
  biographical, x, 23-26, 49, 65, 71, 77, 169
  on Canadian nationalism, 84-85, 125n., 130
  on church organization, 69
  on evangelism, 34, 108
  and men's work, 128

and moral reform, 146-147
on preaching, 106
as Ralph Connor, 66, 131-132, 143, 177-178
and temperance, 139, 152n.
on war, 160-161, 164
on women, 101
Gordon, D.M., 56
Gourlay, R.S., 92
Graingrowers' Association of Manitoba, 158
Grant, A.S., 65, 167-168
Grant, G.M., 1, 56
Gray, R.A., 92
Green, T.H., 4, 25, 31

Haddow, Robert, 65, 148, 165-166
Halifax, 57-66, 144
Hart, Thomas, 65
Hastings, James, xi
Hefner, Phillip, xi
Hegel, G.W.F., 4, 28
Herdman, J.C., 65
Herridge, W.T., 85
Higher Criticism, 8-12, 19n.
Hull House, Chicago, 104
Hume, J.G., 114-115
Hutchison, A.C., 128
Hutchison, W.R., 43
Hutton, Maurice, 25

James, William, 78
Jordon, D.S., 159
Jowett, Benjamin, 4, 25

Kant, Immanuel, 4, 28-29
Keith, Marion, 76
Kilgour, R., 128
Kilpatrick, T.B.:
biographical, x, 23, 49, 71, 77, 119, 169
on Canadian nationalism, 199, 115-116
on the family, 101
on preaching, 106-107
on theology, 27-43, 173-174
on war, 162
King, J.M., 27, 65
King, W.L.M.:
on Hull House, Chicago, 104
on labour, 136, 151n.
on peace, 159
at Rockefeller Foundation, 162
on social sciences, 141-142
Knox, W.J., 117-119, 128-129
Knox College, Toronto:
and Presbyterian progressives, 24-26, 33-37, 49, 134
and social Christianity, 1
and Western missions, 65
Knox College Monthly, 66, 68, 90, 110-112
Knox Presbyterian Church, Toronto, 91-92
Kootenays, 34, 108-109, 145, 146

Labour, 40-42, 130, 132-137, 156
Laurier, Wilfrid, 116, 136, 146-147, 154n., 158
Law, Robert, 86-87
Law Enforcement, 142-147
Laymen's Missionary Movement, 149n.
Legislation, 137-142
Lemieux Act (1907), 136

Liberal Party:
and Presbyterian progressives, 25, 128, 141
and moral reform, 146-147, 154n.
and war, 158
Lord's Day Alliance, 49, 70, 99, 137

MacBeth, R.G., 176
Macdonald, H.J., 145
Macdonald, J.A.:
biographical, x, 23-26, 49, 71, 77, 169
on Canadian nationalism, 125n., 142, 177
on the family, 101, 104
on education, 115
on the Kingdom of God, 86
and men's work, 128
on moral reform, 146-147
on peace, 157-159, 162-164
and the press, 109-114
on urban missions, 91-92
on women, 101-102
Macdonnell, D.J., 56
MacDougall, John, 129
MacGregor, D.C., 166
MacGregor, Malcolm, 113, 115
Mackay, John, 156, 162
MacKay, R.P., 65, 84, 159
MacKinnon, Murdoch, 86
MacLaren, William, 25
MacLeod, Norman, 56
MacVicar, D.H., 26, 173
Magill, Robert, 141
Manitoba College, Winnipeg, 27, 49, 65
McAinsh, D.T., 66
McCurdy, J.F., 9, 157
McFadyen, J.E., 9-12, 20n., 27, 111-112, 118
McIntosh, W.R., 78, 119
McKillop, A.B., 23
McTavish, Daniel, 78, 91
Mead, Edwin, 159
Methodists:
and Canadian nationalism, 51
and church union, 89
and social reform, xii, xivn., 129, 156
and revivalism, 24, 55
as an urban institution, 64
Mill, J.S., 31
Mitchell, J.B., 157
Moir, J.S., 56
Montreal, 57-66, 167
Moody, D.L.:
and Canadian Presbyterians, 24
and T.B. Kilpatrick, 33-34, 107
and Scottish evangelical liberals, 2, 9, 12-13
and Sunday Schools, 118
Morgan, W., xi
Morris, J.L., 50
Mott, J.R., 159
Mowat, O., 51
Murray, J. Clark, 26
Murray, W. Clark, 117, 128
Myers, A.J.W., 129
Myers, C.A., 118

Nesbitt, Dr. Beattie, 113-114
Nettleship, R., 4
New College, Edinburgh, 4
Nicholson, J.W.A., 88
Nicol, P., 90-91
Niebuhr, H.R., 51

Oliver, John, 114
Oxford University, 4
Patrick, William, 27, 131, 150n.
Peace Manifesto (1913), 156-158
Pidgeon, G.C.:
  biographical, x, 26-27, 49, 71, 77, 164, 165, 169
  on law enforcement, 143
  on preaching, 105-106, 107-108
  and Sunday Schools, 119
  on temperance, 139-140
Preaching, 105-109
Presbyterian Brotherhood, 128-130
Presbyterian Church in Canada, x, 49-71
  Board of Foreign Missions, W.D., 65
  Board of Home Missions, x, 65, 156, 165-168
  Board of Social Service and Evangelism, x, 34, 70-71, 76, 81, 83-84, 90, 93, 103, 129-130, 137-142, 142-144, 145-146, 156, 165-169
  Commission on Religious Education, 117-119
  Commission on the War, 162
  Pre-Assembly Congress (1913), 79-80, 84-90, 100, 137, 145
Presbyterian College, Halifax, 1, 26, 49
Presbyterian College, Montreal, 1, 26-27, 49
Presbyterian College Journal, 27
Presbyterian Record, 133
Press, 109-114
Prophets, 11-12, 111-112
Proudfoot, J.J.A., 122n.
Proudfoot, William, 25
Psalms, 10-11
Public Schools, 114-118, 127

Queen's University, Kingston, 23, 68, 128

Rauschenbusch, Walter, 77-78
Reid, J.R., 128
Reid, W.D., 89
Religious Education Association, 118-119
Riddell, W.A., 129
Ritschl, Albrecht, xi
Robertson, F.W., 107
Robertson, James, 64-65, 67
Robertson, J.C., 65, 118
Robinson, C. Blackett, 66
Robinson, F.A., 166
Robson, Justice H.A, 144
Roman Catholics, 53, 116
Rowell, N.W., 51

Scott, Ephraim, 65-66
Secessionists, 24, 51-55
Settlements, 90-94, 104, 166
Shearer, J.G.:
  biographical, x, 23-25, 34, 49, 70-71, 77, 162, 165-169
  on evangelism, 85-86, 108-109
  and labour, 1432-134
  on law enforcement, 144
  and men's work, 148
  on public opinion, 99
  on urban reform, 79-80, 90-91
Shortt, Adam, 141
Simpson, P.C., 2
Sinclair, A.G., 100, 145
Skelton, O.D., 81-83, 142

Smart, J.D., 8
Smith, G.A., xi, 9, 11, 26
Smith, W.H., 135-136, 137, 141-142
Smith, W.R., 2, 8, 11
Social Reform, xi-xiii, 35-43, 70-71, 77-95
Social Service Congress (1914), 130, 149n., 169
Social Service Council of Canada, 138-139, 141, 160n., 180
Social Surveys, 129
Socialism, 41-43, 82, 135, 157
Spurgeon, Charles, 107
St. Andrew's Presbyterian Church, King St., Toronto, 68
St. James Square Presbyterian Church, Toronto, 167
St. Stephen's Presbyterian Church, Winnipeg, 49, 161, 167
Stead, W.T., 158-159
Steele, R.C., 92
Stelzle, Charles, 78, 131-134, 165
Strong, Josiah, 68, 75n., 80, 103
Stuart, Alexander, 128
Sunday Schools, 118-119

Taschereau, Justice, 145
Taylor, Bruce, 88
Taylor, Graham, 82
Temperance, 138-140
The Canada Presbyterian, 66
The Presbyterian:
  on evangelism and social reform, 165-166
  on the family, 104-105, 110
  founding, 65, 110
  on J.A. Macdonald, 112, 113
  on peace, 157, 158
  on socialism, 135
  and Sunday Schools, 119
  on temperance, 138
  on urban reform, 880-81, 93
  on war, 160
The Westminster, 66, 80, 110, 112
Thompson, John, 100-101
Toronto, 56-66, 80-84, 90-94, 167, 173
Toronto Presbyterian Union, 92-93
Toynbee Hall, London, 103

University College, Toronto, 24
Urban Reform, 80-84, 90-94

Wallace, W., 4
Watson, John, 1, 7, 27, 33, 37
Westminster Company, 49, 66
Westminster Hall, Vancouver, 105, 156
Westminster Standards, 62-63
Winnipeg, 49, 57-66, 69, 161, 167
Winnipeg Vice Commission, 144-145
Woodsworth, J.S., 77
World Congress on Internationalism (1915), 1163-164
World Peace Foundation, 159
World War I, xiii, 155-165

Yinger, Milton, 51-53
Young, G.P., 26-28, 114

SR SUPPLEMENTS

Note: Nos. 1, 3, 4, 5, 7, 8, 10, and 15 in this series are out of print.

2. ***Martin Heidegger's Philosophy of Religion***
   John R. Williams
   1977 / x + 190 pp.
6. ***Beyond Mysticism***
   James R. Horne
   1978 / vi + 158 pp.
9. ***Developments in Buddhist Thought: Canadian Contributions to Buddhist Studies***
   Edited by Roy C. Amore
   1979 / iv + 196 pp.
11. ***Political Theology in the Canadian Context***
    Edited by Benjamin G. Smillie
    1982 / xii + 260 pp.
12. ***Truth and Compassion: Essays on Judaism and Religion in Memory of Rabbi Dr. Solomon Frank***
    Edited by Howard Joseph, Jack N. Lightstone, and Michael D. Oppenheim
    1983 / vi + 217 pp.
13. ***Craving and Salvation: A Study in Buddhist Soteriology***
    Bruce Matthews
    1983 / xiv + 138 pp.
14. ***The Moral Mystic***
    James R. Horne
    1983 / x + 134 pp.
16. ***Studies in the Book of Job***
    Edited by Walter E. Aufrecht
    1985 / xii + 76 pp.
17. ***Christ and Modernity: Christian Self-Understanding in a Technological Age***
    David J. Hawkin
    1985 / x + 181 pp.
18. ***Young Man Shinran: A Reappraisal of Shinran's Life***
    Takamichi Takahatake
    1987 / xvi + 228 pp.
19. ***Modernity and Religion***
    Edited by William Nicholls
    1987 / vi + 191 pp.
20. ***The Social Uplifters: Presbyterian Progressives and the Social Gospel in Canada, 1875-1915***
    Brian J. Fraser
    1988 / xvi + 212 pp.

EDITIONS SR

Note: No. 3 in this series is out of print.

1. ***La langue de Ya'udi : description et classement de l'ancien parler de Zencircli dans le cadre des langues semitiques du nord-ouest***
   Paul-Eugène Dion, O.P.
   1974 / viii + 511 p.
2. ***The Conception of Punishment in Early Indian Literature***
   Terence P. Day
   1982 / iv + 328 pp.
4. ***Le messianisme de Louis Riel***
   Gilles Martel
   1984 / xviii + 483 p.
5. ***Mythologies and Philosophies of Salvation in the Theistic Traditions of India***
   Klaus K. Klostermaier
   1984 / xvi + 552 pp.
6. ***Averroes' Doctrine of Immortality: A Matter of Controversy***
   Ovey N. Mohammed
   1984 / vi + 202 pp.
7. ***L'étude des religions dans les écoles : l'expérience américaine, anglaise et canadienne***
   Fernand Ouellet
   1985 / xvi + 666 p.

8. *Of God and Maxim Guns: Presbyterianism in Nigeria, 1846-1966*
Geoffrey Johnston
1988 / iv + 322 pp.

9. *A Victorian Missionary and Canadian Indian Policy: Cultural Synthesis vs Cultural Replacement*
David A. Nock
Spring 1988 / 200 pp. estimated

10. *Prometheus Rebound: The Irony of Atheism*
Joseph C. McLelland
Fall 1988 / 360 pp. estimated

STUDIES IN CHRISTIANITY AND JUDAISM / ETUDES SUR LE CHRISTIANISME ET LE JUDAISME

1. *A Study in Anti-Gnostic Polemics: Irenaeus, Hippolytus, and Epiphanius*
Gérard Vallée
1981 / xii + 114 pp.

2. *Anti-Judaism in Early Christianity*
Vol. 1, *Paul and the Gospels*
Edited by Peter Richardson with David Granskou
1986 / x + 232 pp.
Vol. 2, *Separation and Polemic*
Edited by Stephen G. Wilson
1986 / xii + 185 pp.

3. *Society, the Sacred, and Scripture in Ancient Judaism: A Sociology of Knowledge*
Jack N. Lightstone
1988 / xiv + 126 pp.

THE STUDY OF RELIGION IN CANADA / SCIENCES RELIGIEUSES AU CANADA

1. *Religious Studies in Alberta: A State-of-the-Art Review*
Ronald W. Neufeldt
1983 / xiv + 145 pp.

2. *Les sciences religieuses au Québec, 1972-1984*
Louis Rousseau et Michel Despland
Printemps 1988 / 146 p. estimé

COMPARATIVE ETHICS SERIES/ COLLECTION D'ETHIQUE COMPAREE

1. *Muslim Ethics and Modernity: A Comparative Study of the Ethical Thought of Sayyid Ahmad Khan and Mawlana Mawdudi*
Sheila McDonough
1984 / x + 130 pp.

2. *Methodist Education in Peru: Social Gospel, Politics, and American Ideological and Economic Penetration, 1888-1930*
Rosa del Carmen Bruno-Jofré
1988 / xiv + 223 pp.

Available from / en vente chez:
Wilfrid Laurier University Press
Wilfrid Laurier University
Waterloo, Ontario, Canada N2L 3C5

Published for the
Canadian Corporation for Studies in Religion/
Corporation Canadienne des Sciences Religieuses
by Wilfrid Laurier University Press